INTERPRETATION
Making a Difference on Purpose

INTERPRETATION
Making a Difference on Purpose

SAM H. HAM

FULCRUM
GOLDEN, COLORADO

Interpretation—Making a Difference on Purpose
Sam H. Ham

Fulcrum Publishing
Golden, Colorado

Library of Congress Cataloging-in-Publication Data on file.

Printed in the United States of America

0 9 8 7 6 5 4 3

Design by Barbara Ham

Cover image: Interpretation provoking thought and illuminating the world.

Fulcrum Publishing
4690 Table Mountain Dr., Ste. 100
Golden, CO 80403
800-992-2908 • 303-277-1623
www.fulcrumbooks.com

For Maleia, Vincent, and Miles

And to the memory of David L. Larsen (1960–2011)

Contents

Foreword

You may already be familiar with Sam's original *Environmental Interpretation: A Practical Guide for People with Big Ideas and Small Budgets*. It was published in 1992 and became a valued text in college classrooms around the world and a key resource for working interpreters everywhere.

In *Environmental Interpretation*, Sam first explained the use of a thematic approach to communication. He has always been thoughtful in explaining that Bill Lewis, author of *Interpreting for Park Visitors*, encouraged his original interest in themes. Bill once told me that he got the idea of using themes from Aristotle, so the idea of thematic communication isn't new. But as a psychologist and former frontline interpreter, Sam realized how important it was to connect practice in the field back to research. At every step of the way he has explained the studies that support a thematic approach to interpretation, making the reasoning behind the use of themes accessible to all.

In *Interpretation: Making a Difference on Purpose*, Sam brings a new level of understanding to the real power that thematic communication has for the interpretation profession. To talk about the value of this book, I must share a personal story. In the 1980s, I was the director of a community nature center in Pueblo, Colorado. A member of the board of directors once stopped me midsentence when I was explaining that we were involved in "values education." He was so upset that he eventually resigned from the board, disgusted with the "propagandistic" direction we seemed to be taking. At that time my defense of our approach was enthusiastic, but it lacked key points that might have changed his understanding of a nature center and the positive influence it hopes to have in a community.

Thinking later about the unhappy board member, I realized he worked as marketing director of the city's major hospital, which was heavily engaged in programs to curtail the use of tobacco and unprotected sex. The hospital had programming to encourage weight loss and exercise—essentially stewardship of the human body. Why is stewardship of the environment more controversial than "values education" about the human body and lifestyles? The board member saw a nature center's role solely as imparting factual information about nature, not influencing attitudes, beliefs, and behaviors about conservation and stewardship in the community and beyond. I might have compared our work to the hospital's work with health, but my thoughts were not fast enough to soothe the anger of the unhappy board member, and I could not have provided any significant research to back up my assertions.

Sam's new book provides the underpinning for our current understanding of interpretation and its vital role in influencing attitudes, beliefs, and behaviors in many settings, including parks, zoos, museums, aquariums, nature centers, wildlife refuges, historic sites, and communities. He explains in the preface his intent to help practitioners understand how and why interpretive principles work as an approach to communication. He rightfully suggests that we "own" our beliefs and practices when we can explain how they work.

For many years, Sam has emphasized that a major objective of interpretation is to get the visitor or guest to *think*. That sounds simple enough, but it is in fact far from simple. He has pointed out that Tilden (1957) made a similar point in restating a quote from a National Park Service administrative manual: "Through interpretation, understanding; through understanding, appreciation; through appreciation, protection." This is the same social marketing construct the National Association for Interpretation (NAI) trainers have taught since 2000 and a model I first saw at the National Park Service's Mather Training Center. Information is just that, but interpretation has a purpose. As interpreters, we provide access to experiences—both intellectual and emotional—that encourage understanding. We trust that having a greater understanding will lead to more respectful behavior. People can memorize information through repetition or mnemonic devices, but understanding implies a deeper grasp based on analysis. That drive toward thoughtful analysis is what differentiates interpretation from the easier—but far less effective—method of simply providing information.

In my role as the executive director of the NAI for more than seventeen years, I witnessed a great deal of change in this profession as we moved from relying on information-heavy lecture-style programs or fun but unrelated gimmicks and gadgets to more engaging, thought-provoking thematic interpretation. NAI's certification and training programs rely heavily on Sam's approach to thematic interpretation, and the recognition of those programs around the world speaks to the value of that approach.

If I could go back in time, I could now discuss the finer points of "values education" with the unhappy board member. Interpretation helps people understand the world, important stories, other cultures, the universe, or beer. Our subject matter could be anything at all, but the process remains. We do not need to teach "values." We have no need for propaganda. As interpreters, we can encourage a thought process whereby people can reach their own conclusions based on better understanding. And that understanding may lead them to discover new ways of relating to the world around them.

Sam has been around the world many times, including dozens of trips to Australia alone. He is respected by guides working on their own in remote protected areas and by professors teaching at major universities. He has been an interpreter to the interpreters and to their teachers at the same time. I daresay, no one could have done it better. All who know him are energized by his enthusiasm and his very real desire to make a difference.

A profession does not grow and mature at a steady rate. It develops in spurts as key events drive change. *Environmental Interpretation* had a tremendous influence on the profession as tens of thousands of interpreters added it to their personal libraries. With this book, *Interpretation: Making a Difference on Purpose,* Sam will most definitely make a difference for the profession, again.

Tim Merriman
Past Executive Director
National Association for Interpretation
Fort Collins, Colorado, United States

Preface

When I wrote *Environmental Interpretation* twenty years ago, I had a specific purpose in mind. At the time, there simply were no other books written for people in the interpretation field that told them in much detail how to actually do practical things—such as how to plan and present a talk, lead guided tours, design exhibits, or produce audiovisual programs. And outside of Bill Lewis's *Interpreting for Park Visitors* (1980), which introduced the concept of a theme to the interpretation profession, no sources existed that showed interpreters how to apply thematic reasoning to their work. Since I emphasized all these topics in my own classes at the University of Idaho in those days, I simply decided one day to write a textbook for *myself*—one that matched the way I wanted to teach interpretation. That was my purpose, and I'd have to say it worked out well.

But even as I was putting the finishing touches on that book, I already knew I had to write this one. And just as I was two decades ago, I'm again encouraged by the prospect that this volume might serve some useful purposes—albeit they different ones. I hope those of you who turn these pages will notice (and appreciate) that, although *Interpretation—Making a Difference on Purpose* has a practical "how-to" focus, it's as much a book on how to *think about* interpretation as it is a book on how to *do* interpretation. There's a reason for that, and the reason is made explicit in the subtitle—*Making a Difference on Purpose*.

In order to make a difference on purpose—as opposed to crossing one's fingers and hoping to get lucky—an interpreter needs to think strategically about how to approach interpretation. This means, first and foremost, knowing where a principle comes from and *why* it makes sense. If you have success applying a principle you can't explain, you don't yet "own" it, and you'll be hard-pressed later—when audiences, circumstances, and media have inevitably changed—to apply it again with the same success. To me, for example, it simply isn't enough to "know" that interpretation should aim to provoke thought in an audience; an interpreter must know *why* it's necessary. Similarly, it isn't enough simply to "know" that a theme title is required if a museum exhibit is going to be capable of reaching its largest audience—the designer and writer must know *why* a theme title is needed. And it just isn't sufficient to "know" that you don't necessarily have to articulate the theme of every talk or guided tour to the audience—you need to know *why* that is.

The whole point of this book's ten chapters is that interpretation isn't magic (meaning it's not a collection of tricks and gimmicks that defy logical explanation). On the contrary, interpretation is treated in this book as *strategy*—the purposeful design and delivery of communication that stands a better chance of making a difference on purpose with the kinds of audiences most interpreters encounter.

Of course, to be strategic, you need to know not only what you're doing, but also why you're doing it that way. You need a reason and a rationale that are based not simply on intuitive guesses about what works but also on reliable evidence that only a body of consistent research findings can provide. I've tried to make sure that every chapter of *Interpretation—Making a Difference on Purpose* draws on that kind of evidence.

I've also wanted to put in writing a formal statement of the theory and cognitive science that lies behind my understanding of thematic communication. I hope the documentation I've offered provides a useful source for researchers and academics developing their own approaches to understanding interpretation, and that it serves as a point of departure for master's and doctoral students who need a place to start. Although the theory and research I use to substantiate my approach to thematic communication constitute only one professor's formulation, I thought it was high time I put these ideas in writing—if for no other reason than for someone else to find holes in them. If this volume serves even just that purpose, it will have made one of its most important contributions.

I want to draw every reader's attention to the "Additional Thoughts" section I've included at the end of each chapter. I know a lot of us don't bother to read the fine print of footnotes and endnotes because we assume they'll just list a bunch of bibliographic citations along with the occasional ibid, op. cit., and et al. that we academics use to tell other academics we're not just making stuff up. The notes I've compiled for my reader here, however, are nothing of that sort. Rather they're exactly what the heading says—additional *thoughts*. In many cases I've used these notes to explore new angles or offer different perspectives on something I mentioned in the main text. Some of them introduce wholly new issues I wanted my reader to think about, but which I thought might interrupt the flow of ideas in the body of the chapter. And—as readers who know me personally might expect—some of my notes contain humorous commentary or personal anecdotes. Although I have indeed relegated most of my bibliographic citations to these notes (yes, so you can see I'm not just making stuff up), in some ways my "Additional Thoughts" constitute another small book within this book. I truly hope you will enjoy reading them and that they add depth to your understanding of thematic interpretation and how you might increase your chances of making a difference on purpose.

The ten chapters start with a sort of refresher and update on the TORE model (formerly the EROT framework, with which many readers will be familiar). This update (in Chapters 1 and 2) is shaped mainly by a now vast body of consistent research findings showing just how important audience thinking is in the "making a difference" business. Many of these studies were conducted after *Environmental Interpretation* was published, so readers familiar with that earlier presentation of thematic interpretation principles will find some important new wrinkles. However, readers familiar with Freeman Tilden's (1957) assertion that interpretation isn't instruction but rather "provocation" will understand intuitively why this update was needed. Indeed, Tilden was nearly thirty years ahead of theory and research when he made his famous claim, and the first two chapters of this book serve in large part to put his provocation principle front and center in the TORE approach to thematic interpretation. It's what the *audience* does (think) and not so much what the interpreter does (communicate information) that tells us when we've achieved excellence in interpretation—provocation, not instruction, indeed.

One of the first to appreciate why I decided to do this was my dear friend and close colleague David Larsen, who saddened the world when he died unexpectedly on January 17, 2011. For five years—from March 2005, when I first began work on this manuscript, until November 2010—David and I talked almost monthly by phone as he read draft chapters of this book (some still too rough to show a less heady or less compassionate critic). Our conversations, typically lasting from thirty minutes to three hours, were nothing short of intellectual catharses for both of us. This was because the two of us had quite independently arrived at an almost identical understanding of interpretation, but via two very different ways of knowing. In one of our last exchanges, I confessed to David that I was more impressed with his journey than my own because mine required the weight of empirical evidence provided by the research I'd been following for years, whereas David and his astute team of colleagues in the US National Park Service, simply "knew" and "saw" the same things—much the way Freeman Tilden also appears to have simply seen them. It is for this reason that I've dedicated *Interpretation—*

Making a Difference on Purpose to four important people in my life: my three grandchildren and David Larsen. Although nearly every chapter in this volume has been informed in some way by David's brilliance, the first three chapters (along with Chapter 8) were the ones we talked about most.

In Chapter 3 ("The Endgame of Interpretation"), I ask an important question about what interpretation should aim to accomplish, and I invite readers to explore what their answers to that question might mean—not only for determining whether interpretation succeeds or fails but also for our long-term pursuit of excellence in interpretation and interpretive training.

Chapters 4 and 5 explore what it means to make a "difference" via interpretation and what those differences might look like. In Chapter 4 ("Can All Interpretation Make Some Kind of Difference?"), we'll see that it's unrealistic to think just anything called "interpretation" should necessarily be capable of making such differences. But in Chapter 5 ("Making a Difference on Purpose"), we'll consider evidence suggesting that interpreters can indeed increase their chances of making purposeful differences if they arm themselves with solid principles and apply them strategically in their design and delivery of interpretive products.

Chapters 6 and 7 focus on themes and the rationale behind thematic communication, which today is considered best practice in many parts of the world. In Chapter 6 ("Two Sides of Theme and Sentences in the Head"), we'll see that to harness the thematic approach to the best advantage requires us to understand not only a theme's value to an *interpreter* but also how a well-developed theme can impact an *audience's* thinking. In Chapter 7 ("Not All Themes Are Equal"), we'll see that the hallmark of a strong theme is that it alone provokes thought—even without further development. We'll see how strong and weak themes differ from one another and consider several ways interpreters can add interest and thought-provoking appeal to their themes.

Chapter 8 ("The Zone of Tolerance") presents what will probably be a new idea for many readers. In its simplest form, an interpreter's zone of tolerance is her or his subjective "happy zone." When you provoke an audience to think thoughts that make you happy (i.e., thoughts you're satisfied with), you can think of them as falling within your zone of tolerance. However, if people in your audience think thoughts you'd rather they didn't think (such as those that simply miss your point or those that are factually incorrect or which you find morally opposed to what you are trying to say), those thoughts fall outside your zone of tolerance. In this important chapter, we'll see that because the primary goal of interpretation is provoking audiences to think their own thoughts, being able to determine whether their thoughts fall predominantly within or outside your zone of tolerance is important—not only because it will tell you whether your interpretation is accomplishing what you want it to accomplish—but, even more important, because it will help you know how to improve it.

In the final two chapters of the book, we explore ways to develop a theme. In Chapter 9 ("Sequential Theme Development"), we consider the many communication strategies available to you when *you* (not the audience) determine the order of information they'll receive. Sequential theme development ordinarily applies to personal, face-to-face communication activities such as talks, oral presentations, and guided tours. In Chapter 10 ("Nonsequential Theme Development"), we consider strategies for developing themes through nonpersonal interpretive products such as exhibits, panels, posters, brochures, websites, and many smartphone apps. In this kind of theme development, individuals in the audience (not the interpreter) determine what they'll pay attention to and in what order. For this reason, the strategy for nonsequential theme development is necessarily much different from that for sequential communication.

In each chapter, you'll find selected words in **boldface**. These are glossary terms—words that require a formal definition. At the end of the book, you'll find a glossary containing these definitions. In addition, many of the chapters refer to one or more of four appendixes. For readers with advanced interests, Appendix 1 contains some additional detail about the two main theories that underpin thematic communication—the elaboration likelihood model of persuasion and the reasoned action model. These two theories are among the most applied and best substantiated theories in the history of communication science.

Appendix 2 contains around 2,500 interesting verbs—active, "visual" verbs—that you might use to strengthen not only your themes but also an entire interpretive commentary. Appendix 3 contains an example of a "thought-listing" procedure, which is a useful technique for exploring whether the thoughts your interpretation provokes lie within or outside your zone of tolerance. And finally, at the request of some of my colleagues in Spain, I've included in Appendix 4 an invited article I wrote a few years ago for the Spanish Association for Heritage Interpretation. It tells the story of how the idea of "captive" and "noncaptive" audiences first occurred to me some four decades ago.

It amazes me when I realize this book has been in the making for seven years. The ideas it contains have steadily evolved and thickened over that period in concert with the research that informs them. David Larsen remarked to me in one of our email exchanges a few years ago that "some readers will never see interpretation the same way after reading this book." I think he meant that in a good way. Anyone who knew David knows he often made bold proclamations that turned out to be true. I'm counting on this being another one of them. I hope you enjoy *Interpretation—Making a Difference on Purpose*. I doubt it will fundamentally change everything you know about the premise and promise of interpretation. But if it provokes you to think more deeply about ways to increase your own odds of making the kinds of differences you want to make, we'll both be happy.

Sam H. Ham
February 7, 2013
Moscow, Idaho, United States

Acknowledgments

When writing a book spans a seven-year period, you can bet it involved a lot of people. Indeed this one has. Some have read and commented on draft chapters, others have allowed me to bother them by phone or email to ask questions or explore issues, some have helped with photographs or illustrations, and still others have provided much-needed data or resource material. Literally dozens of colleagues from across the world have lent me their brilliance in the form of a comment that made me think, a reply to a question I hadn't considered, or a way of looking at something I especially appreciated and later adopted. To all of you goes my deepest gratitude. I could not have written this book without *you*.

The only person who has read literally *every* word, of *every* draft, of *every* chapter (and some suffered through as many as seventeen drafts) is my wife of four decades, Barbara. She was the *only* person I allowed to see the truly first draft of a chapter—mainly because she had such a nice way of telling me when to start over. But much more visible to readers will be the talent Barbara brought to the artistic design and layout of this book—struggling with me through dozens of decisions about placement, illustration, and visual flow. The result is beautiful and entirely a product of Barbara's critical eye and artistic sense. You are my best friend, the center of my life, and every bit as much a part of this book as I am. Like so many things, we've done this together.

Over a period of years, I entrusted a very small group of especially close colleagues to read and comment on early drafts of chapters I wasn't yet ready to share with the "outside" world. For these people, reviewing a chapter meant not only reading and commenting on one to several drafts but also following up with me by phone or email to work out problems or resolve questions they had raised. I took *significant* amounts of their time, and yet they gave it freely—in fact, enthusiastically—because they believed in what I was trying to do and took a personal interest in helping me get there. Needless to say, I'm deeply grateful to all of you (in alphabetical order): Lisa Brochu, Dave Bucy, Troy Hall, David Larsen, Tim Merriman, and Malcolm Montgomery. Your resonant responses to ideas that still needed help, and your encouragement to stay the course, played an important role in my completion of the manuscript. I'm indebted, to say the least.

Writing a book such as this one is ultimately a selfish act because it requires putting research and writing first, and everything else—including your family—second. I can't count the number of times I stole away during family events to work on the manuscript or attend to some other task related to this book. And I selfishly spent far too many nights and weekends in writer's hibernation when I could have been enjoying time with the people I care most about in life. To all of you, thank you once again for your understanding and for giving me the space I needed to finish this important project: my son, Jared Ham; my daughter, Alison Vega; my brother, Fred Ham; and three amazing grandchildren who have turned my life upside down in the best possible way—Maleia Ham, Vincent Vega, and Miles Vega—I'm happy to report that I'm now back full time.

An especially personal, heartfelt thanks goes to Susan Journell, who kindly provided the photo of her late husband, David Larsen, for my dedication page. Susan, David was a trusted friend and valued colleague. He also was perhaps the most brilliant interpreter I've ever had the pleasure to know. Thanks to your efforts, my book and his genius will be forever linked. As you know, it's how David and I both wanted it.

I'm deeply grateful to many colleagues from around the world who gave me their constructive criticisms of draft chapters and whose insightful suggestions led to important improvements in this manuscript. I want to extend special thanks to four colleagues who generously accepted my invitation to write special commentaries in three of the chapters: Larry Beck and Ted Cable (celebrated authors who wrote the invited commentary in Chapter 3), Shelton Johnson (acclaimed interpreter who authored the invited commentary in Chapter 2), and one of the world's most eloquent voices for sustainable travel, Sven-Olof Lindblad (owner of Lindblad Expeditions who authored the invited commentary in Chapter 5). Thanks to your generosity, my readers will find the ideas presented in those chapters much clearer and more poignant than they otherwise would have been.

Although literally hundreds of friends, colleagues, and former students have contributed something important to my work on this book, I want to single out a couple of groups that have figured into things in especially prominent ways. First among these is the amazing team of communicators in the Integrated Sustainability Services branch of the Townsville City Council in Queensland, Australia. Behind the extraordinary vision and leadership of Greg Bruce, a small but savvy band of thematic communication specialists is making an increasingly visible difference in the way people in that community think about sustainability and how it manifests itself every day in their lives. I've been nothing short of privileged to have been part of their journey the past many years. How incredibly gratifying it has been watching them take thematic communication principles and apply them in such an important context and at such a high level of professionalism.

I also want to thank my new colleagues at the Swedish Centre for Nature Interpretation (SCNI), both for inviting me to spend a couple of months a year for the next three years working with them and for their keen interest in my work. I owe all of you a debt of gratitude not only for reviewing drafts of several chapters but also for convening truly stimulating discussions around those ideas. The SCNI is based at the Swedish University of Agricultural Sciences in Uppsala, as part of one of Europe's strongest academic programs in environmental communication. Thank you, one and all (in alphabetical order): Anders Arnell, Lars Hallgren, Eva Sandberg, Per Sonnvik, and Nadarajah (Sri) Sriskandarajah.

Along the way, many colleagues offered not only their time but much needed photographs and other images—many of which I've included in the book to illustrate or punctuate key ideas. Among these organizations and individuals, I'm especially indebted to (in alphabetical order): Abu Dhabi Tourism and Culture Authority (with special thanks to Ahmed Abdulla Al Mehairbi and Michelle Sabti), Arkansas State Parks (with special thanks to Kelly Farrell), California Academy of Sciences (with special thanks to April Rand), Lindblad-National Geographic Expeditions (with special thanks to Pamela Fingleton, Bennett Goldberg and Scott Kish), Monterey Bay Aquarium (with special thanks to Jim Covel and Kris Ingram), National Association for Interpretation (with special thanks to Paul Caputo), Ochre Learning (with special thanks to John Pastorelli), Parks Canada (with special thanks to Cal Martin and Annique Maheu), Susan Strauss Storyteller (thank you, Susan!), The Shannon Company (with special thanks to Michael Daddo), The Sovereign Hill Museums Association (with special thanks to Glenn Bishop, Barry Kay, and Tim Sullivan), US National Park Service (with special thanks to Dominic Cardea, Stephen Geiger, Bolly Helekahi, Shelton Johnson, Walter Pu, Jay Robinson, and Becky Wiles), and VolcanoDiscovery Hawai'i (with special thanks to Erik Storm, Malia Storm, and photographer Arthur Wierzchos). And finally, I want to thank my friend, colleague, and fellow wine enthusiast, Ron Force, for providing the image from Copán Ruins in Chapter 7.

I am also indebted to Dr. Tom Mullin, Elizabeth Hammack, and their terrific students—respectively at Unity College (Maine, USA) and West Valley College (California, USA)—for giving a draft of this manuscript a "dry-run" in the months just before it went to print. Tom and Elizabeth, thanks for your offer to do this. Although the book is aimed at a broad cross section of readers, including those at intermediate and advanced skill levels, I also want it to connect well with beginning interpreters. Your invitation to give it a go in your introductory interpretation classes helped make sure I wasn't missing that mark. I *know* the book is better as a result. I am forever grateful.

Many more friends and colleagues have helped immeasurably along the way. To each and every one of you go my deepest thanks (affiliations, in most cases, are the ones that were current at the time the individual's contribution was made):

James Absher, USDA Forest Service, USA; **Christiana Admiral**, National Park Service, USA; **Icek Ajzen**, University of Massachusetts, USA; **Melanie Alguire**, Parks Canada; **Adrian Arias**, James Cook University, Australia; **Alberto de Armas Estévez**, Spain; **Dawood Abdulkareem Alwadi**, Saudi Commission for Tourism and Antiquities, Kingdom of Saudi Arabia; **Idelfonso de los Angeles**, National Botanical Garden, Dominican Republic; **Ketut Yudha Anthara**, guide, Bali, Indonesia; **Benoît Aquin**, Parks Canada; **Gregorio Arencibia**, Arqueocanaria S.L., Spain; **Heather Armstrong**, University of Idaho, USA; **Arne Arnberger**, University of Hannover, Germany; **Anders Arnell**, Swedish Centre for Nature Interpretation, Sweden; **Carl Atkinson**, Countryside Council for Wales, UK; **Ana Báez**, Turismo and Conservación Consultores, Costa Rica; **Eduardo Báez**, Secretariat of Tourism, Dominican Republic; **Ann Baillie**, Museums Australia, Australia; **Roy Ballantyne**, University of Queensland, Australia; **Juliane Bauszus**, Department of Conservation, New Zealand; **Larry Beck**, San Diego State University, USA; **Gabriela Benito**, University of Hawai'i-Hilo, USA; **Dan Benjamin**, Parks Canada; **William Bevil**, Fort Collins Museum of Discovery, USA; **Glenn Bishop**, The Sovereign Hill Museums Association, Australia; **Rosemary Black**, Charles Sturt University, Australia; **Ariel Blotkamp**, National Park Service, USA; **Ovini Bokinin**, Tavua Town Council, Fiji; **Richard Bottger**, University of Idaho, USA; **Judy Braus**, National Audubon Society, USA; **Lisa Brochu**, National Association for Interpretation, USA; **Kathy Brown**, National Park Service, USA; **Terry Brown**, Griffith University, Australia; **Greg Bruce**, Townsville City Council, Australia; **Dave Bucy**, Dave Bucy Associates, USA; **Tamara Budowski**, Horizonte Tours, Costa Rica; **Robert Burns**, University of Hannover, Germany;

Lee Burton, Queensland Indigenous Family Violence Legal Service, Australia; **Ray Burton**, Townsville City Council, Australia; **Trey Byus**, Lindblad Expeditions, USA; **Ted Cable**, Kansas State University, USA; **Amy Cadge Berquist**, Lindblad Expeditions, USA; **Brian Cahill**, California State Parks, USA; **Roz Cameron**, Charles Darwin Research Station, Ecuador; **Doug Capra**, National Park Service, USA; **Paul Caputo**, National Association for Interpretation, USA; **Dominic Cardea**, National Park Service, USA; **James Carter**, communication consultant, Edinburgh, Scotland, UK; **Beth Case**, University of Idaho, USA; **Catherin Cattafesta**, International Resources Group, Dominican Republic; **Eric Cline**, Lakehead University, Canada; **Theresa Coble**, Stephen F. Austin State University, USA; **Fiona Colquhoun**, Department of Conservation, New Zealand; **Kerry Cooper**, New South Wales National Parks and Wildlife, Australia; **Jim Covel**, Monterey Bay Aquarium, USA; **Peter Crane**, Cairngorms National Park Authority, Scotland, UK; **Ian Cruickshank**, Ergon Energy, Australia; **John Cunning**, Missouri State Parks, USA; **Jim Curtis**, Monash University, Australia; **Michael Daddo**, The Shannon Company, Australia; **Ron Dale**, Parks Canada; **Jean Devlin**, Pennsylvania State Parks, USA; **Jan Dook**, University of Western Australia; **Scott Eckert**, Fish and Wildlife Service, USA; **Mike Edginton**, Department of Conservation, New Zealand; **Steve Edwards**, Conservation International, Ecuador; **Betsey Ellerbroek**, Columbia River Maritime Museum, USA; **Claire Ellis**, Tourism Tasmania, Australia; **Cristina Simó Espinosa**, Association for Heritage Interpretation, Spain; **John Falk**, Oregon State University, USA; **John Farrell**, Federal Hotels and Resorts, Australia; **Kelly Farrell**, Arkansas State Parks, USA; **Sue Ellen Fast**, Interpretation Canada, Canada; **James Fazio**, University of Idaho, USA; **Rich Fedorchak**, National Park Service, USA; **Fen Luo**, Central South University of Forestry and Technology, China; **Fidelina Fernández**, Secretariat of Environment and Natural Resources, Dominican Republic; **Gil Field**, Western Australia Department of Conservation and Land Management, Australia; **Pamela Fingleton**, Lindblad Expeditions, USA; **Martin Fishbein**, US Centers for Disease Control, USA; **Phil Fitzpatrick**, Hierophant Communications, Australia; **Juan Flaim**, Lindblad Expeditions, USA; **Ron Force**, Moscow, Idaho, USA; **Jennifer Fry**, Parks and Wildlife Tasmania, Australia; **Dylan Furnell**, Townsville City Council, Australia; **Jim Gale**, National Park Service, USA; **Kathy Gatenby**, Tourism Tasmania, Australia; **Stephen Geiger**, National Park Service, USA; **Michael Glen**, Touchstone Heritage Management and Interpretation, UK; **Owen Glendening**, National World War II Museum, USA; **Bennett Goldberg**, Lindblad Expeditions, USA; **Peter Grant**, Parks and Wildlife Tasmania, Australia; **Guo Xiren (Daniel)**, Guidemap Pty., China; **Julie Haar**, University of Idaho, USA; **Evan Hall**, Leilani's on the Beach, USA; **James Hall**, Northwest Linen, USA; **Jill Hall**, Northwest Linen, USA; **Patricia Hall**, Family Matriarch, USA; **Robert**

Hall, Family Patriarch, USA; **Troy Hall**, University of Idaho, USA; **Lars Hallgren**, Swedish University of Agriculture Sciences, Sweden; **Barbara Ham**, University of Idaho, USA; **Jared Ham**, Young's Market Company, USA; **Elizabeth Hammack**, California State Parks, USA; **Anne Hardy**, University of Northern British Columbia, Canada; **Pamela Harmon-Price**, Queensland Parks and Wildlife Service, Australia; **Julie Harris**, Sustainability Victoria, Australia; **Melissa Hartley**, University of Idaho, USA; **Julie Heath**, Ergon Energy, Australia; **John Hecht**, Bureau of Reclamation, USA; **Bolly Helekahi**, National Park Service, USA; **Olga Garcia Hernández**, Association for Heritage Interpretation, Spain; **William Darío Hernández**, Secretariat of Environment and Natural Resources, Dominican Republic; **Kristy Hewitt**, Parks Canada; **Phil Hewitt**, Texas Parks and Wildlife Department, USA; **Pat Hine**, University of Idaho, USA; **Steven Hollenhorst**, University of Idaho, USA; **Jon Hooper**, Chico State University, USA; **Sarah Hopkins**, Pennsylvania State Parks, USA; **Anna Housego**, Communication Consultant, Australia; **Karen Hughes**, University of Queensland, Australia; **Sven Hultman**, Swedish Care Dog Training School, Sweden; **Will Husby**, EcoLeaders Consulting, Canada; **José Infante**, Secretariat of Environment and Natural Resources, Dominican Republic; **Kris Ingram**, Monterey Bay Aquarium, USA; **Jane James**, Flinders University, Australia; **Frida Jaremark**, Tyresta National Park, Sweden; **Cindy Johnson**, University of Idaho, USA; **Shelton Johnson**, National Park Service, USA; **Bradley Jorgensen**, La Trobe University, Australia; **Susan Journell**, Loudoun County Public Schools, USA; **Susan Jurasz**, Sea Reach Ltd., USA; **Nopparat Kaipeth**, Department of Marine and Coastal Resources, Thailand; **William Kaschak**, International Resources Group, Dominican Republic; **Barry (Baz) Kay**, The Sovereign Hill Museums Association, Australia; **Scott Kish**, National Geographic Expeditions, USA; **Jon Kohl**, PUP Global Heritage Consortium and University of Costa Rica; **Ed Krumpe**, University of Idaho, USA; **Mathew Lachesnez-Heude**, Lindblad Expeditions, USA; **Brenda Lackey**, University of Wisconsin-Stevens Point, USA; **Allison LaDuke**, National Park Service, USA; **David Larsen**, National Park Service, USA; **Rebecca Lee**, Townsville City Council, Australia; **Stuart Lennox**, Tasmania Parks and Wildlife Service, Australia; **Deb Lewis**, Tourism Tasmania, Australia; **William Lewis**, University of Vermont, USA; **Mavi Lezcano**, Association for Heritage Interpretation, Spain; **Sven-Olof Lindblad**, Lindblad Expeditions, USA; **Emilio Molero López-Barajas**, Jaén County Council, Spain; **Bob Loudon**, USDA Forest Service, USA; **Thorsten Ludwig**, Bildungswerk Interpretation and Interpret Europe, Germany; **Annique Maheu**, Parks Canada; **Lisa Malouf**, New South Wales National Parks and Wildlife, Australia; **Mauricio Manzione**, National Park Service, Argentina; **Julie Marshall**, Federal Hotels and Resorts, Australia; **Antonia Marte**, Secretariat of Environment and Natural Resources, Dominican Republic; **Cal Martin**, national chair,

Interpretation Canada, Canada; **John Martin**, La Trobe University, Australia; **Luz del Carmen Martínez**, Secretariat of Environment and Natural Resources, Dominican Republic; **Rosendo Martínez**, National Protected Areas Center, Cuba; **Charles (Corky) Mayo**, National Park Service, USA; **Nicky McKibben**, Tourism Tasmania, Australia; **Debbie McLaughlin**, University of Idaho, USA; **Tom Medema**, National Park Service, USA; **Ahmed Abdulla Al Mehairbi**, Abu Dhabi Tourism and Culture Authority, United Arab Emirates; **Tim Merriman**, National Association for Interpretation, USA; **Jay Miller**, Arkansas State Parks, USA; **Malcolm Montgomery**, Washington State University, USA; **Jorge Morales**, Heritage Interpretation Consultant, Spain; **Gianna Moscardo**, James Cook University, Australia; **Matilde Mota**, Secretariat of Environment and Natural Resources, Dominican Republic; **Bradley Muir**, Parks Canada; **Tom Mullin**, Unity College, USA; **Ralph Naess**, City of Seattle, USA; **Rosalind Newlands**, World Federation of Tourist Guides Associations, Scotland, UK; **Eliezer Nieves**, University of Puerto Rico, Puerto Rico; **Patrycja O'Brien**, Lindblad Expeditions, Spain; **Tom O'Brien**, Lindblad Expeditions, Spain; **Clara Olagüe**, Association for Heritage Interpretation, Spain; **Paul Ollig**, National Park Service, USA; **Jerry Ostermiller**, Columbia River Maritime Museum, USA; **Adam Paredes**, Secretariat of Environment and Natural Resources, Dominican Republic; **Joy Passanante**, University of Idaho, USA; **John Pastorelli**, Ochre Learning, Australia; **Katie Payne**, University of Idaho, USA; **Virginia Pina**, Association for Heritage Interpretation, Spain; **Primoz Pipan**, University of Primovska, Slovenia; **Santo Alejandro Plata**, Secretariat of Environment and Natural Resources, Dominican Republic; **Robert Powell**, Clemson University, USA; **Walter Pu**, National Park Service, USA; **Jim Quiring**, USDA Forest Service, USA; **Nunila Ramírez**, CDEEE, Dominican Republic; **Fernando Ramos**, INECO, Spain; **April Rand**, California Academy of Sciences, USA; **Jim Reece**, University of Idaho, USA; **Peter Reedijk**, Sea Reach, Ltd., USA; **Emma Ridley**, Lindblad Expeditions, Ecuador; **Scott Riener**, University of Idaho, USA; **Jay Robinson**, National Park Service, USA; **Mark Robinson**, Townsville City Council, Australia; **Joe Roggenbuck**, Virginia Tech University, USA; **Kerri Rollins**, Larimer County Department of Natural Resources, USA; **Bolívar de la Rosa**, Punta Cana Ecological Foundation, Dominican Republic; **Ethan Rotman**, IspeakEASY, USA; **Matthew Rowe**, Loan Solutions, USA; **Nancy Rowe**, Heartwood Extended Healthcare, USA; **Robert Rowe**, Heartwood Extended Healthcare, USA; **William Rowe**, Heartwood Extended Healthcare, USA; **Michelle Sabti**, Abu Dhabi Tourism and Culture Authority, United Arab Emirates; **Wendy Sailors**, Alaska Wilderness Recreation and Tourism Association, USA; **David Salisbury**, James Cook University, Australia; **Vickie Salisbury**, Umbrella Studios, Australia; **Eva Sandberg**, Swedish Centre for Nature Interpretation, Sweden; **Elizabeth Sande**, South Peace Centennial Museum,

Canada; **Gloria Santana**, Secretariat of Environment and Natural Resources, Dominican Republic; **Nick Sanyal**, University of Idaho, USA; **David Saunders**, Parks Canada; **Claire Savage**, Savagely Creative, Australia; **Pam Scaggs**, Texas Parks and Wildlife Department, USA; **Kara Scharbach**, University of Idaho, USA; **Laurie Schwartz**, Parks Canada; **Fred Sheppard**, Parks Canada; **John Shultis**, University of Northern British Columbia, Canada; **Kim Sikoryak**, National Park Service, USA; **Fernando Silva**, Institute for the Suarez Canal, Puerto Rico; **Ken Soderberg**, Montana State Parks, USA; **Liam Smith**, Monash University, Australia; **Gerry Snyder**, Kansas State University, USA; **Per Sonnvik**, Swedish Centre for Nature Interpretation, Sweden; **Rita Spadafora**, US Agency for International Development, Panama; **Celese Spencer**, University of Washington, USA; **Jeremy Spoon**, Oregon State University, USA; **Nadarajah (Sri) Sriskandarajah**, Swedish University of Agriculture Sciences, Sweden; **Paulina Starkey**, National Park Service, USA; **Patricia Stokowski**, University of Vermont, USA; **Erik Storm**, VolcanoDiscovery Hawai'i, USA; **Malia Storm**, VolcanoDiscovery Hawai'i, USA; **Linda Strand**, Colorado Open Space Alliance, USA; **Susan Strauss**, Susan Strauss Storyteller, USA; **Marc Stern**, Virginia Tech University, USA; **Tim Sullivan**, The Sovereign Hill Museums Association, Australia; **Damien Sweeney**, Swinburne University of Technology, Australia; **Paula Tagle**, Lindblad Expeditions, Ecuador; **Bill Taylor**, Heritage Tourism Consultant, Norway and Scotland; **Jonathan Tourtellot**, National Geographic Society, USA; **Adrian Turnbull**, Warringah Council, Australia; **John Van Miert,** Dunkin and Bush Inc., USA; **Kelsey Van Miert**, Anderson Daymon Worldwide, USA; **Debbie Van Winkle**, National Park Service, USA; **Faustina Varela**, Secretariat of Environment and Natural Resources, Dominican Republic; **Alison Vega**, Ascent Audiology, USA; **Vern Veitch**, Townsville City Council, Australia; **Tracey Verishine**, Parks Canada; **Vàngelis Villar**, Association for Heritage Interpretation, Spain; **Maria Jose Viñals**, Universidad Politécnica de Valencia, Spain; **Eick von Ruschkowski**, University of Hannover, Germany; **Frank Wadsworth**, USDA Forest Service, Puerto Rico; **Per Wallsten**, Tyresta National Park, Sweden; **Carolyn Ward**, Blue Ridge Parkway Foundation, USA; **Betty Weiler**, Southern Cross University, Australia; **Kelly Wendland**, University of Idaho, USA; **Arthur Wierzchos**, VolcanoDiscovery Hawai'i, USA; **Rebecca Wiles**, National Park Service, USA; **Gary Williams**, University of Idaho, USA; **Lars Wohlers**, University of Lüneburg, Germany; **Homer Wu**, National Taichung University of Education, Taiwan; **Naoko Yamada**, Pusan National University, South Korea; **Natalia Zamora**, Instituto Nacional de Biodiversidad, Costa Rica; **Catherine Zehr**, Ballets with a Twist, USA; **Ron Zimmerman**, University of Wisconsin-Stevens Point, USA.

Organizations That Contributed

I also want to thank the many organizations that in one way or another contributed to the writing of this book. I'm grateful for your help:

Abu Dhabi Tourism and Culture Authority, United Arab Emirates; Arkansas State Parks, Little Rock, AR, USA; Asociación para la Interpretación del Patrimonio, Spain; California Academy of Sciences, San Francisco, CA, USA; California State Parks, Sacramento, CA, USA; Columbia River Maritime Museum, Astoria, OR, USA; Dave Bucy Associates, Corvallis, OR, USA; Department of Conservation, Wellington, New Zealand; Ergon Energy, Townsville, QLD, Australia; Fort Collins Museum of Discovery, Fort Collins, CO, USA; Interpretation Australia; Interpretation Canada, Red Deer, AB, Canada; Lindblad Expeditions, New York, NY and Seattle, WA, USA; Melbourne Zoos, Melbourne, Australia; Monash Sustainability Institute, Melbourne, Australia; Monterey Bay Aquarium, Monterey, CA, USA; Museums Australia, Canberra, ACT, Australia; Museum of New Zealand, Te Papa Tongarewa, Wellington, New Zealand; National Association for Interpretation, Fort Collins, CO, USA; National Geographic Expeditions, Washington, DC, USA; National Geographic Society, Washington, DC, USA; National World War II Museum, New Orleans, LA, USA; New South Wales National Parks and Wildlife, Sydney, NSW, Australia; Northwest Trek Wildlife Park, Eatonville, WA, USA; Ochre Learning, Sydney, NSW, Australia; Parks Canada, Cornwall, ON, Canada; Sea Reach, Ltd., Sheridan, OR, USA; The Sovereign Hill Museums Association, Ballarat, VIC, Australia; Susan Strauss Storyteller, Bend, OR, USA; Sustainability Victoria, Melbourne, VIC, Australia; Swedish University of Agricultural Sciences, Uppsala, Sweden; Swedish Centre for Nature Interpretation, Uppsala, Sweden; Tasmania Parks and Wildlife Service, Hobart, Tasmania, Australia; The Shannon Company, Melbourne, VIC, Australia; Tourism Tasmania, Hobart, TAS, Australia; Townsville City Council, Townsville, QLD, Australia; Tyresta National Park, Sweden; University of Hannover, Institute of Environmental Planning, Hannover, Germany; Unity College, Unity, ME, USA; University of Idaho, Moscow, ID, USA; USDA Forest Service, Washington, DC, USA; US Fish and Wildlife Service; Washington, DC, USA; US National Park Service, Washington, DC, USA; VolcanoDiscovery Hawai'i, Volcano, HI, USA; Wadi El Gamal National Park, Marsa Alam, Egypt; West Valley College, Department of Parks Management, Saratoga, CA, USA.

CHAPTER 1
Interpretation and Communication

Interpretation attempts to communicate in a thought-provoking way to an audience that's completely free to ignore it.

Interpretation is simply an approach to communication. Like all forms of communication (for example, teaching, advertising, or political campaigning), we can define interpretation according to the places or contexts in which it usually occurs, the kinds of audiences it's trying to reach, and the types of outcomes it aims to produce.[1] Interpretation traditionally involves communication with a pleasure-seeking audience in such places as museums, parks, historic sites, zoos, aquariums, and botanical gardens as well as on cruise ships, in wineries, breweries, cheese and chocolate factories, and just about any place visitors go to have a good time and possibly learn something of interest. But in recent years, the practice of interpretation has been applied in many other ways that have little to do with tourism or leisure (e.g., municipal sustainability programs, marketing, advertising, and philanthropy campaigns).

In the interpretation field, we frequently refer to our audiences as "visitors," but this isn't always the case (as when the audience consists of households or businesses, someone surfing the web at home or reading a travel guide prior to visiting a place). Obviously, interpretation can reach many audiences right in their own communities, not just those that are "visiting" someplace. Still, it's their openness to learning (an intellectual and sometimes emotional dimension of their experience) that sets audiences of interpretation apart from most others.

Although the outcomes we hope to produce through interpretation can vary widely, they usually involve at a minimum enhancing someone's experiences. This happens, for example, when park visitors make personal connections to the places, features, or ideas someone interprets for them. The more they're stimulated to think about things, the more connections they make, and the deeper their experience with those things is. Most interpreters I know consider this interpretation's highest purpose.

Another outcome of interest to a lot of interpreters is audiences having a positive attitude about the things that are interpreted for them (e.g., the place, feature, concept, and so on). Often interpretation strives to leave its audiences with an appreciation or positive evaluation of something. This "something" might be the organization or agency that manages the place (i.e., good public relations), but it also almost always includes appreciation of the things that were interpreted (the historic place or person, the time period or era, the valley or mountain, the river, the plant community, the geologic history, the wine, or the wildlife). People in the interpretation profession often refer to this sort of appreciative attitude as caring (Larsen, 2003), although similar terms such as mattering, liking, or even loving are sometimes used. Central

Interpretation's highest purpose—provoking thought. *Photo courtesy of the Monterey Bay Aquarium, USA.*

to this outcome of interpretation is the goal of facilitating some sort of emotional or affective response within the visitor.

A third but less common outcome of interpretation is behavioral. Among the visitors to interpretive settings, we sometimes encounter a special subset of people whose behavior is somehow at odds with management or protection objectives. Sometimes a relatively few visitors do things that cause damage to protected resources or fragile settings, and other times they may unknowingly put themselves in danger. When their actions are due mainly to naïveté, misinformation, or misconception, we often use interpretation in the form of persuasive communication to promote proper or preferred behavior.

These three outcomes of interpretation (enhancing experiences, facilitating appreciation, and influencing behavior) are closely related, and together they define the kinds of differences interpretation is capable of making. As we'll see in later chapters, there's a sequence to them that is underpinned by quite a lot of research on how communication affects human beings. The first person to highlight the steps in this sequence was Freeman Tilden (1957: 38) whose phrase "through interpretation, understanding; through understanding, appreciation; through appreciation, protection" has become nothing short of a mantra for practicing interpretation professionals around the world.

As I've pointed out elsewhere (Ham, 2009a), only in the half century following Tilden's bold claim has the research evidence behind his assertion actually materialized (an indication, perhaps, that he was well ahead of his time). Yet studies today do indeed show that when people are able to make their own connections (e.g., enhancing visitors' experiences), they're inclined to appreciate one way or another what was interpreted (positive attitudes), and when they have an appreciative attitude about something, they're likely—when given the opportunity—to act toward it in a respectful or protective way (appropriate behavior). As the US National Park Service (2012) aptly put it: "People will only care *for* what they first care *about*."

Three Important Terms

So who actually does interpretation? In this book, I'll call them **interpreters**. I use "interpreter" to refer to anyone who does *any* kind of interpretive work through *any* communication medium (face-to-face or nonpersonal). Among these are speakers, writers, designers, and artists; employees of or volunteers for parks, zoos, museums, historic sites, tour operators, cruise ship companies, science centers, gardens, forests, aquariums, wineries, breweries, theme parks, and manufacturing plants; as well as guides, expedition leaders, docents, storytellers, composers,

Interpreter—
anyone who
does any kind
of interpretation

*Interpretive
encounter—*
any act of
interpretation

*Interpretive
product—*
any finished
interpretive
program or device

dramatists, directors, actors, and performers of all kinds. Whew, that's quite a list. And, if nothing else, it reflects the sheer diversity of the interpretation profession across the world.

I'll use the term **interpretive encounter** to refer to any *act* of interpretation—both personal (face-to-face) and non-personal (self-guided)—in order to avoid continually repeating these two possibilities. Interpretive encounters happen at the point of communication. They can involve a park interpreter talking or interacting with one or more visitors; they can occur while a person surfs the web at home; they take place when a motorist stops to read a wayside exhibit, when a museum visitor ponders a display, or through virtually any communication medium aimed at achieving one of the three outcomes earlier described. How interpretive encounters can be orchestrated to produce these outcomes is the topic of this book.

Finally, I'll use the term **interpretive product** to mean any finished interpretive program or device. A museum theatrical performance is an interpretive product; a community sustainability education event is an interpretive product; a park ranger's evening program is an interpretive product; a tour through a wildlife park is an interpretive product; and displays, smartphone apps, wayside exhibits, brochures, information kiosks, and websites are all interpretive products, too. Interpretive encounters take place whenever the product is being delivered to an actual audience.

A Working Definition of Interpretation

I said at the beginning of this chapter that interpretation is an approach to communication. I'll outline in more detail what this approach entails later in this chapter, but for now the term *interpretation* is probably new to some readers and needs a working definition. The first author to define interpretation formally was Freeman Tilden (1957: 8) in his classic, *Interpreting Our Heritage*. Tilden wasn't a scientist, a naturalist, a historian, or a technician of any kind. Rather, he was a journalist, playwright, and philosopher. He was not academically grounded in history,

(a)

(b)

(c)

(d)

(e)

Examples of face-to-face interpretive products: (a) museum docent presentation, Hands On Childrens Museum (Olympia), USA. *Photo by Barbara Ham*; (b) interpretive theater. *Courtesy of Sovereign Hill Museums Association, Australia*; (c) storytelling performance. *Courtesy of Susan Strauss Storyteller, USA*; (d) visitor information desk encounter, Haleakala National Park, USA. *Photo by Barbara Ham*; (e) guided nature walk. *Courtesy of Arkansas State Parks, USA*.

(a)

(b)

(c)

(d)

(e)

Examples of nonpersonal interpretive products:
(a) interpretive brochures. *Photo by Barbara Ham*;
(b) interpretive website. *Photo by Barbara Ham*; (c)
interpretive wayside exhibit, Haleakala National Park,
USA. *Photo by Barbara Ham*; (d) science center exhibit.
Courtesy of California Academy of Sciences, USA; (e)
interpretive smartphone app. *Photo by Barbara Ham.*

biology, or the physical sciences—frequent subjects of interpretive programs—but he was an unusually sensitive person with a profound intuitive understanding of how humans communicate best. This understanding guided his view of interpretation, which he defined as

> an educational activity which aims to reveal meanings and relationships through the use of original objects, by firsthand experience, and by illustrative media, rather than simply to communicate factual information.

As his definition suggests, Tilden saw interpretation as an approach to communicating in which the primary aim is the construction of meanings and the revelation of relationships in the visitor's mind rather than the mastering of isolated facts and figures. Although any interpreter will use factual information to illustrate points and clarify meanings, according to Tilden, it's the points and meanings that interpreters should care about most—not the facts.

It sometimes escapes the casual reader of *Interpreting Our Heritage* that Tilden's definition was not saying that it's the interpreter who does the "revealing of meanings and relationships." On the contrary, he was making the case that the interpreter's role is one of facilitating or stimulating visitors to make these connections for themselves. In his view, the meanings and relationships are self-revealed in visitors' minds as a result of the thinking that good interpretation can provoke them to do—rather than somehow being "put" there by the fact-bearing interpreter. Tilden saw in the 1950s what it took nearly three decades of research to demonstrate later: that the only meanings a visitor can attach to a place, thing, or concept are those that he or she makes in his or her own mind. The interpreter's job, as he saw it, is to orchestrate and catalyze the thinking—what he called "provocation." We'll give special attention to this idea in Chapter 3 ("The Endgame of Interpretation") and will return to it repeatedly throughout the book.

In the fifty years following the publication of *Interpreting Our Heritage*, a number of other definitions of interpretation have made Tilden's meaning-making view of things even more explicit. I think the best of these is the one advanced by the National Association for Interpretation (NAI):[2]

> Interpretation is a mission-based communication process that forges emotional and intellectual connections between the interests of the audience and meanings inherent in the resource.

Although philosophers and wordsmiths might debate this or that word choice, what's significant about NAI's definition is that it clearly distinguishes interpretation from other forms of communication. Most important is its emphasis on connection making and the audience, since these two elements are at the heart of the difference interpretation can make, at least if it's done well. The definition is consistent with dozens of studies that have demonstrated that the more an audience is provoked to do its own thinking and make its own connections, the stronger and more enduring their attitudes about related things will be as a result (see Ham, 2009a and 2007 for reviews of some of this research). So, as NAI's definition says, connection making is the single most important outcome of interpretation. In addition, NAI has taken the necessary step of linking the role of interpretation to the missions of the organizations that provide interpretive services. This makes interpretation core business for these organizations and not simply an add-on customer entertainment function as it has sometimes erroneously been seen.

Therefore, taking the heart of NAI's definition and applying it explicitly to Tilden's focus on provocation, I've adopted the following working definition of **interpretation** for this book:

> Interpretation is a mission-based approach to communication aimed at provoking in audiences the discovery of personal meaning and the forging of personal connections with things, places, people, and concepts.

For the purposes of the chapters that lie ahead, this definition captures what I believe makes interpretation both different from other forms of information transfer and deserving of special treatment in a book such as this one. First, it's a way of communicating—an *approach*—that is necessary given the settings in which interpretation is normally practiced and the mindset of the pleasure-seeking audiences that are reachable there. Second, it follows NAI's lead in seeing interpretation as purposeful and relevant within an organization's core mission. Third, it's consistent with Tilden's and NAI's notion that the hallmark of successful interpretation lies in the *thoughts, meanings, and connections* made in the audience's minds. And finally, it makes clear that the meanings and connections we're most interested in are those that pertain to the things interpreters actually show and explain to their audiences.

Interpretation versus Formal Instruction

You'll notice that all three of these definitions (Tilden's, NAI's, and mine) clearly set interpretation apart from traditional instruction. In the classroom, the teacher's goal sometimes is to communicate facts alone, a process necessary in the long-term education of students.[3] In interpretation, however, the facts are a means to an end, rather than the end itself. Interpreters carefully select and present only those facts that help the audience relate to and appreciate what they're trying to show or explain. In instruction, presenting facts may sometimes be the teacher's ultimate objective; in interpretation, it virtually never is. Carefully selected facts can be supportive, illustrative, and illuminating—but they're rarely ends in themselves. In interpretation, as we'll see shortly, our bigger goal is to communicate a message—a message that answers the question "so what?" or "big deal?" with regard to the factual information we've chosen to present. In this respect, there's always a "moral" to an interpreter's story. We'll return to this idea in much more detail in Chapters 2 and 6.

One of the difficulties some interpreters have is understanding that their job is not to "teach" their audiences in the same sense they were taught in school. Many interpreters enter their jobs without formal training or prior experience, and they're understandably unsure just how they should approach their role as communicators. The only role models many interpreters have are their former teachers. There is nothing inherently wrong with this because there are some very good teachers, but as we shall see, communication methods appropriate in the classroom may not always be acceptable to audiences outside of the formal education system.

> Interpretation is a mission-based approach to communication aimed at provoking in audiences the discovery of personal meaning and the forging of personal connections with things, places, people and concepts.

Some of You Might Remember This Guy

Mr. Jones (Figure 1-1) made his public debut in 1992 when I chose him as a figurehead for explaining what I called the "interpretive approach to communication." Some of you might recall that he's a secondary school science teacher during the school year and works as a park interpreter every summer. Mr. Jones is fascinated with rocks and minerals and tends to emphasize them in his science classes as well as in his talks at the park.

Notice Mr. Jones's classroom teaching methods. He tells his students to read from a geology book, so they'll learn terms he feels they should know in order to identify several kinds of rocks. Among these terms are *cleavage, silicates, tetrahedral bonding, volcanism, metamorphosis,* and *sedimentation.* Whether or not you know much about rocks, you might agree that these are important terms for Mr. Jones to teach his students. He also gives lectures using his extensive notes, and he writes and draws a lot on a whiteboard. Meanwhile, the students know it's their role to copy the material from the whiteboard and take notes on everything Mr. Jones says during his lectures. There will be an exam soon, and they'll be expected to know everything they've read and everything Mr. Jones has said. In other words, the students will have to demonstrate to Mr. Jones that they remember the facts he taught them about rocks. But they don't mind; although Mr. Jones demands a lot of work from them, he's a nice man, he tells a lot of jokes in class, and he gives fair exams. Most students enjoy his classes.

Now look at Mr. Jones, the interpreter. He likes to give talks about geology to visitors at the park. He photocopies pages from the geology book—the same pages his students read—so that the people in his audiences can learn terms such as cleavage, *silicates, tetrahedral bonding, sedimentation*, and the rest. He passes these out to the visitors and then presents his talk using a portable whiteboard he borrowed from the school. He didn't have to work too hard preparing the talk because he was able to rely on some of the lecture notes he uses in his classes. The only trouble is that, unlike his students who usually enjoy his lectures, the park visitors attending his talks always seem bored. Mr. Jones can't understand why. He decides that people who visit

Figure 1-1. *Contrasting formal education and interpretation. Drawings by Jeff Egan.*

his park simply aren't interested in rocks, and he considers changing the topic of his talk to something that would interest them more.

The problem, of course, wasn't with the visitors and certainly not with the topic. No topic is inherently boring or interesting. There are only people who make them that way. Mr. Jones's problem was that he failed to understand that what made Mr. Jones, the teacher, effective would not necessarily make Mr. Jones, the interpreter, effective. He needed a different approach for the park visitors. As we'll see, they were a different kind of audience than his students, and Mr. Jones needed to change his communication methods to suit his audience.

Captive versus Noncaptive Audiences

Let's further analyze the problem in Figure 1-1, this time in terms of the audience Mr. Jones is trying to communicate with in each setting. It's probably already clear to you that his error at the park was that he treated his audience like students. Why should this make a difference? Are his students different kinds of people from visitors at the park? If some of his students attended his talk at the park, would they be interested in his presentation even when the rest of the audience wasn't? The answer is probably not.

People act according to the environment or situation they're in. Where we are influences much of our behavior, including how we talk, how we conduct ourselves, what we're interested in, and what kinds of behavior we expect from other people. If you and a close friend were at the beach together, you'd behave and expect others to behave much differently than if the two of you were in a place of worship, at a restaurant, or at a wedding. Your ideas about what's interesting, funny, out of place, and so forth would probably be very different in each of these settings. What might seem funny at the beach or restaurant, for example, might seem terribly inappropriate at the place of worship or the wedding. In the classroom, Mr. Jones's students expect certain kinds of behavior from him—behaviors that are consistent with his role as Mr. Jones, the teacher. But at the park, they'd expect a different Mr. Jones. The reason is that, at the park, the students probably don't see themselves as students but rather as *visitors*.

Interpreters who understand why and how audiences such as these differ, and even more important, how to tailor communication methods to suit them, have a distinct advantage over interpreters who don't. Although there are many physical differences in the two settings, there's one overriding *psychological* difference. The classroom is a setting in which the audience has to pay attention. The park is one in which it doesn't.

Boiled down to a single defining characteristic, it may be said that the students in the classroom are a **captive audience** because they're forced to stay and pay attention if they want to get good grades or avoid the trauma of getting poor ones. They've come to expect and to accept certain forms of information transfer that they associate with the classroom setting. On the other hand, the visitors at the park are a **noncaptive audience** because they don't have to worry about grades. If they decide to stay and pay attention, it will be only because they want to. If the interpretive product isn't interesting, if it seems too academic, or if it requires too much effort to follow, they probably won't pay attention. In the classroom, of course, students will try to pay attention regardless of how boring or difficult the information is. They have to. There will be an exam. (If you're interested in how the idea of captive and noncaptive audiences originated, see Appendix 4.)

Figure 1-2 lists the key differences between captive and noncaptive audiences. Although the most common captive audience is the student in a classroom, there are many kinds of noncaptive audiences: visitors in museums or at historic sites, forests, parks, zoos, botanical gardens, breweries, and so forth, and people who use the Internet, read text messages on their phones, watch television, listen to radio, and read magazines and newspapers. As Figure 1-2 suggests, any audience that has the option of ignoring the information without punishment or loss of a potential reward is a noncaptive audience. Noncaptive audiences are driven to pay attention not by some external reward (such as a grade or qualification) but rather by their own intrinsic satisfaction with what they're hearing, seeing, or reading. The only reward noncaptive audiences seek is internal. As long as the information they're receiving continues to be more interesting and engaging than other things around them, noncaptive audiences will pay attention to it. However, if the information loses its interest or entertainment value, the audience will switch attention to something more immediately gratifying. This response may be overt, as when someone closes the website, puts down the magazine, switches the television channel, turns off the radio, or walks out of the movie theater early. It may also be quite involuntary, as when we find ourselves daydreaming in the middle of a conversation.

The mind tends to go where it finds the most gratifying information. Psychologists have linked

> The mind tends to go where it finds the most gratifying information.

this tendency to two kinds of chemicals called endorphins and dopamine that the brain produces. Some of these chemicals are a lot like morphine in their chemical makeup, and like morphine, they're addictive. Pleasurable thought stimulates the brain to produce endorphins and dopamine. Boring or excessively difficult information causes the brain to look for more gratifying information elsewhere. This is essentially what hap-

Differences between Captive and Noncaptive Audiences	
Captive Audiences	**Noncaptive Audiences**
Involuntary audience Time commitment is fixed External rewards important Must pay attention Will accept a formal, academic approach Will make an effort to pay attention, even if bored	Voluntary audience Have no time commitment External rewards not important Do not have to pay attention Expect an informal atmosphere and a nonacademic approach Will switch attention if bored
Examples of motivations: grades diplomas certificates licenses jobs/employment money advancement success	**Examples of motivations:** interest fun entertainment self-enrichment self-improvement a better life passing time (nothing better to do)
Typical settings: classrooms job training courses professional seminars courses required for a license (e.g., driving)	**Typical settings:** parks, museums, zoos, aquariums, etc. informal education programs at home watching television, listening to radio, reading a magazine

Figure 1-2. *Typical characteristics of captive and noncaptive audiences.*

pens when we daydream.

Consider the student, part of a captive audience, who knows he absolutely *must* pay attention in a class on a certain day because the next exam will stress the information that's being covered. Subconsciously, perhaps, he's saying to himself, "Okay, brain. We've got to pay attention today. *Please* pay attention today—there's going to be an exam!" With determination to commit to his notes every piece of information the teacher presents, our student finds himself an hour later being awakened from one of his better daydreams by the sound of his own name. It's his teacher telling him that he should pay better attention if he wants to do well on the exam.

Make no mistake about it. Your brain is in control of your attention. So powerful is its tendency to find pleasure that even a student consciously trying to pay attention to an important lecture is unable to do it if the presentation isn't interesting. Going back to Mr. Jones's experience at the park, it's easy to understand why the people in his audience weren't able to pay attention. They didn't even try; they didn't *have* to.

The Interpretive Approach to Communication

If Mr. Jones had been aware of the differences between his captive classroom audience and his noncaptive park visitor audience, what changes might he have made in his approach? What might he have done to hold his audience's interest and make them want to pay attention to his talk? Although there are many possible answers to these questions, all of them would boil down to four general qualities that Mr. Jones should try to give his presentation. Taken together, these qualities define what I have called the "**interpretive approach** to communication." They are:

1. Interpretation has a theme (*T*).

2. Interpretation is organized (*O*).

3. Interpretation is relevant (*R*).

4. Interpretation is enjoyable (*E*).

A Bit of History

Some readers will recognize these four qualities (thematic, organized, relevant, and enjoyable) as the **EROT framework** in reverse (Ham, 1983, 1992, 2002b). And they're right. The four qualities (*E*, *R*, *O*, and *T*) came from a very large body of research on how humans respond to communication when it's done well.[4] Emerging from those studies were two important lessons about successful communication that every interpreter can understand and apply. These are that communication is successful when it (1) attracts and holds an audience's attention long enough to make a point and (2) makes the point in a compelling way. That is, to be a successful interpreter you have to achieve *both* outcomes. The *E*, *R*, *O*, and *T* are simply abbreviations for the four qualities your interpretation must have in order to accomplish these two ends. This remains as true today as it was in 1992 when the EROT framework first appeared in *Environmental Interpretation*. So nothing has changed on that front.

But was there a reason for introducing the four letters in that order? Well, the fact is that it doesn't really matter which order you put them in. They'd be just fine as ROTE or OETR or TREO, as long as your interpretation has all four qualities. The original EROT resulted mainly from taking the perspective of the audience as I explained the interpretive approach to communication. I reasoned simply that audiences first had to pay attention during an interpretive encounter before anything else could happen. If they didn't attend to the interpreter or the interpretive product, no point (regardless of how compelling it might be) was going to be made.

So that's why the *E*, *R*, and *O* came first. They specialize in *engaging* audiences by capturing and holding attention (literally entertaining them). They make interpretation enjoyable to process (*E*); they cause it to connect to things that already matter to an audience (*R*); and they make it easy for audiences to follow along without a lot of work (*O*). In this sense, you can think of the entertainment industry as an ERO industry. It's designed mainly to attract and hold our attention, and it usually doesn't care much about making any sort of point. A good suspense movie, a talented stand-up comic, or a *Guinness World Records* book are judged by how much they attract us (and our business), not by whether they impart some important conclusion or moral of the story.

In interpretation, the *E*, *R*, and *O* work together to engage the minds of the audience and to hold their attention—a task every accomplished interpreter knows is critical to success. Obviously, since three of the four required qualities have to do with capturing and holding attention, it's fair to say that three-fourths of an interpreter's job is purposeful entertainment. But the same accomplished interpreters will be quick to add that entertainment alone isn't sufficient to be successful in their work. Something more is needed. What's lacking, of course, is the compelling point they hope to make while all that attention is being held, and that's why the *T* was added to turn ERO into EROT.

I've been happy to see that the EROT framework has served practicing interpreters well, and in many places it's considered a defining framework for best practice. In the past few years, some of interpretation's leading thinkers have appropriated the framework (see, for example, Colquhoun, 2005; Morales, 1998; and Moscardo, Ballantyne & Hughes, 2007), and some of them have extended the four-letter framework to create memorable acronyms that offer additional practical value for interpreters. In the second edition of *Personal Interpretation* (2008), Lisa Brochu and Tim Merriman discuss the framework as **POETRY**, adding a *P* for *purposeful* to make the very important point that interpretation should be driven by an objective or mission, and a *Y* for *you*, the interpreter who must adapt approaches to varied audiences and continue to grow professionally. In *Conducting Meaningful Interpretation*, Carolyn Ward and Alan Wilkinson (2006) rework the framework into **CREATES**, wherein a C (for *connects*), an *A* (for *appropriate*), and an extra *E* (for *engaging*) are added to the *E* and *R* (note that the *S* for *structure* is substituted for the *O* in EROT). And finally, Anne Ross, Greg Siepen, and Sue O'Connor (2003)—following in the footsteps of many before them who observed that EROT is phonetically two-thirds of *erotic*—added the inevitable *I* (for *involving*) and *C* (for *creative*) to form **EROTIC** as a framework for delivering excellent distance education programs.

Each of these acronyms (POETRY, CREATES and EROTIC) is a valuable framework for practicing interpreters because each is wrapped around the core of what more than a century of research has taught us about successful communication. Yet each is customized in its own way to give interpreters additional practical insight into their work. But the fact that all of them retain their own version of *E*, *R*, *O*, and *T* is important because these four qualities together capture what every interpreter must do in order to be successful: hold attention and make a compelling point. As we'll see throughout this book, the more skillful you become in infusing each of the qualities into your interpretive products, the more successful you're going to be as an interpreter. That much seems pretty clear.

From EROT to TORE

Today, I prefer to present these four qualities of successful interpretation as TORE. Shifting perspective from what goes on in the audience's mind to what the *interpreter* must do to develop a successful interpretive product, it makes sense that the theme really must come first. In many ways, it's the *T* that gives purpose and strategy to the *O*, *R*, and *E*. In other words, without an overarching idea to develop, the attention held by the *O*, *R*, and *E* is pointless, except in its purpose to keep an audience entertained. But entertained to what end? As Larsen (2003) and Brochu and Merriman (2012) have convincingly argued, entertainment as an end in itself is not interpretation. Rather, it's simply "**infotainment**," "**edutainment**," or what Bob Roney (see Larsen, 2003) has aptly called "**interpretainment**." But when the *T* is added at the front, the interpreter's attention is focused on how to apply ORE in a purposeful and strategic way. So for these reasons, EROT has given way to TORE.

In Chapter 2, we'll review the **TORE model** of thematic communication in more detail and look at practical ways an interpreter can infuse an interpretive

---

Cornerstones of the interpretive approach to communication:

T (thematic)

O (organized)

R (relevant)

E (enjoyable)

product with each of the four essential qualities. That will set the stage for us to consider what "making a difference" through interpretation might actually entail and prepare us for a closer examination of how to apply the interpretive approach to communication in personal, face-to-face interpretive products (such as oral presentations, performances, and guided tours) as well as in nonpersonal interpretation (such as exhibits, panels, brochures, smartphone apps, and websites).

Glossary terms: captive audience, CREATES, edutainment, EROT framework, EROTIC, infotainment, interpretainment, interpretation, interpreter, interpretive approach, interpretive encounter, interpretive product, noncaptive audience, POETRY, TORE model (of thematic communication)

Additional Thoughts for Chapter 1

1   We often use these three characteristics (context, audiences, and outcomes of interest) to distinguish among different types of strategic communication. For example, interpretation, teaching, sales, advertising, political campaigning, and courtroom argumentation are all forms of communication, but they vary quite a lot in terms of the settings or circumstances in which they're practiced, the kinds of audiences they're interested in reaching, and the kinds of results they're after.

2   In 2007, a groundbreaking project facilitated by the US-based National Association for Interpretation (NAI) and funded by the US Environmental Protection Agency brought together representatives of professional associations, federal agencies, and other major employers of interpreters to define and accept common usage of terms in the field. It was through NAI's Definitions Project that this definition of interpretation was developed. You can find NAI's Definitions Project online at www.definitionsproject.com.

3   Examples might include teaching the alphabet and how to construct words from those symbols, memorizing multiplication tables, what a negative exponent means, what happened on important dates in history, the formula to calculate velocity or surface area. Educators will recognize memory-based learning as the "Knowledge" tier of the cognitive domain in Benjamin Bloom's Taxonomy of Learning Objectives. Interpreters are only rarely interested in this sort of learning outcome unless there is some very good reason to "teach" audiences isolated facts. In formal school curricula, however, teaching such facts is considered necessary to prepare students for higher-order learning that relies on those facts. Good teachers usually instruct at all levels of Bloom's Taxonomy. For more on Bloom's Taxonomy, see http://en.wikipedia.org/wiki/Bloom's_Taxonomy.

4   I reviewed much of this research in *Environmental Interpretation* (Ham, 1992) and previously in Ham (1983). Ham (2002b) applies research from cognitive psychology primarily to the museums field. You can find good literature reviews related specifically to thematic interpretation in Morales (1998—in Spanish); Tarlton and Ward (2006); and Ward and Wilkinson (2006). See also Chapter 2 ("TORE") in this volume.

CHAPTER 2
TORE

Successful interpretation has a strong theme, is easy to follow, matters to the audience, and is enjoyable to process.

In this chapter, we'll take a closer look at the TORE model of thematic communication. You'll recall from Chapter 1 the mishaps of Mr. Jones, the star of our illustrative example. Mr. Jones—like a lot of interpreters who don't yet fully appreciate that their audiences are noncaptive—was frustrated because the instructional methods that worked so well in his science classes fell flat when he tried them out on visitors at his park. His example led us to recognize that captive and noncaptive audiences are different psychologically, and it prompted us to draw on what more than a century of communication research tells us Mr. Jones might do to be more successful as an interpreter. The lessons learned from all those studies can be summarized in four letters (T, O, R, and E), each of which corresponds to a different quality or characteristic that communication must have if it's going to succeed consistently in holding attention and making some kind of point. Together, these four qualities define the interpretive approach to communication, which simply says that successful interpretation:

has a *theme* (T);

is *organized* for easy processing (O);

is *relevant* to the audience (R); and

is *enjoyable* to process (E).

In the following pages, we'll examine each of these qualities a little more closely and consider some very basic ideas for how interpreters can consciously incorporate them into their interpretive products. Let's begin with the theme.

Quality 1: Interpretation Has a Theme

Your interpretation is thematic if it has a **theme**; that is, if you build it around some major point you'd like to make. It really is that simple. Bill Lewis (1980), who's the person I credit for bringing the word *theme* to the interpreter's vocabulary, has traced its origin back to Aristotle. So there's really nothing new in the concept. Today, almost every author who writes about interpretation places the concept of theme somewhere near the center of the discussion (just a few examples are Beck and Cable, 2002; Brochu and Merriman, 2012; Caputo, Lewis and Brochu, 2008; Colquhoun, 2005; Ham, 1992; Knudson, Cable and Beck, 1995; Kohen and Sikoryak, 2005; Larsen, 2003; Levy, Lloyd and Schreiber, 2001; Morales, 1998; Moscardo, Ballantyne, and Hughes, 2007; Pastorelli, 2003; Ward and Wilkinson, 2006).

The fairly universal acceptance of thematic interpretation stems mainly from its practical value to interpreters. Having a theme in mind makes your job easier because it helps you see what to include, what to exclude, what to emphasize, and what to deemphasize in your interpretive product. It gives you a sort of rule for making what would otherwise be a daunting decision: "From all my knowledge about this topic, what few bits of it should I bring to the forefront with this audience today?" When you allow a theme to guide your thinking, this decision is much easier. In Chapter 6 ("Two Sides of Theme and Sentences in the Head"), we'll consider in a lot more detail why this approach to interpretation is important, and in Chapter 7 ("Not All Themes Are Equal"), we'll look at ways to express themes so that they stand a good chance of provoking your audiences to think.

Themes Are Not Topics

It's important to convince yourself that a theme is not the same as a **topic**, even though some people use the two interchangeably in everyday discourse. Virtually any presentation of ideas can—and should—have both a topic and a theme. Their major difference is that the topic is merely the subject matter of the presentation, whereas the theme is the main point or idea a communicator is trying to convey about that topic.

As a simple example, look at the topics and themes in Figure 2-1. Notice that each topic is a sentence fragment, whereas each of the themes is either a single complete sentence with a

---

Theme ≠ Topic

The topic of an interpretive product isn't the same as its theme. The topic is simply the subject matter (it's what the interpretation is "about"). The theme, on the other hand, is the overarching conclusion about the topic you'd like your audience to consider—to think about.

Look at the following list of topics. Notice that each could be a *part* of a sentence, but none of them is a *whole* sentence. It simply tells the subject matter. Now look at the list of themes. Even though each theme relates in some way to the topic of architecture, each takes your mind in a very different direction than do the other themes. That's because any topic can have any number of themes depending on what the interpreter wants to communicate to the audience about it.

Examples of Topics

Architecture	Fourteenth-century castles	Indigenous views of the land
Nocturnal birds	Chocolate	Dinosaurs

Examples of Themes for the Topic of Architecture

- Ancient Egyptians solved architectural problems in ways people today are still trying to understand.
- Gothic architecture wasn't just about pointed buildings and arches; it was about projecting power and inspiring awe in people.
- Chuck Berry was one of the most ingenious architects of all time; he designed rock and roll.
- Ants could teach present-day miners a thing or two about underground architecture.
- In the United States, Thomas Jefferson was in many ways the architect of democracy.

Figure 2-1. *Examples of topics and themes.*

subject and a verb or a couple of *closely related* sentences. I've found that the most important characteristic of a theme is that it captures a *single whole idea*, regardless of the number of grammatical units it takes to express it smoothly or effectively. When a theme is fairly simple, it's usually easy for an interpreter to express it in a single sentence. But sometimes themes are more complicated than a single phrase can capture without sounding like a run-on sentence. When you encounter this problem, try expressing the same whole idea in two closely related sentences. Some interpreters like to use semicolons between the sentences as a way to show they're related. But however you decide to write your theme, remember that it should express one whole idea, even if it takes a couple of sentences (or more) to articulate it. We'll revisit the old "one-sentence rule" in Chapter 7 ("Not All Themes Are Equal").

Themeless Interpretation Is Doomed to Infotainment

Finally, notice that although each of the five themes listed in Figure 2-1 relates in its own way to the general topic of architecture, each one would require a different approach and entirely different information to flesh out or develop. Imagine you work at a museum, and one day you're asked to give a thirty-minute talk on architecture to a local group. That's all you know in advance—the amount of time available and your subject matter. Specifically: you have thirty minutes and your topic is architecture. As you ponder how to approach preparing this talk, you might well be thinking:

> Hmm, now let me see. I have thirty minutes to talk about architecture. What should I say first, then second? What should I say last? When I go to the library or surf the web to do some research for this talk, what should I look for?

You probably can see that your answers to these questions could be quite arbitrary. At best, you could adopt an ORE (infotainment) approach, reasoning simply that since you have thirty minutes to talk, you need to find thirty minutes of interesting things to say about architecture (much like a comedian in search of enough material to fill a thirty-minute gig). And when you arrive at the library or go online, your search for information will be guided mainly by your need to find interesting or entertaining things to say about architecture. In other words, when you know only your topic and the size of your "communication container" (e.g., the amount of speaking time you need to "fill," the size of the panel you're designing, and so on), about the only creative approach available to you is infotainment. This is because you have no other rule or tool for making decisions about the content of your presentation. Online, you could do

ORE = infotainment

a search using key words such as "amazing architectural facts," and at the library, perhaps you'd do well to find any book on the topic of architecture and look in the index under the *F*s (for "Fun Facts" about architecture). Any experienced interpreter will see the grain of truth in this dramatized scenario.

Now look again at Figure 2-1 and imagine that you had one of the five themes in mind as you prepared your talk. Can you see how much easier your job is now, both in terms of the research and deciding what information to include? One of the main advantages of having a theme is that it not only shows you where to start in preparing a new interpretive product, it tells you when you're *done*. As this example illustrates, applied communicators will find few more helpful friends than their themes.

The Story's the Thing

In discussing the characteristics that make interpretation different from other ways of communicating, Tilden (1957) said: "The story's the thing." By this he meant that presentations—whether written, spoken, or conveyed by some device—should have the qualities of a story. That is, they should have a beginning, an end, and most of all, a message, main point, or moral.[1] The message may be short and simple: "Indigenous views of the land have a lot to teach us." Or it might be more involved: "Indigenous views of the land paint a picture of people serving nature as much as nature serving people."

As you probably noticed in the two examples, each theme requires its own set of facts, concepts, and main points. That's because every theme involves telling a different story than other themes would tell, even if they share the same topic. Although both of these example themes stemmed from the topic of "indigenous views of the land," the development of each would require a fundamentally different approach. With a theme clearly in mind, a communicator enjoys the luxury of seeing more clearly what he or she needs to say, write, or show in order to flesh that idea out for the audience. Obviously, a mere topic does not provide that kind of insight.

> The trouble with a lot of interpretation is that it's guided only by a topic.

A problem with a lot of interpretation is that it's guided only by a topic (for example, major historical events, architecture of the period, birds, mountains, castles, and so on), and since there's almost no limit to the number of themes one could develop around a given topic, such a presentation proceeds without focus or direction, as if it were trying to say everything and nothing at the same time. It also, as we've just seen, leaves the interpreter with no other creative approach than sheer infotainment (ORE). When there's *no story* to tell and *no point* to make from it, what else *could* you do?

Your Theme Answers the Question "So What?"

Think of the teachers you've had in school. Were there any that you just couldn't seem to take notes from? Were you ever frustrated because you would sit for an hour, listening and understanding what you were hearing but still unable to write it in your notebook? Did you walk out some days asking yourself "so what?" after listening to what seemed to be an endless list of unrelated facts? Contrast those teachers with the ones you found it easy to take notes from. What do think accounted for the difference?

Presentations that don't have themes beg the question "so what?," and unfortunately, most of us have read or listened to information that has left us asking this question. But presentations that do have themes seem to be "going somewhere," and it's easy for us to organize all the facts and supportive details in our minds because we can "stick" them to the theme. This is what the plot does for a movie or story. When audiences don't know where a presentation is going, they have nothing to stick all the facts to, and they become lost in a sea of irrelevance. The theme of a presentation helps provide the adhesive.

All interpretive encounters ought to be able to stand up to the question "so what?," and good stories, poems, songs, dramas, and classroom lectures offer an answer. So do good talks, web-pages, exhibits, brochures, signs, and other interpretive media, if they've been developed with some overarching idea in mind. You may know it by other words: *the big picture*, *the moral to the story*, *the main idea to be cohesively developed*, and so forth. But all these words mean about the same thing, and regardless of which term you prefer, you should make sure each of your interpretive products is built around one.

> Presentations that don't have themes beg the question, "so what?"

Going back now to our example of Mr. Jones in Chapter 1, what might he do to make his talk on geology more thematic? By now the answer is probably obvious: he should select a theme from his topic—one he thinks will matter to the audience—and then he should develop his talk to bring out the important aspects of that theme. As we'll see later, this might or might not involve Mr. Jones actually telling his audience what his theme is.[2] This is usually a matter of personal style. But regardless of whether he actually puts his theme into exact words while presenting his talk or presents it in a more implicit way, he'll want to make sure that whatever he does leads his audience to think thoughts that hover somewhere around that theme.[3] As we'll see throughout this book, your theme expresses the overriding conclusion you hope your audience will think about when the interpretive encounter has ended. But, of course, you also realize that the actual ideas they take away might vary a little or even a lot. Either way, it will be the thoughts you provoked in each person that will shape their own personal morals of your story. For them, each thought is a personal answer to the question "so what?"

In Chapter 8 ("The Zone of Tolerance"), we'll take a closer look at how this works in practice, and in Chapter 9 ("Sequential Theme Development"), we'll see there's a bit more to consider in developing a presentation like Mr. Jones's talk. For now, however, it's important simply to see that having a theme in mind will make your work as an interpreter a lot easier, and furthermore, that presenting your audience information that supports this important theme will make you more successful in developing virtually any type of interpretive product.

Your Theme Makes Your Job Easier

As I mentioned earlier in this chapter, the most basic value of having a theme in mind as you develop an interpretive product is that it helps you make decisions that would otherwise be a lot more difficult. Your theme not only gives you a clear view of the information you should include and exclude, it also makes it a lot easier for you to research your topic and gather information. Consider this segment from Mr. Jones's talk:

> *Sediment* is just another word for the mess. In a river, the mess comes from small particles of rock that have been rubbed off by the water and, of course, all the soil and other material that washes in from the sides of the river. Over time, the mess piles up, and the whole process is called "sedimentation." If you're like me, you're thinking that one of the best things about rivers is that you don't have to clean up after them. Or do you? Where do you suppose all the sediment goes?

His topic seems to be geology, and more specifically, soil erosion and sedimentation. But what do you think his theme might be? Of course, it's difficult to tell from such a small piece of his talk, but Mr. Jones seems to be building up to the idea that we do, in fact, have to "clean up" the mess that sedimentation can cause. His statement about the "soil and other material that washes in from the sides of the river," along with the question he poses to his audience at the end of the paragraph, provide a clue to his thinking. Where's he taking us with this question? Perhaps to the realization that the sediment ends up in the river where it fouls and contaminates our drinking water, spoils our fisheries, and potentially blocks shipping channels. If so, Mr. Jones's theme is easy to see. He's trying to tell his audience that *soil erosion threatens not only agriculture, it threatens our water, our fisheries, major shipping corridors, and eventually all of us.*

If this were Mr. Jones's theme, what information would he want to include that would help flesh out the idea for his audience? This would depend on Mr. Jones's interests, knowledge, and beliefs about the topic he's dealing with, wouldn't it? If you and two other people were each

> Your theme expresses an overriding conclusion you hope your audience will think about.

independently developing a talk around Mr. Jones's theme, you'd probably come up with three different ways to do it, and all three of you would probably end up giving very different talks from the one Mr. Jones presents.

But what's important to notice here is that once you know for yourself what your theme is, you're led automatically to consider what you *really* need to say or show so that your audience leaves thinking thoughts that hover—more or less—around your theme. In this way, your theme becomes a set of eyeglasses through which all of your knowledge is filtered, culminating in a clear picture of what's important and not important for developing the theme. As thematic interpretation pioneer Bill Lewis (1980) advised, if you have a clear theme in mind, you'll find that most everything else will fall into place.

Quality 2: Interpretation Is Organized

Interpretation is **organized** when it's presented in a way that's easy to follow. Another way of stating this idea is that interpretation, at its best, doesn't require a lot of effort from the audience. Noncaptive audiences will switch attention if they have to work too hard to follow a train of thought. In advertising, this relationship is well known. Mass media experts have even developed a formula to express it:

$$\frac{\text{Probability that a noncaptive}}{\text{audience will pay attention}} = \frac{\text{Reward (potential benefit)}}{\text{Effort (amount of work required)}}$$

The formula, developed four decades ago by Wilbur Schramm (1971), says that audiences that don't have to pay attention, won't—if they have to work too hard. As the amount of work they have to do increases, the likelihood that they'll continue to pay attention decreases.[4] Put another way, the best interpretation is easy for its audience to follow.

What Does Organization Really Do? An Example

Think of the last time you entered a movie theater after the show had already started. If you're like most people, your first concern was trying to figure out what was going on in the movie, so you could make sense out of what you were hearing and seeing on the screen. If you weren't too late, you were probably able to sort things out pretty quickly. But if you missed more than fifteen minutes or so, you probably missed the introductions of the key characters, and even more important, the plot.

Undoubtedly, you then spent the next several minutes trying to piece things together. When you thought you'd finally figured it all out, you probably felt you could relax; that is, until one of the characters said or did something that didn't fit with what you thought was going on. Then you had to start all over again trying to figure things out.

If you paid a lot of money to see the movie, you probably continued this trial-and-error process as long as it took to get things straight. If you were home watching television free of charge, however, you probably switched channels or turned off the TV long before you spent a lot of effort. Likewise, if you were at a museum viewing an exhibit, reading a brochure, watching a video, or listening to a talk, you probably either started to daydream or just got up and left altogether. Why?

> When interpretation is organized (*O*), it's easy to follow.

The reason, of course, is that noncaptive audiences won't spend a lot of time and effort to follow a difficult presentation. As our formula suggests, they usually decide early on whether the benefits of paying attention are going to be worth the effort required, and a major factor in their estimate of the effort is how well the message is organized. If the ideas being presented follow a logical train of thought, little effort is needed to keep things straight. A movie's plot, the introduction of a talk or audiovisual program, and the title, headings, and subheadings of an exhibit, brochure, or webpage all help provide this logic. The result is that the information presented is easier to follow because it can be put into categories and therefore not seem like so much.

But, as in our movie example, if the ideas being presented can't be attached to some organizational framework, they become mere isolated facts. And, as we shall see shortly, humans have definite limits in their ability to keep unorganized information straight in their minds. If too much information builds up out of context, we become hopelessly confused and eventually quit trying to sort it out. With noncaptive audiences, this can happen in a matter of seconds.

Organizing information is like putting a piece of tape or Velcro on every idea and fact that you're presenting and then sticking each one to some larger idea. When we can connect a piece of information to some idea (such as a plot or major point) that we already have in our memory, that information seems easier to remember. If we keep the main ideas to a manageable number, we can present an amazing amount of information within them without losing the audience. But what exactly does "manageable number" mean?

The Magical Number Revisited

The answer to the above question is four or fewer, and some argue it's even less. That is, talks, exhibits, publications, audiovisual programs, and so forth that try to present four or fewer main ideas will be more interesting and more understandable than those that try to communicate more. The reason is that they simply require less effort from the audience.

The number four comes from studies on just how much information we humans are capable of handling all at one time. Prior to 2001, the most famous of these studies was published by George Miller in 1956. His article, "The Magical Number Seven, Plus or Minus Two," reported that on average, we humans are capable of making sense out of only five to nine separate and new ideas at one time.[5] But since some of us can handle only as many as five (that is, seven minus two), I advised in *Environmental Interpretation* (Ham, 1992) that interpreters should keep their actual number of main points (or **subthemes**) to five or fewer. This advice was later adopted by a number of other writers and over the past couple of decades became more or less best practice in interpretation (see, for example, Beck and Cable, 1998; Brochu and Merriman, 2008; Field and Lente, 2000; Levy, Lloyd and Schreiber, 2001; Morales, 1998; and Ward and Wilkinson, 2006).

The "no-more-than-five" guideline was considered solid advice until 2001 when our views about the capacity of human working memory changed quite dramatically. That was when psychologist Nelson Cowan, utilizing a newer methodology, revisited Miller's research and discovered that Miller's rough average had *overestimated* people's actual memory capability. Cowan found that the limiting number in most cases is closer to three or four, and this has since been supported by other studies (if you're interested, you'll find good reviews in Cowan, 2005 and Klingberg, 2009).

While virtually everyone agrees today that four is an absolute upper limit, some psychologists claim the "magical number" is probably only three (or even fewer) for certain kinds of situations (see, for example, Gobet and Clarkson, 2004). Still, the evidence pointing to four as the so-called magical number is so widespread that interpreters can feel fairly certain they won't overtax their audiences if they keep the number of subthemes they're presenting to four or fewer. For this reason, we'll refer in later chapters to the **magical number 4** (see Figure 2-2).

In 2001, the "magical number" became four.

This important guideline applies to all types of presentations, whether they're spoken or written, auditory or

In Interpretation, It Pays to Keep Your Main Ideas to Four or Fewer

People have definite limits in their ability to make sense out of new information. Research has shown that the sheer amount of information, as well as how it's organized, make a difference in how well we're able to sort it out and use it. Studies have shown that most people are capable of handling about four different pieces of information at a time in most situations. Yes, some people can keep more than four different ideas or facts straight in their heads, but others become lost when the number exceeds four. Studies show that this relationship has less to do with the person's intelligence than it does with the amount of prior experience he or she has with the topic at hand. It stands to reason, then, that since some people in your audiences will have difficulty when the number exceeds four, you should limit the number of main ideas in your presentations to four or fewer. Doing so will make it easier for people in your audience to follow your ideas, and this will increase the likelihood that they'll continue paying attention to you.

Some examples:

If you limit yourself to no more than one second, which group is easier to count, A or B?

A	B
****	********

How about this one: A or B?

A	B
********	++++****

Notice how organization can make a difference. Even though B has the same amount of information as A, it's easier to sort out because it's organized into two easy-to-see categories. So actually, there are only two pieces of information in B (two groups of four), whereas A contains eight. In communication, good organization reduces effort.

Now try this one:

A	B
FBIPHDIBMCIA	FBI PHD IBM CIA

Obviously, if your ideas are organized around things your audience already can relate to, your presentation will be that much easier for them to follow.

Figure 2-2. *The importance of organization in interpretation.*

visual. The only two requirements are that: (1) the audience can easily distinguish between the main points and the subordinate information you attach to them, and (2) the number of main points you present doesn't exceed four. Intelligently applied, this principle will help make any presentation easier to follow, more understandable, and more thought provoking. In fact, many studies have shown that making interpretation easy to process is one of the two main prerequisites for provoking thought in an audience.[6]

A Misconception about Subthemes

I've found that some interpreters think that if you're "allowed" to have up to four subthemes, then it's best to have exactly four. They reason that four must be better than three, or two, or no subthemes, and they automatically try to develop any interpretive program or device around four main ideas. But this is probably a mistake. In communication, simple is almost always better than complicated, and my experience has been that most interpretive products don't need any (yes, that's *zero*) subthemes. Unless your theme is inherently multifaceted or complex, there's a good chance you can develop it effectively without breaking it into smaller subthemes. But like so many things in interpretation, this is often a matter of personal style.

> Don't go looking for subthemes. If you need them, they'll find you.

Still, experienced interpreters usually find that their **global theme** is all they need as they decide how to present their ideas. Arbitrarily force fitting subthemes in such a case will serve only to fragment your creative planning and probably your audience's attention. Although the main purpose of organization is to make it easier for your audience to follow your ideas, the additional structure you create when you impose unnecessary subthemes on your organization might actually make more—rather than less— work for your audience.

So my advice is to begin developing a new interpretive product under the assumption that you *won't* need to organize your presentation of ideas around subthemes. If, however, you run into difficulty making your ideas flow, or you find that there are gaps in the logic you want your audience to grasp, then you might want to consider developing one to four subthemes to make things easier for them. Put differently, you might say it's best not to go looking for subthemes; if you need them, *they'll find you.*

Returning to our example, how could Mr. Jones improve the organization of his talk so that his audience might follow him more easily? A key will be that he first decides whether he needs subthemes at all. If he determines he does need them, he should carefully select one to four of them based on the global theme he's trying to develop for his audience. The method is really that simple.

Quality 3: Interpretation Is Relevant

Information that's relevant to us really has two qualities: it's **meaningful** and it's **personal**. Although related, being meaningful and being personal are different things. As we'll see, information that's meaningful isn't necessarily personal. When we succeed in giving interpretation both of these qualities, we've made it **relevant** to our audiences.

What Does Being "Meaningful" Mean?

When information is meaningful it's because we're able to connect it to something already inside our brains. Meaningful information is said to have "context" since we understand it only in the context of something else we already know. Some psychologists say that we humans have a lot of words floating around in our heads, and that when something we hear or see reminds us of one or more of them, we attach a meaning to it that's based on the words it awakened in our minds. When something we hear or see doesn't connect with anything we already know, it's meaningless to us. The trouble with a lot of interpretation is that it's not very meaningful to its audiences.

Going back to our example in Chapter 1, Mr. Jones could probably do at least two things to make his talk more meaningful to the visitors at the park. First, he could avoid using technical terms unless they're necessary for his audience to understand some important concept or idea he's trying to get across. In the example, however, it appears Mr. Jones is simply trying to teach his audience terms such as *tetrahedral bonding*, *silicates*, and *sedimentation*, just the way he teaches his science students the same terms. But because few non-geologists have words in their heads that would be awakened by such terms, they probably aren't very meaningful to Mr. Jones's audience. Second, he could try to bridge the unfamiliar world of geology to things that his audience is likely to already know something about. He might do this by using **examples**, **analogies**, **contrasts**, **similes**, and **metaphors**. Common everyday things make the best "bridges" (see Figure 2-3).[7]

> Interpretation is relevant (R) when it's both meaningful and personal.

Some Ways to Bridge the Familiar and the Unfamiliar

Examples: Quickly refer to something or someone that is like or in some way represents the kind of thing or person you're talking about.

"This boomerang is a good example of Aboriginal ingenuity."

Analogies: Show many similarities of the thing you're talking about to some other thing that is highly familiar to the audience.

"To understand how volcanoes work, you can think of a covered pot of boiling water and an agitated bottle of champagne."

Contrasts: Compare the major similarities and/or differences between the thing you're talking about and something else that can easily be related to it. The result is that one or both of the objects become clearer in relation to the other.

"These two pine trees are a lot alike. Both have three needles to a group, and they grow in the same kinds of places. But if you smell the bark, you'll notice that one of them smells like vanilla and the other like turpentine."

Similes: Compare some characteristic of two things using the words *like* or *as*.

"At this stage of his life, van Gogh appeared more as a troubled soul than as the creator of the beautiful art he would later unveil."

"This tree has spines like daggers on every limb."

Metaphors: Describe something with a word or phrase usually used to describe something very different. That is, using one thing to mean another.

"Chuck Berry's genius produced the *blueprint* that gave rise to rock and roll."

"The canoe *plowed* through the rapids."

Figure 2-3. *Some techniques for making information more meaningful.*

What Does Being "Personal" Mean?

Being meaningful is only half the challenge if interpretation is going to be relevant. The other half is being personal. In his first principle of interpretation, Tilden (1957: 11) captured the essence of this idea when he said, "Any interpretation that does not somehow relate what is being displayed or described to something within the personality or experience of the visitor [audience] will be sterile." By this he meant that interpreters must not only find a way to link the information being presented to something their audiences know about but also to something they *care* about. This is especially important with noncaptive audiences because they'll almost always ignore information that seems unimportant, even if they understand it perfectly. Consequently, we can understand why it's difficult to sit through presentations we've heard before or to read something we've read before. Although the information is very meaningful, it lacks the promise of new insight and is therefore unimportant to us.

The reverse is also true. That is, noncaptive audiences can be expected to switch their attention to any information that is highly personal. Highly personal things include ourselves, our families, our health, our well-being, our quality of life—our deepest values, principles, beliefs, and convictions.

One of the most helpful ideas for increasing the relevance of interpretation came from the US National Park Service (Larsen, 2003), which advanced the important idea of **universal concepts**. Universal concepts are intangible or symbolic connections to notions that (as far as we know) have always had special significance to humans everywhere, and for all time. They include extreme emotions such as love, hate, fear, elation, and sorrow; basic biological imperatives such as birth, death, hunger, and thirst; human fascinations with uncertainty, the cosmos, mystery, and suspense; and many other linkages such as the few examples listed in Figure 2-4. You'll find that just about any good story, screenplay, or stage play revolves around one or more universal concepts.[8] Linking your interpretation to them is a very good way to make

Interpretation is relevant when it connects to something the audience cares about. *Photo courtesy of California Academy of Sciences, USA.*

A Fast-Track to Relevance—Universal Concepts

Anger	Hunger	Sorrow (sadness, remorse)
Birth	Integrity	Spiritual (cosmic)
Blood	Irony	Starvation
Bravery (courage)	Isolation	Strength
Conflict	Jealousy	Struggle
Cruelty	Joy	Suffering
Danger (peril)	Justice	Supernatural power
Darkness	Killing	Survival
Dark side of people	Lies (lying)	Suspense
Death (dying)	Loneliness	Sweat
Deceit	Longing	Tears
Defeat	Love	Tension
Elation	Loved ones	Thirst
Embarrassment	Martyrs (martyrdom)	Threat
Equality	Misunderstanding	Tyranny
Evil (versus good)	Morality	Uncertainty
Fairness (social equity)	Mortality	Underdog
Family (blood relatives)	Mystery	Valor
Fear	Pain	Victory
Fight	Patriotism	Vindication
Freedom	Power	Violence
Good (versus evil)	Regret (remorse)	Virtue
Guilt	Revenge	Visionaries
Happiness (elation)	Sadness (sorrow)	Weakness
Hate	Saving (someone/something)	Worry
Heroines (heroes)	Sex	You (yourself, us)
Hope	Shame	
Humiliation	Slavery	

Figure 2-4. *Just a few examples of universal concepts.*

what you're saying or showing instantly more relevant to your audience. As Fudge (2003) and others have recommended, when the theme of an interpretive product is wrapped around one or more universal concepts, it often becomes inherently interesting in and of itself. You might recall Mr. Jones's theme from earlier in this chapter:

> Soil erosion threatens not only agriculture; it threatens our water, our fisheries, major shipping corridors, and eventually all of us.

In this theme, it appears Mr. Jones is making connections to at least two universal concepts: threats and all of us. While he might want to continue looking for ways to strengthen his theme (an issue we'll take up in Chapter 7), this is a good start. If you were giving your own talk on geology, what are some universal concepts you might be able to work into your theme? Power? Mystery? Violence? Survival? Others?[9]

Interpretation that connects *strongly* with universal concepts is often moving to an audience, particularly when humans are themselves part of the story. Artfully presented, this kind of interpretation is visceral; it somehow touches the soul of the audience and profoundly affects them. A performance depicting the life of a "Buffalo Soldier" by Shelton Johnson, acclaimed interpreter at Yosemite National Park in the United States, is one of the best contemporary examples of how the skillful use of universal concepts can powerfully impact an audience.[10] In his invited commentary (Figure 2-5), Shelton explains the thinking behind his approach and discusses the sensitivities, risks, and rewards involved in this style of interpretation.

> Universal concepts are intangible or symbolic meanings that hold special significance for humans.

Any communication that connects itself to things that matter in our lives will capture and hold our attention more so than other kinds of information. And as we'll see next, our tendency to pay attention to personal information is so powerful that we do it even when we're consciously trying *not* to.

The Power of Being Personal

The best communicators always try to connect their ideas to the lives of their audiences. The power this gives their presentations has been shown repeatedly in laboratory experiments utilizing a technique called "shadowing." In these experiments, a person wears stereo headphones and is given very different recorded messages in each ear. In the left ear the person might hear

Touching the "Soul" of an Audience with Universal Concepts

The hardest stories to tell are the ones that no one wants to hear—the stories that make us squirm in our seats; the ones that bend our minds and touch something within our souls. These are the stories that make us grow silent or scream, sigh or cry, lower our heads in shame or jut chins in defiance. There's no mistaking this kind of story because each is mirrored on the faces of those who have the courage to listen, and sometimes to listen in spite of themselves. This is the kind of story I tell through interpretive theater at Yosemite National Park, USA.

But I'm not the only interpreter who tells such stories. Indeed, this is the world that awaits any interpreter who successfully engages audiences with a profound injustice—the Holocaust, the centuries of African Slave Trade, or the mistreatment of indigenous people all across the world. It's a universe without humor, and yet there can be laughter. It's a place without compassion, and yet there are people who will tearfully embrace you. It's a room where you feel alone awaiting the judgment of your audience, and yet the risk you've taken is almost always rewarded because you have given them a priceless gift—hope.

Shelton Johnson
Park Ranger and
Freeman Tilden Award Recipient
Yosemite National Park, United States

No food is more sustaining than hope. You can have all of the nourishment a body requires, but without hope, the body will waste away and die. Hope is never more powerful than when it's rendered as a story, and no tale is more powerful to us than our own history.

History is Truth viewed from afar. You're looking back over your shoulder. The sun is blinding you, but you can still make out the world that once was. With all its beauty and ugliness, it is there where you can see, feel, smell, and taste it. Do you swallow or spit it out? Do you breathe it in deep or hold your breath? Do your hands reach out to softly touch or do they tighten into fists? Do your eyes open wide in recognition, or do you simply shut down in defeat?

A good interpreter can influence how people respond to the Truth. But a great interpreter can profoundly influence that response. Hard stories are the bread and butter of great interpreters because the pairing of poignant narrative and a talented soothsayer can result in real, demonstrable change in people.

How does one accomplish this? I think it's by pulling the audience's attention away from the superficial differences that pull us apart and appealing instead to the profound similarities among people that bind us together. I do this by utilizing universal concepts such as what it feels like to be a child in an adult world, to be a member of a community that is both disenfranchised and politically powerless, the meaning of family, what "home" means, the idea of making sacrifices for your family, and what it feels like to be around people who look at you in a negative way, to feel unloved, vulnerable, and alone.

I engage my audience directly through storytelling, but I also pull some of them onto the stage and make them part of the history I'm unfolding. In this way, everyone can experience that history, but from the inside looking out rather than the outside looking in. My strategy is to move my character from the status of being an "other" from the past to the status of being a "brother" here and now. "You know me, and I know you." I engage the intellect, but my efforts are rooted in the heart. Nothing that I do matters if people aren't emotionally engaged, and every great interpreter knows that strong universal concepts are a fast track to human emotions.

I want my audience to walk away after 90 minutes feeling as if they'd been briefly in the presence of a Black Indian from South Carolina named Elizy Boman, a man who was a cavalry sergeant in the US Army, a man who first became a Buffalo Soldier, but ultimately served as one of the first park rangers in Yosemite National Park. What keeps me on track when I'm performing on stage is the thought that the audience itself is my extended family, that they feel for me and support me, that they want to understand and see me as a fellow human being. Consequently, I'm completely blameless in my approach, which helps immensely when you're an African American man speaking, in general, to audiences that are not African American, and you're talking about race in America.

Now, what I've done can easily be applied to any story or subject that involves controversy or tension. Obviously, stories about people caught up in war or great social injustices are fertile ground for such a method, but every kind of story involves some sort of conflict. That's the essence of drama, and if there's no drama, there's no story. And all great stories revolve around universal concepts—that's what makes them great. Your job is to find the universal concepts that are buried like treasure in the stories you tell.

For example, building a vegetable or flower garden in a wilderness area is waging a kind of "war" because those plants don't belong there. However nourishing or beautiful they might be, some would see them as invasive plants in a sacred place. You can't make beer or wine without agriculture, and yet no other human invention has transformed the natural tapestry of our planet more than agriculture has. It's all about perspective, isn't it? War, invasions, planetary transformations—like joy, fear, love, hate, loneliness, and sorrow—are universal concepts one and all.

I tell every good interpreter who wants to be great that they must see everything they do in terms of universal concepts. Proficiency in doing this lies at the very core of what it means to be an "interpreter." This comes much easier when we understand that our job is not just to help people think about these sorts of connections, but to create an environment where feeling something about them is inevitable. Where would the heart be without arteries and veins? Where would any story be without a heart? Yes, you can lead people to the edge of something you think is magnificent—the Grand Canyon, the Pyramids, Uluru, or a tiny beautiful wildflower—but it's up to them to see and feel it. Only they can find that special place where the thing and their souls become one. And wherever that confluence may be, you will find a universal concept. Your role is showing them the way to it.

Figure 2-5. *A master's advice on the importance of universal concepts.*

a story about some city, for example, Paris, while simultaneously hearing a description of a complex process in the right ear, for example, photosynthesis. The person is told to pay attention to the message about Paris, and to ignore the message about photosynthesis. This is a difficult task in itself, but there's more. Besides having to listen to only one of the two messages, the person is told to "shadow" or repeat back the message he or she is listening to as it is heard, all the while trying to ignore the other message. Few mental tasks require as much concentration and sheer effort as shadowing.

Moray (1959) and Cherry (1966) conducted shadowing experiments and found that not only was it difficult for their subjects to shadow, but when tested for their recall of information they were supposed to pay attention to, the subjects could remember very little. Of course, when the researchers tested their recall of the ignored message (in our example, the description of photosynthesis), the subjects remembered even less. In Cherry's experiment, the subjects didn't even notice that the speaker switched from English to German, and in Moray's experiment, they didn't recognize that some words were repeated thirty-five consecutive times. In both studies, however, when the researchers prefaced some part of the ignored information with the subject's actual name (for example, Mary or Jim), the subjects were able to remember what followed it, even though they remembered nothing else. Studies such as these dramatically show why interpretation needs to be personal. We'll always pay attention to information we care about, even if we're trying to concentrate on something else.

As Solso, MacLin, and MacLin (2008) pointed out, most of us have experienced this kind of thing at one time or another: You're at a noisy party or social gathering, and someone on the other side of the room says, "I heard that Sue and Howard…" Until then completely involved in their own conversations, every Sue and Howard in the room now turns an attentive ear to the speaker. Psychologists call this "selective attention," and it's something that all audiences have. They'll predictably switch their attention to things they care about and, as we saw, even when they're consciously trying not to.

> We always pay attention to information we care about.

But how else might Mr. Jones make his presentation on geology more personal? Certainly, he couldn't mention the names of all the people in his audience. Even if he knew them, there'd probably be far too many. But he might try two other simple techniques that are almost as effective. These are self-referencing and labeling (see Figure 2-6).

Self-Referencing

Self-referencing is getting people in the audience to think about themselves and their own experiences as you give them new information. This causes them to connect the new ideas you're giving them with something they already care about—themselves. Mr. Jones could do this by using simple phrases such as, "Think of the last time you…," "Have you ever…?," or "At one time or another, most of you have probably…" Self-referencing phrases are simple, and research has shown that using them will often increase the interest level of your communication.[11]

You might have noticed that self-referencing often relies on the word *you*. This is a powerful word in all languages (especially when it's combined with direct eye contact), and the best interpreters use it frequently. But variations can also be effective. For instance, try substituting other words for *you* in the examples provided in the previous paragraph. You'll see that although the effect is different, the new phrases still help personalize the information that follows them. For example, "Think of the last time a person you know did such and such…," "Have your kids ever…," or "At one time or another, most of us have probably…"

How could Mr. Jones use self-referencing to make his talk on geology more personal? If he were trying to explain the process of sedimentation, for example, he might say something such as the following:

> How many of you like to skip stones across water? Have you ever noticed that the best skipping stones are found near rivers? Why is that, do you think? That's right, they're smooth and polished from the water's current, just the way wood is

Self-Referencing and Labeling
Two Ways to Make Communication More Personal

Communication that appeals to things we really care about—such as ourselves, our loved ones, our strongest beliefs, values, and deepest convictions—attracts our attention. Information that is somehow related or connected to this inner circle of our lives will seem more important to us than it otherwise might. That's because it's more personal, and therefore, more relevant. Interpreters can make their communication more personal in many ways. Two simple techniques are self-referencing and labeling.

1. *Self-referencing* means getting people in your audience to think momentarily about themselves as you give them some new piece of information. This makes them relate to that information at a personal level and, according to research, increases the likelihood that they will pay attention to it, understand it, and be able to remember it later. You can use self-referencing by issuing a simple phrase (the self-reference) and then relating to it the information you want your audience to remember. For example:

- "Think of the last time you…"
- "Have you ever…?"
- "How many of you have ever…?"
- "At one time or another most of us have…"
- "How many of you can remember the very best teacher you ever had? Think about that person for a second. What do you suppose made him or her such a good teacher? One thing you probably noticed was that…"

2. *Labeling* is classifying people (or kinds of people) in either a positive, negative, or neutral way. When the label is issued, most people in your audience will either associate themselves with it or disassociate themselves from it. Either way, they'll have to identify themselves in relationship to the label. Information that you relate to the label therefore will seem more personal to them.

- Examples of positive labels: "People who can fathom the horrors of war know that…,""If you're the kind of person who cares about wildlife, then you probably…," "If you consider yourself a lover of beer, then you most likely…,""Parents who worry about…"
- Examples of negative labels: "The worst criminals are the ones who commit crimes against nature,""The biggest headache for land managers are people who think that…,""If you don't care about protecting endangered species, then you probably don't believe that…"
- Examples of neutral labels: "Canadians…,""People who live in Hawaii…,""We Scots…,""Children…,""Parents… "

Figure 2-6. *People pay attention to things they care about.*

smooth after you rub it with sandpaper. And if you've ever used sandpaper on a piece of wood, you know that all that rubbing can cause quite a mess. *Sediment* is just another word for the mess. In a river, the mess comes from small particles of rock that have been rubbed off by the water and, of course, all the soil and other material that washes in from the sides of the river. Over time, the mess piles up, and the whole process is called "sedimentation." If you're like me, you're thinking that one of the best things about rivers is that you don't have to clean up after them. Or do you? Where do you suppose all the sediment goes?

In this statement, Mr. Jones did two important things to make his description of sedimentation more personal to his audience: he used three self-referencing phrases, and he used the word *you* ten times (eleven, counting *you've*). He also made sedimentation more meaningful to his audience by using an analogy (comparing wood sanding to sedimentation), and he tried to be lighthearted and informal in his tone. It appears that Mr. Jones is more interested in helping his audience understand how the process of sedimentation works than he is in teaching them the terminology and facts he might expect his high school students to know. Contrast the above description with the more formal definition Mr. Jones gives to his students from his lecture notes:

> Sedimentation is the process by which particulate matter is freed from parent material by the erosive power of water, and subsequently deposited as strata at a point downstream directly proportional to the mass of the particles and the velocity of the stream.

Had Mr. Jones, the interpreter, relied on his class lecture notes instead of on his knowledge of techniques such as self-referencing and analogies, his audience would have received a very different (and no doubt poorer) presentation.

Labeling

A second technique for making interpretation more personal is **labeling**. It's based on the idea that people will pay attention to things that remind them of themselves. Used frequently in advertising, a label is simply a statement that's made about a "kind" of person or group of people in relation to some idea, point, or object that an interpreter is trying to describe. A successful peanut butter advertisement from a few years ago used the tagline, "Choosy mothers choose (this brand of peanut butter)." The message in the slogan is that mothers who really care about their children will select the brand, presumably because it's better. The label is "choosy mothers." Since most mothers like to think of themselves as being careful about the food they give their children, they paid attention to the advertisement. By contrast, an agricultural extension agent once said to his audience, "If you really care about the water, air, and soil you'll leave for your children, then you'll be very interested in what I'm going to show you this afternoon. However, if these things don't interest you, then perhaps you should leave now and send me your *children*. Certainly, *they* will care."

Although it was probably too strong a statement, you can see in the latter example that labels can be negative as well as positive. The idea is that people like to see themselves as having good qualities, and they'll often pay attention to a negative label in order to reassure themselves that they're not like the people being described. Another example is a ranger giving an evening program in Grand Teton National Park, United States who told his audience, "The worst criminals are the ones who commit crimes against nature."

Labels can also be neutral and nonjudgmental: "People who live in a warm climate…," "People from the United States…," "We Australians…," "British men over the age of thirty…," and so forth. As in the case of positive and negative labels, neutral labels can help you personalize the information you're presenting because when the label is issued, most people will either associate themselves with it or disassociate themselves from it. In either event, the label requires them to identify in a personal way with the information being presented. A frequent result is that the information is more interesting to them and they pay attention to what follows.

Be thoughtful when using labels. They classify people and therefore have the potential to offend if they're not chosen carefully. In addition, you should be careful not to exclude part of your audience with a label that's too restrictive—unless, of course, that's your intention. Finally, try to select labels that are important to people in your audience. A museum docent might be more effective using the label, "People who value what the past can teach us…," than if she simply said, "People who visit this museum…," Both are good labels, but the first one is better because it refers to something that's probably more important to the docent's audience. Likewise, an interpreter at a zoo might say, "All of us who care about preventing the extinction of this animal believe that…," instead of simply "A lot of people think that…," Practice using labels and self-referencing. The better you become at recognizing and capitalizing on opportunities to use them, the more personal your interpretation will be.

Quality 4: Interpretation Is Enjoyable

All successful communication is **enjoyable** in the sense that mentally pleasing information helps engage audiences and keep them entertained. And for this reason, some have wanted to use these three *E* words (*enjoyable*, *engaging*, and *entertaining*) interchangeably in TORE. It's probably true that two of them (being engaging and being entertaining) can be taken to mean pretty much the same thing because they both refer to attracting and holding an audience's attention. But being enjoyable means something more specific than this in the TORE model (Figure 2-7).

In fact, being enjoyable does only part of the work needed for interpretation to engage and entertain an audience. As I pointed out in Chapter 1, the *O* (organization) and *R* (relevance) are needed to complete the job. In other words, for interpretation to attract and sustain an audience's attention, it must be easy to follow, connect to what matters to an audience, and be mentally pleasing to process (*O*, *R*, and *E*). This is why I don't use *engaging* or *entertaining* to refer to the *E* in TORE. It's also why in Chapter 1, I called the **entertainment** industry an

---

The *E* Words of Interpretation—*Enjoy, Entertain,* and *Engage*

In TORE, I always intend the literal meaning of *enjoy* (from old French *enjoir*, "to rejoice"), in the sense of deriving satisfaction or pleasure as we do, for example, when something captivates us. Clearly, humans can enjoy being captivated, even when it's not very amusing or fun in the ways we typically think of these words (for example, while reading about a tragic event or watching a scary movie). Yes, it's true that some kinds of enjoyment involve amusement, frivolity, or playful fun, but I never mean *only* those things when I use the word.

I also use the literal meaning of *entertain*, which is "to hold attention." Its etymology is old French (*entre*, "between," plus *tenir*, "to hold") and Latin (*inter*, "among," plus *tenere*, "to hold"). In its literal meaning, *entertain* doesn't necessarily imply amusement or fun. Obviously, sad or psychologically disturbing ideas and bodily painful events hold our attention, too. In fact, they captivate us, and anything that holds our attention that strongly is, by definition, entertaining. Likewise, *entertain* can mean "to contemplate," "consider," or "hold in mind." So, for example, in daily conversation we might say, "Let's entertain the possibility of such and such…" or, "Would you entertain a slightly different point of view?" These are the meanings I intend when I use the word *entertain*—literally, "to place something strongly in the mind of another"—to *engage* that person.

Engaging and entertaining are essentially the same thing—that is, being engaged means being entertained in the sense that your attention is being held. When you engage with something, you commit yourself to it as you do, for example, when you pay attention to an interpretive product.

Figure 2-7. *Definitions of enjoyable, entertaining, and engaging.*

All three *E* words—enjoyable, entertaining, engaging. Northwest Trek Wildlife Park, USA. *Photo by Barbara Ham.*

Most audiences enjoy being involved in an interpretive encounter. Lindblad Expeditions, Baja California, Mexico. *Photo by Barbara Ham.*

Humor is one way to add enjoyment to interpretation. *Courtesy of Sovereign Hill Museums Association, Australia.*

"ORE" industry, not just an "E" industry. To be engaging or entertaining—that is, to attract and hold the attention of a noncaptive audience—interpretation must be *all three*: *O*, *R*, and *E*.

So what, exactly, does it mean to say that interpretation should be "enjoyable?" Does it mean interpretation should always be fun or funny or lighthearted? Not necessarily. As we all know, things we enjoy paying attention to can sometimes be sad or scary, shocking or even appalling. Just watching television news is enough to convince us of that. Yet we enjoy paying attention to these things in the sense that they attract our attention, even though they don't make us smile or laugh.

The essential ingredient of enjoyable interpretation is that it's presented in a way that matches the audience's idea of having a good time, even if having a good time means being sad or angry or scared or contemplative. Although some interpretation might not be very uplifting or lighthearted, it simply pleases the mind to pay attention to it,[12] at least for a while. That is, it's enjoyable to process. And this is why the *E* word in TORE must be *enjoyable*. It captures a specific characteristic of successful interpretation (pleasure) that makes it qualitatively different from the *O* and *R* words. And when interpretation has all three qualities (*O*, *R*, and *E*), you can expect it to engage and entertain its audience.

The mind involuntarily goes where it finds the most gratifying information, and this is what enjoyment is all about. As Mr. Jones discovered in Chapter 1, when noncaptive audiences aren't enjoying what's in front of them, they're likely to switch attention to something their minds find more appealing. As we saw in Chapter 1, attention switching might be an involuntary action such as daydreaming, or it can be more blatant such as getting up and walking out in the middle of a presentation. Audiences viewing exhibits or signs might simply stop viewing them; boring publications might end up in a recycling bin, or worse, on the ground.

Ways to Make Interpretation Enjoyable

How to make learning enjoyable will vary depending on the communication medium one is using. Enjoyable exhibits, for example, have different qualities from enjoyable audiovisual programs or enjoyable talks. Yet one thing that seems to stand out in most successful interpretation is that it's informal and not classroom-like.

Interpreters can create an informal atmosphere in many ways. For example, a speaker like Mr. Jones could use a conversational tone of voice rather than the artificial and stuffy tone that some academicians and politicians are known to use, especially when they read from notes.[13] Also, many years of research on exhibits have shown that people will pay less attention if the exhibits utilize media or communication strategies that remind them of formal education, such as Mr. Jones's portable whiteboard. Generally, the best exhibits are those that invite engagement or interaction, are three-dimensional, or that contain movement, changing scenes, or lively colors—all characteristics more commonly associated with entertainment than with traditional classroom media.[14] Likewise, talks, tours, and other kinds of presentations have been found to attract greater attention if they incorporate humor, music, or two-way communication.[15] For similar reasons, an audiovisual program containing background music will often hold an audience's attention longer than one containing only a narrator's voice, and signs and publications that have novel titles, pose intriguing questions, or contain colorful illustrations are more likely to attract attention than those that are less novel or colorful.[16]

> Informality usually adds enjoyment to interpretation.

Contrary to some people's opinions, you don't have to be a gifted communicator to make interpretation of even very technical information enjoyable for a noncaptive audience. A number of straightforward techniques for doing this are listed in Figure 2-8.

There Are Many Ways to Make Technical Information More Enjoyable

Smile: A smiling face indicates pleasure in most cultures. An old Louis Armstrong song goes: "When you're smiling, the whole world smiles with you." This means that your audience will take its cue from you. If you look like you're relaxed and having fun, they'll begin to feel that way, too. Appearing too serious can create a formal atmosphere that works against you.

Use active verbs: Verbs are the power in any language. Don't rob them of their power by making them passive (e.g., "The explorers faced uncertainty every day" not "Uncertainty was faced by the explorers every day"). Academic writing stresses the use of passive verb forms too much. Use powerful, active verb forms. In Chapter 7 ("Not All Themes Are Equal"), we'll return in more detail to the importance of using active-voice verbs.[17]

Show cause and effect: People like to know what things cause other things to happen. Try to show direct relationships between causes and their effects.

Link science to stories about people: Nonscientists are often more interested in science if it can be related directly to people. For example, weaving information about plants into a story of how indigenous people utilized those plants in their diets, art, and religion might be more entertaining than the same information would be by itself. Telling about any aspect of a natural or physical science through the eyes of those who explored it, discovered it, described it, wondered about it, overcame it, succumbed to it, worried about it, died from it, were saved by it, were empowered by it, were hindered by it, or who otherwise affected or were affected by the thing in question will generally make it more interesting to nonscientists.[18]

Exaggerate size: "If we were small enough to actually walk inside of a wasp's nest, you'd be amazed at what you'd see."

Exaggerate timescale: "If time were speeded up so that a thousand years went by every second, you'd be able to stand right here and watch continental drift for yourself."

Use an overriding analogy: That is, an analogy that your entire presentation revolves around (e.g., likening the making of cheese to the making of a fine red wine, comparing the earth to an onion's layered skin in order to tell about certain geologic processes, or relating forest succession to the construction of a house).

Use a contrived situation: Demonstrate the need for forest conservation by making up a story about a town in which there is no such thing as wood or wood products, go forward or back in time, pose a hypothetical problem or set up an illustrative situation (e.g., "What if there were no governments?" or, "What would life on earth be like if its average temperature increased just 5° C?").

Use personification: Give selected human qualities to nonhuman things (e.g., "What might trees say if they could talk?" or "How might ants view humans?"). Give the narrator of an audiovisual program an animal's identity or point of view. Walt Disney made personification famous in his many movies about animals and stories in which the audience experienced certain adventures through the eyes of the animal characters. This technique has been criticized (sometimes rightly and sometimes not) by biologists, because it involves giving human qualities to nonhuman animals. Be careful when using personification. Don't imply that animals and plants really think and act like humans.

Focus on an individual: That is, make up a fictitious but technically accurate story about one particular person or object (e.g., an animal, plant, rock, water molecule, ice crystal, etc.). Give an account of what this person or thing experiences in terms of the technical information you are trying to get across to your audience.

Some examples of focusing on an individual:

- Tell a story about the members of a single indigenous family who fought courageously against an ethnic majority for basic human rights.
- Relate one soldier's loneliness and fears from his or her journal excerpts.
- Recount the mishaps of a bear who became conditioned to human food as a cub and subsequently had various encounters with park rangers leading to tranquilization and relocation and eventually to being euthanized.
- Follow a single water molecule as it goes through the entire water cycle, or a mass of rock as it's changed from sedimentary to metamorphic to igneous states.
- Describe what happens to a particular parrot after it's taken from its tropical forest home and transported with other birds to a pet store in another country.
- Tell about the final days of the last individual of a particular species.
- Describe a specific smuggler's attempt to transport endangered wildlife skins out of a country.
- Follow the journey of an individual grape from growth on the vine to harvest to fermentation to bottling, and decades later when the bottle is opened to commemorate a special event.

Figure 2-8. *Examples of ways to be more enjoyable.*

Where to from Here

In this chapter, we've seen that being thematic (T), organized (O), relevant (R), and enjoyable (E) is important to the success of virtually every interpretive product, if *success* is defined as "holding attention long enough to make a compelling point and then making that point." Together, these four ingredients of the TORE model represent the interpretive approach to communication as I have researched it and taught it. According to many dozens of studies on how humans process communication and how we're affected by it, infusing any type of interpretive product with all four qualities will enhance its chances of success.

We've also seen in this chapter—as well as in Chapter 1—that interpretation's main goal is provoking audiences to think their own thoughts. With this goal in mind, the respective roles of T, O, R, and E become clearer to interpreters in the sense that they see themselves not as teachers or entertaining fact givers, but rather as *facilitators* of something that is ultimately far more important—what we'll call in later chapters "meaning making." In Chapter 3, we'll take a closer look at what this facilitator job entails and why it's so different from seeing interpretation as instruction or pure entertainment.

Glossary terms: analogy, contrast, enjoyable, entertainment, example, global theme, labeling, magical number 4, meaningful, metaphor, organized, personal, relevant, self-referencing, simile, subtheme, theme, topic, universal concept

Additional Thoughts for Chapter 2

1   I'm not using the phrase "moral of the story" in the strict literary sense that it's some sort of message about "right and wrong" or "good versus bad." Rather, I'm using the term in the popular sense of "a lesson learned," "principle extracted," "main conclusion drawn," or "implication seen."

2   In Chapter 9 ("Sequential Theme Development"), we'll see that there are at least three different ways to do this. One of them involves never actually saying your theme (whether orally or in writing) to your audience.

3   This idea (which I call the "zone of tolerance") is a little more involved than I'm presenting here. As you'll see in Chapter 8, the idea of the zone of tolerance is not that people in your audience will be able to repeat back to you ("parrot") your theme. But if you've done a good job of developing and presenting your theme and then later have a chance to talk with people in the audience about their thoughts, what you'd hear from them should please rather than disappoint you. We'll leave it at that for now until we revisit the idea later.

4   In the interpretation field, Bitgood and Patterson (1993) developed a "cost-benefit" model of attention paying by museum visitors in order to explain in more detail how this works. Others, including Moscardo et al. (2007) and Trapp, Gross, and Zimmerman (1994) have offered similar guidelines related to audience effort and attention capture.

5   Ironically, three decades later Miller revealed in an autobiographical sketch (Miller, 1989) that he really offered the seven-plus-or-minus-two range only as a rough estimate and didn't intend for

it to be taken as a precise limit. Not aware of this nuance, many psychologists over the years were openly critical of Miller, claiming that his magical number seven was too high. However, in defending Miller, Nelson Cowan (whose own research had largely been responsible for proving Miller wrong), claimed that Miller's original "magical number seven" article was actually just tongue in cheek, even if everyone else failed to see it (Cowan, 2005). Aside from being one of the truly interesting oddities in the history of psychology, a moral of this story is that, yes, even we academics can have a sense of humor.

6   Specifically, research has shown that ease of processing and message relevance are the two stars that must align for interpretation to stand the greatest chance of provoking an audience to think. Most of these studies have focused on the elaboration likelihood model of persuasion (ELM) or the heuristic-systematic processing model (HSM). See, for example, Chaiken (1980); Petty and Cacioppo (1986); Petty, Cacioppo and Schumann (1983); Petty, McMichael and Brannon (1992); and Petty, Rucker, Bizer, and Cacioppo (2004). I've also reviewed a number of these studies in the specific context of interpretation (Ham 2007; 2009a).

7   See Scherbaum (2008), who offers a useful collection of practical ways to make interpretation more meaningful.

8   Great stories (Strauss, 1996), great stage plays (Egri, 1946), and great screenplays (McKee, 1997) usually hinge on a core of universal concepts. The same can be said for a lot of great songs and poems.

9   If you're interested, a thoughtful discussion by Tardona (2005) discusses why our inherent interest in universal concepts might have played a role in human evolution. Manhart (2005) offers a complementary explanation from evolutionary psychology about the brain's need and capacity for making meaning from things that matter to us. Simply put, universal concepts allow us to make sense of our world in ways that help us survive.

10   Many people know about Buffalo Soldiers from Bob Marley's famous reggae song (1980). To learn more about their place in American history and the US national parks see http://en.wikipedia.org/wiki/Buffalo_Soldier. Shelton Johnson's interpretive brilliance has been widely recognized, including by television icon, Oprah Winfrey, acclaimed filmmaker, Ken Burns, and US President Barack Obama. See http://en.wikipedia.org/wiki/Shelton_Johnson.

11   See especially Barney (2006) and Symons and Johnson (1997).

12   Just about anyone who has visited the Holocaust Museum in the United States or Auschwitz in Poland will attest to the fact that both are grippingly and viscerally entertaining, yet neither produces many smiles.

13   A good speaker avoids reading from notes. In fact, most interpreters don't use them at all. They know that referring to their notes can create not only a formal or academic atmosphere, but it might even make the audience wonder whether the interpreter really knows much about the subject being presented.

14 See, for example, Ames, Franco, and Frye (1997); Bitgood (2000); Dierking, Ellenbogen, and Falk, (2004); Falk and Dierking (2000); Moscardo (1996); Moscardo et al. (2007); Serrell (1999); Shiner and Shafer (1975); Washburne and Wagar (1972).

15 This was the main finding of an early study by Ham and Shew (1979). Other characteristics of entertaining presentations are described in Brochu and Merriman (2012), Field and Lente (2000), Pastorelli (2003), Regnier, Gross and Zimmerman (1994) and Ward and Wilkinson (2006).

16 See examples in Caputo, Lewis, and Brochu (2008); Moscardo (1999b); and Moscardo, Ballantyne, and Hughes (2007). See also Hall, Ham, and Lackey (2010), who compared the ability of various approaches to sign messaging to attract and hold the attention of national park visitors in the USA. Moscardo (1999a) provides a useful summary of attention-getting methods for interpretive texts.

17 If you pay attention to (or eavesdrop on) people's everyday conversations, you'll notice we only rarely use passive voice. What you'll hear in a normal exchange is a string of active-voice sentences. It's as though we instinctively want to be our most interesting selves in everyday discourse, and it's only when we have to communicate about technical topics that we start using a lot of passive voice.

18 This method can work well even when the reference group isn't exactly "human." One of the most celebrated astrophysicists of all time, Carl Sagan, was not only a brilliant scientist but an accomplished teacher and interpreter. One of his former students, a colleague of mine at the Smithsonian Tropical Research Institute in Panama, recounted one of Sagan's lectures in an astronomy class at Cornell University, USA. Sagan's topic for the day was the evolution of the telescope as it would have been perceived by extraterrestrials. "ET go home," indeed. If you're not familiar with the immense accomplishments of Dr. Carl Sagan, a good summary is at http://en.wikipedia.org/wiki/Carl_Sagan.

CHAPTER 3
The Endgame of Interpretation

When you know ahead of time what you're trying to accomplish, succeeding is much more likely.

A man sits in his workshop, busy with an invention of wheels and springs. You ask him what the gadget is, what it is meant to do. He looks at you confidingly and whispers: "I really don't know."

Another man rushes down the street, panting for breath. You intercept him and ask where he is going. He gasps: "How should I know where I'm going? I am on my way."

Your reaction—and ours, and the world's—is that these two men are a little mad. Every sensible invention must have a purpose, every planned sprint a destination.

Lajos Egri (1946: 1), *The Art of Dramatic Writing*

We all know life is full of uncertainty, but two things we can be fairly sure of are that the second guy is still running and the invention remains a work in progress. Without an end in sight, neither can achieve a result, at least not a purposeful one. So it is with interpretation.

This chapter considers the outcomes of interpretation, what results we might be after, what we're trying to achieve in the end, and what we would need to know at a minimum to say whether we're successful at it. I'll call this the "**endgame**," a term chess players use in the final stages of a match when the position of all the pieces makes the outcome certain.[1] In everyday language, it refers to the status or condition of things when some process or event has reached a successful conclusion.

Like the inventor and sprinter in Egri's example, we need to be able to envision the endgame of interpretation in order to give it a *purpose* and a *destination*. Once we're clear on what we're after, our decisions about content, communication approach, and how to evaluate it also become clearer. Likewise, when we've defined the endgame, we'll be able to see more clearly just how we ought to educate, train, and develop interpretation professionals to continually improve their effectiveness. For these reasons, this chapter necessarily begins with the *end*.

Some Possible Endgames of Interpretation

Having worked with a lot of interpreters[2] around the world, I've noticed some patterns in how they see their craft. Particularly interesting to me has been listening to the ideas out there about what constitutes "good" or "effective" or "successful" interpretation. The indicators of success an interpreter emphasizes over others reveal something about her or his philosophy and approach—that person's sense of purpose and destination.

A typical discussion begins with the interpreter either raving or complaining about the quality of interpretation that she, he, or some other person has produced. After listening to the evaluation, I almost always respond with the same question: "Why do you say that?" The conversation that ensues is usually pretty revealing in terms of the endgame my friend has perhaps consciously (although often unwittingly) adopted. Whenever we're forced to explain to someone else the reasons behind our assessment of something as being "good" or "bad," we must come to grips with the criteria we've applied in arriving at that conclusion. That's where the endgame is revealed. In Figure 3-1, I've listed some of the reasons given to me at one time or another to explain why interpretation was good.

As the willing participant in many dozens—if not hundreds—of such exchanges over the years, I've noticed three prevalent endgames. These are not necessarily the only endgames, nor are they necessarily mutually exclusive (in fact, hybrids are common). But they differ enough in the criteria we'd apply in distinguishing between excellent and poor interpretation—or between interpretation that succeeds and that which fails—that they represent fundamentally different points of view about interpretation's endgame. Our sense of how to design interpretive encounters[3] to be effective, and how to train interpreters to be excellent at their craft, will vary depending on which of these endgames we adopt. The ones I see most often are championed by three archetypes—the "provoker," the "teacher," and the "entertainer."[4] Maybe you can see some of these archetypes reflected in the list in Figure 3-1.

Why Do You Say That?
"It was amazing. She held those kids' attention for forty-five minutes!"
"I swear they could *feel* their own heritage! It was a zen thing."
"Afterward, everyone could identify every bird."
"Everyone in that audience saw the connection."
"They could tell me the names of all the architects who designed the main buildings."
"They were laughing like crazy through the whole program."
"His body language was the key to whole thing."
"The colors were incredibly vivid. They almost exploded right off the panel."
"People actually wanted to have their picture taken with me afterward."
"When I got to his campsite the next day, he invited me to eat with them."
"They actually offered me a beer!"
"You could see their wheels spinning. He really had them captivated."
"Those people left so moved they probably didn't even sleep that night."
"I've never had a more motivated audience. It was like they were just eating out of my hand."
"That was a great way to show how the Roman aqueducts were built."
"I'd have to say that this was my most memorable experience as an interpreter. They seemed to respond to everything I said."
"It was creative. The visitors really enjoyed themselves."
"If you wanted to illustrate how evolution works, you couldn't find a better analogy."

Figure 3-1. *Interpreters' explanations of why an interpretive encounter was successful.*

Interpretation as Provocation

Defining the endgame of interpretation seems to have been Freeman Tilden's purpose in his fifth chapter of *Interpreting Our Heritage* (1957). He was emphatic that we mustn't see interpretation as some sort of "instructional" or "teaching" exercise in the academic sense. Borrowing from Ralph Waldo Emerson, he gave us a now famous dichotomy, "not instruction, but **provocation**," as a basic framework to show what interpretation is and is not:

> It is true that the visitors…frequently desire straight information, which may be called instruction, and a good interpreter will always be able to teach when called upon. But the purpose of Interpretation is to stimulate the reader or hearer toward a desire to widen his horizon of interests and knowledge, and to gain an understanding of the greater truths that lie behind any statements of fact…to search out meanings for himself. (1957: 32-33, 36)

When a skilled interpreter provokes thought, an audience will make personal meaning. Hawai'i Volcanoes National Park, USA. *Photo by Stephen Geiger. Courtesy of US National Park Service.*

In this way, Tilden was telling us that the main thing interpretation should aim to accomplish is provoking people to think for themselves, and in doing so, to find their own personal meanings and connections.[5] Furthermore, he cautioned against seeing interpretation as serving some sort of academic teaching function. If you're already familiar with Tilden's philosophy, you'll know that his formula for success hinged on two *R*s, *relevance* and *revelation*. The best (most successful) interpretation, as he envisioned it, would connect to what people care most about (themselves and their own experience in life), and it would be presented in such a way that the thing being interpreted would "reveal" its inner meanings (or "greater truths") to the people—that is, they themselves would find their own personal meanings in the thing. Two generations later, I think this is still pretty good advice. The archetype interpreter in this endgame could be called the "provoker."

Interpretation as Teaching

However, Tilden observed then, as we do now, that interpreters sometimes can lose sight of the provocation endgame, a danger (or temptation) that appears to grow in proportion to their own knowledge about the things they interpret. When this happens, they run the danger of becoming more like unskilled teachers—where the mastery of facts, rather than the potential meanings audiences might themselves make from those facts—becomes the center of their focus. Tilden recounted his own experience as a member of the audience:

> When getting facts across becomes the primary focus, interpretation takes on a teaching-like quality.

> Thus, in so many cases that we have observed, the provocation to the visitor to search out meanings for himself, and join in the expedition like a fellow discoverer, was sometimes submerged in a high tide of facts, perfectly accurate, perfectly ineffectual…And as a participant in such groups I have so many times had my enthusiasm wilted by an interlocutor who mistook information for interpretation—who became a poor instructor when he could have been an inspiring guide. (1957: 36)

We probably have to forgive interpreters who succumb to a desire to tell everything they know (the "encyclopedists"), since in many cases their weakness stems directly from an admirable and necessary source—their own passion. And, of course, it's probably impossible to interpret anything without facts, maybe even lots of them. But despite their good intentions, when getting those facts across becomes the primary focus of an encounter, interpretation takes on a teaching-like quality.[6] In this endgame, success is an audience learning, recognizing, or being able to remember the facts presented during an interpretive encounter. We might label this archetype the "teacher."

Interpretation as Entertainment

A third endgame arises from the obvious fact that most audiences of interpretation are plea-sure-seekers who want to be entertained. Success in this endgame is making each interpretive encounter enjoyable and holding audience attention. Toward this end, we design and deliver interpretive encounters that emphasize the "wow factor"—superlatives, unusual and extraor-dinary facts, dynamic presentation styles, and novel media—a sort of information carnival, if such a thing exists, in which interpretation becomes an ad hoc collection of "cool facts" and interesting linkages presented in a clever way. Seeing interpretation through this endgame, we gauge its effectiveness mainly by whether our audiences enjoy it and whether we're able to keep them entertained for an allotted time. You might recall the literal meanings of *entertainment* and *enjoyment* I provided in Chapter 2 (Figure 2-7).

Appropriately, Dave Larsen (2002, 2003) labeled this kind of interpretation "interpretain-ment." Its older siblings, infotainment and edutainment,[7] respectively refer either to entertain-ment that's intended to be informative and educational, or education that's supposed to be entertaining. Either way, the "tainment" in each of them signals the defining quality of their endgame: holding attention.

As we saw in the first two chapters, the first and necessary task of every interpretive en-counter is to capture and maintain the audience's attention; until we've done that, we're truly wasting our time trying to do anything more. There are probably hundreds of ways to do this, some of which we'll discuss in later chapters, but the success of any one of them depends on matching your method with the audience's notion of enjoyment (what to them is appealing, interesting, attractive, and so forth). Since audiences can vary a lot in what they enjoy, we have to know something about them in order to entertain them, whether in face-to-face or nonpersonal interpretation. When we guess wrong, it's doubtful we'll be success-ful in achieving much else. Recognizing this, some interpreters focus most—or even all—of their attention on the entertainment value of their interpretation. These are the archetypes of this endgame—let's call them the "entertainers."

An inherent risk of the entertainer's endgame is that the entertainment itself can steal the show, and whatever other outcome the interpreter had in mind is lost in the bells and whistles of the performance. As the Canadian philosopher Marshall McLuhan warned, the medium itself can become the message an audience takes away.[8] This, for example, is what occurred to travel writer Bill Bryson, while watching an interpretive performance, "Ned Kelly's Last Stand," which chronicled the demise of a famous Australian bad guy:

> We bought tickets and shuffled through a door into a dim room where the spectacle was to begin…Before us, in a deep gloom, we could just make out the shapes of furniture and seated dummies. After a few minutes, the lights dimmed altogether, there was a sudden very loud bang of gunfire, and the performance began. Well, call me a Whimp, drop a brick shithouse on me, but I can honestly say that I have never seen anything so wonderfully, so delightfully, so monumentally bad as "Ned Kelly's Last Stand." It was so bad it was worth every penny. Actually, it was so bad it was worth more than we paid. For the next thirty-five minutes we proceeded through a series of rooms where we watched homemade dummies, each with a frozen smile and a mop of hair that brought to mind windblown pubis, reenacting various scenes from the famous Kelly shoot-out in a random and deliriously incoherent way. Occasionally one of the dummies would turn a stiff head or jerk up a forearm to fire a pistol, though not necessarily in synch with the narrative. Meanwhile, around each room lots of other mechanical events were taking place—empty chairs rocked, cupboard doors mysteriously opened and shut, player pianos played…Do you know those fairground stalls where you fire a rifle at assorted targets to make an outhouse door swing open or a stuffed chicken fall over? Well, this reminded me of that, only much worse. (2000: 166)

As we all know, most audiences are eager to reward clever and creative communication styles with their attention and applause, and to the well-intentioned "interpertainer," this feedback is irresistible and motivating. So it's not surprising that evaluations of interpretation have often stressed audience attention and enjoyment as the primary indicators of success. In this way, audiences, interpreters, and evaluators alike have

> When holding attention is the only prominent concern, the distinction between interpretation and pure entertainment is pretty fuzzy.

joined forces in validating the infotainment endgame, and a view of interpretation as fact-based entertainment persists today in some places.

But while any interpretation must succeed in holding the attention of its audience, when attention holding becomes our only significant concern, the line of distinction between interpretation and sheer entertainment is pretty hard to find. And, as Bryson's account reminds us, when the message is lost altogether, what could have been interpretation can come across more like a carnival act.

What Is "Excellence" in Interpretation?

We've seen that three prevalent archetypes (the provoker, the teacher, and the entertainer) represent very different views about interpretation's purpose and destination. Although I've stressed that they're not necessarily mutually exclusive, in presenting them separately I've accentuated their individual qualities and differences, as if they were separate and distinct windows through which the endgame of interpretation can be viewed. And a lot of us have indeed known interpreters, or have seen interpretation, that falls exclusively in one or another of these categories. In reality, however, probably not one of the archetypes *alone* represents an endgame that's both achievable and of interest to most interpreters. The would-be provoker who lacks the knowledge to make connections between a place and his or her audience will come across as a shallow naïf, the teacher short on showmanship will bore, and the entertainer who fails to see beyond the show will leave audiences smiling but clueless about what it all might mean to them.

Common sense should tell us that to some degree an ideal interpreter would probably embody aspects of all three endgames: a skilled communicator, armed with knowledge, who knows how to get between other people's ears and provoke them to think on their own. Provocation, as we've already seen, is a necessary goal of virtually all interpretation, but we can't succeed in provoking an audience to think without a factual foundation of some kind, and if we fail to capture and hold the audience's attention, we'll just be talking to ourselves. So each of the three endgames has its virtues.

Where the endgames strongly diverge from one another, however, is in the notion of excellence each of them gives us. As I suggested at the beginning of this chapter, we need to be able to envision the endgame of interpretation in order to give it a *purpose* and a *destination*. Until we're clear on what we're trying to achieve, having a view of excellence in interpretation—seeing how to get there and how to evaluate whether we've arrived—isn't even possible. In Figure

3-2, I've attempted to compare the main purposes and some of the evaluative criteria that seem to characterize each of the endgames. The point of it is simply to show that there are real differences between and among them, and that each endgame potentially takes interpreters on a different path to professional excellence.

We've already seen how each endgame brings to mind its own evaluative criteria:

The provocation endgame wants to leave people thinking and discovering their own meanings and connections.

The teaching endgame strives to leave them knowledgeable; informed about the facts surrounding a phenomenon, place or thing; and capable of remembering those facts later.

The entertainment endgame stresses the act of interpretation more than its outcome, where providing enjoyment and holding attention are the main evaluative criteria, in hopes that audiences will leave satisfied and with a fond memory of time well spent.

So you can see that each of them focuses our attention on different kinds of indicators that might tell us how we're progressing on the road to excellence. Were we to evaluate the accomplishments of an interpretive encounter according to any one of the endgames, we'd probably be interested in indicators that are unlike those in the other two categories.

Although, in practice, interpreters might give little thought to the criteria an evaluation uses in judging the success of a given interpretive encounter, we should be acutely aware that, over time, the direction professional interpretation travels in its pursuit of excellence hinges *entirely* on these criteria. Each evaluation produces results. If the magnitude of this or that is used to make judgments about interpretation's achievement (e.g., did people score high or low on the knowledge test, did they or did they not pay attention and rate an activity as enjoyable, or were they provoked to have many or just a few thoughts?), then those judgments should lead us to make decisions about improving the thing being evaluated. If knowledge gains are low, then shouldn't we devise a strategy to get better knowledge scores next time? If people didn't pay attention or rate the interpretation as enjoyable, then shouldn't we find ways to make the interpretation more appealing to them? And if they aren't being provoked to thought, then shouldn't we explore means of achieving that?

I hope you can see there's an almost inescapable conclusion we can draw from this discussion. Not only does our view of the endgame lead us to different indicators of success, but these criteria themselves define excellence in interpretation. Depending on the indicators we pay attention to, each sends us down a different path, both in terms of improving interpretation and in educating the next generation of interpretation professionals. For example, if knowledge acquisition is truly the indicator of interest, then we'll certainly want to train interpreters in methods that will help their audiences better remember the information presented. However, this might well lead us to train them in methods we associate more with uninspired teaching than with interpretation. It's well established, for instance, that techniques such as repetition, reinforcement, and fact rehearsal produce superior knowledge test scores, and yet these same methods are known to kill audience attention in interpretive settings (Moscardo, 1996).[9] Nevertheless, if better knowledge gain is what we want to produce, then shouldn't we be trying to produce the largest gains possible? And shouldn't we be recruiting and hiring interpreters who already possess such pedagogic skills? If not, then why are we using knowledge-based scores to evaluate interpretation? We could apply this logic, of course, to any criterion of success in any of the three endgames.

Primary Endgame		
	Interpreter as "teacher"	**Interpreter as "entertainer"**	**Interpreter as "provoker"**
Main purpose	Make people learn and understand established facts	Entertain people and provide a good time	Make people think and find personal meaning
Usual indicators of success	Correct recall of facts Knowledge recognition	Amount of enjoyment Attention capture and holding power	Number and kinds of thoughts provoked

Figure 3-2. *Purposes and typical evaluative criteria of three interpretive endgames.*

You might be thinking at this point that the endgames really aren't all that different, and that if you can be successful in one then you can assume success in the others as well—for example, that if you hold people's attention long enough they'll be provoked to think and will remember things later, or if you succeed in provoking them to a lot of thought, they'll also do well on a test of knowledge about the main points you were trying to make. As tempting as these assumptions might be, there's little evidence to back them up.

Although you've certainly got to attract and hold your audience's attention to achieve success in any of the three endgames, holding attention doesn't guarantee that anything more will result. Similarly, studies show that provoking people to thought doesn't necessarily mean they'll be able to remember much about the main ideas you presented. And on the flip side, even if they're able to remember or recognize a lot of the facts you presented, it doesn't mean you provoked them to think about anything beyond those facts.[10] So you really do have to decide for yourself which of the endgames you believe in most if you're going to improve your interpretation and achieve excellence over the long haul. That much seems fairly clear.

Therefore, even though none of the three endgames necessarily precludes the others, they are, in fact, *choices* when it comes to our notion of success, what we evaluate, and how we will educate and train interpreters years and decades from now to be capable of achieving excellence. Each gives

The endgame defines excellence in interpretation.

Interpretive guide training at the spectacular Sheikh Zayed Grand Mosque, United Arab Emirates. *Courtesy of Abu Dhabi Tourism and Culture Authority.*

us a set of eyeglasses through which we can see interpretation's purpose and ultimate destination. It determines what we selectively pay attention to, what outcomes matter most, and what it will take to realize them. Returning to the beginning of this chapter, if the sprinter and inventor in Egri's story had a sense of their endgames, they'd not only be able to finish what they set out to do, they'd be able to do it even better next time.

So Which Endgame Is Best?

We've already seen that all three endgames capture something important about an interpreter's job—holding attention, transferring information, and provoking thought. And we just saw that accomplishing any one of these important tasks doesn't necessarily mean that the other two will happen. So maybe it's fair to ask whether one of them is simply a more fundamental endgame than the other two. Is it possible, for example, that one is the ultimate endgame, whereas the other two are a means to that end? I think so.

Of the three archetypes we considered in this chapter, it's the "provoker" who emerges as most indispensable when it comes to interpretation's potential to make some kind "difference" in the audiences it reaches. In Chapter 1, we discussed three categories of these differences (enhancing experiences, promoting appreciative attitudes about the things interpreters interpret, and sometimes influencing the behavior of certain audience segments). Although we won't go into a lot of detail yet about individual studies that have examined the relationship between provoking thought and the likelihood of producing each of these types of outcomes,[11] it's a fair summary to say that achieving any and all them depends first on provoking the audience to think.[12] According to much research conducted since the 1980s, when interpreters are able to accomplish that much, their chances of being able to do all three things is significantly improved. Consider the following:

Experience, it has been argued, is nothing more than what a person thinks. That is, your experience with something resides within the thoughts you think about it. Therefore, provoking members of your audience to think will simultaneously enhance their experiences (provided, of course, you give them pleasurable thoughts to think).[13]

Many dozens of studies have looked at the effect of effortful thought (what in psychology is called "**elaboration**") on people's attitudes. A consistent finding is that the more communication provokes audience thinking, the stronger, more enduring, and more resilient are the attitudes that result.[14] So interpretation that provokes thought in an audience stands a greater chance of promoting appreciative attitudes about the things being interpreted than does interpretation that fails to provoke thinking (again, provided the thoughts people have are themselves appreciative in nature).

Finally, one of the important implications from these elaboration studies is that the strong attitudes resulting from a lot of thinking are also more predictive of future behavior than are attitudes that aren't the result of so much thinking.[15] In studies evaluating the use of interpretation to influence visitor behavior in protected areas, interpretive products designed to provoke thinking were found to be successful in impacting visitors' attitudes about desired behaviors and in bringing about those behaviors.[16]

Studies have not, however, shown any relationships between these three important categories of outcomes and the entertainment value of a communication event or audience recall of program content. Thinking, elaboration, effortful thought—or if you prefer, provocation—appears to be the lynchpin in all three categories.

Therefore, according to the weight of much evidence, you can be confident that if your interpretation succeeds in provoking your audience to think, you're going to have a far better chance of making the three kinds of differences interpretation is capable of making. This—what I've called "making a difference on purpose"—is both the premise and promise of interpretation when it's done exceedingly well. And, it's the subject we take up again in Chapters 4 and 5.

Glossary terms: elaboration, endgame, provocation

Additional Thoughts for Chapter 3

1   *Endgame* became a popular word in 1958 with the publication of Samuel Beckett's play, *Endgame*.

2   Recall from Chapter 1 that I use *interpreter* to refer to anyone who does *any* kind of interpretive work through *any* communication medium (face-to-face or nonpersonal). Among these are writers, designers, and artists; employees or volunteers for parks, zoos, museums, historic sites, tour operators, cruise ship companies, science centers, gardens, forests, aquariums, wineries, breweries, theme parks, and manufacturing plants; and guides, expedition leaders, docents, storytellers, composers, dramatists, directors, actors, and performers of all kinds.

3   Likewise, I'll use *interpretive encounter* to refer both to personal (face-to-face) and nonpersonal (self-guided) interpretation in order to avoid continually repeating the clarification.

4   Other far less common archetypes are "interpreters-as-cops" (which is self-explanatory), "interpreters-as-reproachers" (who blame and shame their audiences for how they think or behave), "inter-

preters-as-preachers" (who impose their own spirituality on their audiences), and "interpreters-as-encyclopedists" (a special breed of "interpreters-as-teachers," who focus not just on important facts but on all facts).

5   Note how similar this view of interpretation is to our working definition in Chapter 1. This is a "constructivist" perspective. Constructivists argue that communicators (whether interpreters, teachers, or courtroom lawyers) do not "put" knowledge in other people's heads. Rather, their role is to stimulate learners (whether museum visitors, students, or a jury of women and men) to think for themselves. Through the process of their own thinking, these people construct their own knowledge (hence, the word *constructivist*). Tilden was obviously a constructivist long before the word was even used outside of esoteric academic circles. He believed that if interpreters could succeed in provoking their audiences to think, then those people would establish their own personal meanings for things—what he referred to as "personal truths." In interpretation today, we often call this "meaning making." Moscardo (1999b) referred to it as "mindfulness," drawing on the mindfulness theory of Langer (1989).

6   Stern, Powell et al. (2012), who studied face-to-face interpretation in US national parks, found that when an interpreter's primary goal was to increase visitors' knowledge about something, it detracted from positively impacting their experiences and appreciation of a park's resources.

7   "Infotainment" (information plus entertainment) was originally used in television journalism to mean "soft news" (a mixture of news and entertainment features). "Edutainment" (education plus entertainment) is more popular in the world of computer games, science centers, and theme parks. It often implies the use of high-tech media or gadgetry.

8   See McLuhan's (1967) classic, *The Medium Is the Message*.

9   See, for example, Bitgood (1988); Falk, Koran, Dierking, and Dreblow (1985); Moscardo (1996); and Serrell (1977).

10 Research on the elaboration likelihood model has shown that people will usually remember things a presentation actually makes them think about. But when there's a difference between what an interpreter wants an audience to remember and what those people actually think about, the relationship doesn't work. See, for example, Cacioppo and Petty (1989), who found that a message with "high provocation potential" actually led to audiences being able to recall less of the information they were presented than did a message with less provocation potential. That's probably because the people thought less about what the communicator expected them to remember than they did about what the information being presented actually meant to them personally. Had the knowledge test asked them about the things they'd actually thought about, they probably would have done a lot better. Not surprisingly, studies in outdoor interpretive settings (one involving a wayside exhibit

and the other a self-guided trail) by Bucy (2005) and Rand (2010) found no relationship between how much audiences could remember and the number of new thoughts they were provoked to think. Meaning making can be high even when audience recall of factual information is low, and vice versa.

11 If you're interested in learning more about some of these studies, I've discussed them elsewhere (Ham, 2007, 2009a). In Chapter 5 ("Making a Difference on Purpose"), we'll look at ways interpretive products have been used successfully to influence a range of behaviors.

12 Gianna Moscardo (1996, 1999b) was the first academic to develop formal principles for making interpretation thought provoking. Her book *Making Visitors Mindful* remains what I think is the single best reference on this topic both for practicing interpreters and researchers.

13 See, for example, Ham (2008) and Powell and Ham (2008).

14 Good reviews are in Griffin (2000); Petty, McMichael, and Brannon (1992); Petty, Rucker, Bizer, and Cacioppo (2004); and Petty and Cacioppo (1986). Moscardo (1996, 1999b) and Ham (2007, 2009a) discuss ways in which this research applies to interpretation.

15 See Fazio (1995); Fazio and Towles-Schwen (1999); and Petty, Rucker, Bizer, and Cacioppo (2004).

16 See studies by Brown, Ham, and Hughes (2010); Ham and Ham (2010); Ham, Weiler, Hughes, Brown, Curtis, and Poll (2008); and Hughes, Ham, and Brown (2009).

CHAPTER 4
Can All Interpretation Make Some Kind of Difference?

If you're trying to make a difference with any sort of consistency or regularity, your interpretation must be TORE-quality.

I've had the great fortune to work with interpreters in many parts of the world. Everywhere I go, it seems they all look a little different, dress a little differently, and speak different languages; they listen to different kinds of music and eat different kinds of food; they watch different kinds of television, laugh at different kinds of humor, and sometimes they even smell different. But despite all these superficial outward appearances, when we sit down together and talk about what's really important to us—what really matters—we find instantly that we share far more similarities than differences.

When the conversation turns to what we care most about in life—I mean that subset of three or four or five key values that a lot of us have wrapped our personal and professional lives around, the lessons we live by, raise our children by, vote by, and shop by—we discover just how alike we really are. Few professional groups are as defined by their values as interpreters are, whether they interpret heritage, nature, history, art, industry, science, or beer.

Here are a few telling questions. If you answer yes to most or all of them, you might well be an interpreter of something:

> If you had to choose between a commercial development that would provide 1,000 jobs for

your community and the preservation of a new archeological discovery, would you question the development?

Do you feel it's your moral responsibility to leave a clean and healthy environment for humans you don't know and who aren't even born yet?

Do you think that preserving and perpetuating the great lessons history has taught us is one of the most important things human society does?

Do you believe that protecting and preserving biodiversity is a worthy end in and of itself, even if some species don't have obvious utilitarian or economic value?

We could go on and on with similar questions related to art, science, heritage, culture, wine-making, agriculture, beautiful scenery, and so forth, but by and large, your answers probably would set you apart from a lot of other people—which makes you different. Indeed, most interpreters I know have committed their personal and professional lives to advancing these kinds of things in some way or to promoting the kinds of values they reflect. Like most professions, interpreters want to *make a difference* about something. But what might set them apart from a lot of other professional groups is that the differences they strive to make are inside the minds of other people, particularly when it comes to things such as heritage, nature, culture, and environmental protection.

In Chapter 8 ("The Zone of Tolerance"), we'll look more closely at the ethical side of wanting to "make a difference" in somebody else's mind, but interpreters all over the world will tell you that they see their ultimate endgame as exactly that. Just a quick look at what some of the world's leading professional organizations say about interpretation's highest purposes or context makes this pretty clear (Figure 4-1). Nearly every one of them refers to making some sort of difference by raising awareness, creating understanding, or advancing appreciation of natural or cultural heritage, and most refer explicitly to a *hope* of protection, conservation, or preservation. Larry Beck and Ted Cable offered this eloquent view of the challenge faced by interpreters who want to be a positive force for change in the world:

> To give hope, interpreters themselves must possess hope to share with others. Interpreters without hope in the future would offer a hollow message. They would lack the motivation and passion that comes from believing people have the power to change things for the better. (2000: 166)

Interpretation is a make-a-difference kind of profession. Individual interpreters might vary in their personal convictions or in the kinds of differences they see themselves capable of making, but whenever I ask a roomful of interpreters if they want to make some sort of difference in the world through their work, virtually every hand goes up.

Interpreting to Make a Difference

Interpretation is an effective management tool…for reducing impacts and instilling positive attitudes and behaviors toward our heritage (including the social environment).

Asociación para la Interpretación del Patrimonio (2012), Spain

Interpretation can bring meaning to…cultural and environmental resources, enhancing… appreciation and promoting better understanding. As a result, [audiences] are more likely to care for what they identify as a precious resource

Association for Heritage Interpretation (2012), UK

Heritage interpretation is a means of communicating ideas and feelings which help people understand more about themselves and their environment.

Interpretation Australia (2012)

We create learning experiences and feelings of connection and stewardship.

Interpretation Canada (2012)

Interpretation helps to raise awareness of [a] site's significance and win community support regarding conservation and management.

Interpret Europe (2012)

Our vision is for natural and cultural heritage to be valued, sustained, and communicated as it represents the shared histories, heritage, and identities of all Australians.

Museums Australia (2012)

We connect people with their cultural and natural heritage to promote stewardship of resources.

National Association for Interpretation (2012), USA

Interpretation aims to improve visitors' understanding and enjoyment through provoking interest, relating to experience, and revealing something new.

Scottish Interpretation Network (2006)

The Interpretive Development Program encourages the stewardship of park resources by facilitating meaningful, memorable visitor experiences. The program is based on the philosophy that people will care for what they first care about.

US National Park Service (2012)

[Our long-term goal] is ensuring that the huge potential of zoos and aquariums throughout the world to contribute to species and habitat conservation and sustainability is fully realised.

World Association of Zoos and Aquaria (2012)

Figure 4-1. *Interpretation's goals as viewed by major professional organizations.*

So what, then, is this "difference making" all about? Recall that we concluded Chapter 3 by looking at the three main kinds of **differences** interpretation is *said* to make.[1] These are that:

1. "Interpretation" can enhance audience experiences (where audiences might be visitors, attendees at an event, web users, consumers of print and broadcast media, and so on).

2. "Interpretation" can impact attitudes and promote appreciation (or caring) about a place, thing, or concept.

3. "Interpretation" can strengthen protection of important, rare, or fragile resources by influencing how audiences behave with respect to them.

In this chapter, we'll ask ourselves whether we should expect *all* interpretation, or just some, to be capable of making these kinds of differences. The questions we have to ask are not at all rhetorical. They underpin the very idea that interpretation can be more than just entertaining fact-giving for pleasure-seeking audiences.

In Interpretation, TORE = Success

You might wonder why I put the word "interpretation" in quotation marks in describing each of the three differences. My reason was simply to say that we must agree on what we mean by the word before the rest of each sentence can make any consistent sense to us. Here I'm not referring to defining interpretation conceptually, as I did in Chapter 1. That definition, like Tilden's and the National Association for Interpretation's, explains what interpretation is *attempting* to do (i.e., provoke thought and reveal meanings) and how this aim makes interpretation different from other kinds of information transfer. However, in discussing how interpretation might actually lead to certain kinds of outcomes, we have to be a lot more specific about what we mean when we use the word.

> There's no reason to expect poor interpretation to accomplish anything beyond sheer entertainment, if even that.

This is important because, whereas an interpretive product might aim to provoke thinking and facilitate meaning making in an audience, unless it actually succeeds in doing so, there's little chance it can actually make any of the three kinds of differences I listed. In other words, if by using the general word *interpretation* we mean both successful and unsuccessful interpretation, then we have no basis for claiming that interpretation can make any sort of difference. That's simply because there's no justifiable reason to expect poor interpretation to accomplish anything at all beyond sheer entertainment, if even that.[2]

You can consider this a sort of postulate in the making-a-difference-on-purpose business. That is, if you want to be able to make the kinds of differences discussed in this chapter, then you have to be confident your interpretation is successful, which, as we saw in Chapter 2, means holding attention (ORE) and making a compelling point (*T*).

That is, making *any* of the three differences requires interpretation that is thematic (*T*), easy to follow (*O*), relevant (*R*), and enjoyable to process (*E*). And therefore, in order to make sensible claims about what interpretation can or cannot achieve, we have to be clear that when we say "interpretation" we specifically mean interpretation that we can objectively verify has all four qualities (see Figure 4-2).

To make a purposeful difference, interpretation must be T, O, R, and E. Heritage interpretation at Lachine National Historic Site, Canada. *Courtesy of Parks Canada.*

Making a Difference—What Interpreters Should Demand of Research

At the end of the day, if we're going to make sensible claims that interpretation can enhance experiences, impact attitudes, and influence behavior, then we really must *specify* that we mean "excellent" or "successful" interpretation that is T, O, R, and E. If we don't specify this, then we really don't have much basis to make any claims at all. According to what research has taught us about successful communication (see Chapter 2), if we can't verify whether each of the four qualities is inherent in a particular interpretive product, then we really don't have any reason for thinking it can accomplish any of the three outcomes.

Interpreters—and those who want to be interpretive researchers—must understand and appreciate this basic logic. Anything short of TORE cannot be considered "good" or "successful" interpretation. So when we talk about the differences interpretation can make, we always have to be sure we're talking about excellent interpretation. And when overzealous researchers make bold claims that "interpretation" *can* do this or *cannot* do that, interpreters must demand that the researchers clarify just what kind of interpretation they're talking about and that they explain how they *know* it has the four required qualities. Unless interpreters insist on answers to these questions, and unless researchers can provide them, our use of the general word *interpretation* will create meaningless discussions about what "it" ("interpretation") can and cannot do.[3]

Figure 4-2. *Avoiding baseless claims and pointless discussions.*

> Unless interpretation accomplishes its basic aim of provocation, it can't hope to produce any other kind of outcome consistently.

Why is this so important? It matters because we know from much research that all four qualities are necessary for interpretation to stand the greatest chance of doing what it's intended to do—provoke thought and meaning making in an audience. And unless interpretation accomplishes its basic aim of provocation, it can't hope to produce any other kind of outcome, at least not with any consistency or regularity. We'll return to this important idea later in the chapter.

TRE, ORE, Tore, tORE, ToRe, tOrE, tore—You Get the Picture

To reiterate, *all four* qualities (TORE) must be in place for us to claim that interpretation can necessarily lead to any of the three main outcomes. In other words, TOE would fail (because

TORE at a high level of professional quality. *Courtesy of Monterey Bay Aquarium, USA.*

the interpretive product lacked relevance to the audience), and so would TRE (a random collection of bells and whistles that was difficult to follow and went nowhere in particular) and ORE (which we know from Chapters 1 and 2 is simply infotainment). Obviously, for interpretation to be successful, it must have all four qualities. And unless we can verify that it has all four, we shouldn't call it "interpretation" or even be talking about making some kind of purposeful difference. That's simply because communication that doesn't contain all four ingredients hasn't been shown to make such differences. So when we talk about interpretation that can make a difference on purpose, we should be very clear that we're talking about good, successful, **TORE-quality** interpretation. Otherwise, the discussion really is pointless.

Likewise, to be successful as an interpreter your programs and presentations must have all four ingredients at a *high level* of professional quality. That is, you have to do all four well, not poorly or in a mediocre way. For example, TOrE would probably have a hard time succeeding, depending on how weakly relevant the interpretive encounter was to the audience. For the same reason, tORE would stumble because, although the presentation might entertain and connect in various ways to things that matter to the audience (ORE), if the theme itself is weak, not much thinking will be provoked and the audience will be left with a vexing question: "So what?" (or "Big deal?"). Of course, we can extend this notation system to all possible combinations of the four letters in upper and lower case, and the *only* one that will allow us to say with any degree of confidence that interpretation can enhance experiences, impact attitudes in positive ways, or influence audience behavior, is TORE.

> To be successful, you need all four ingredients at a high level of professional quality.

As you can see, TORE signifies that all four qualities are infused into the interpretive product at a high level of accomplishment. A *T* means that the product not only has a theme, but it has a *strong* theme (which as we'll see in Chapter 7, means a theme we know is *easy to follow* and *strongly relevant* to the intended audience). A *t*, on the other hand, means that the interpreter is trying to develop a theme, but not one that is easy to understand or which matters much to the audience. Such a weak theme might even be presented in an easy-to-follow, relevant, and enjoyable (ORE) way, but if the main idea itself doesn't matter to the audience, little provocation will result.

In the same way, an *O* means almost effortless information processing by the audience, whereas an *o* means the audience gets overloaded with information or confused in places. An *R* means that the interpreter's presentation of information consistently links to things the audience already cares about. In this sense, a *T* and an *r* would together indicate that the interpreter had a theme with a lot of potential but developed it poorly. And finally, an *E* signifies that the audience found the whole presentation pleasing to process. An *e* would indicate that the presentation bored or repelled the audience even if all three of the other qualities (TOR) were in place.[4]

Next Steps

With these basic points in mind, Chapter 5 considers each of the three claims about the differences interpretation can make. These are that (1) interpretation can enhance audience experiences, (2) it can lead to appreciation by impacting audience attitudes about things in positive ways, and (3) it can strengthen protection by influencing audience behavior. Our analysis will help us see some fairly clear pathways through which TORE-quality interpretation can indeed make a difference on purpose.

Glossary terms: difference, TORE-quality

Additional Thoughts for Chapter 4

1   Obviously, it's one thing to say interpretation can produce these kinds of outcomes, and it's quite another to demonstrate it with real evidence that makes sense in the context of communication theory and research. Unless good, well-conceived studies based on a plausible theoretical rationale and backed up with real data provide this kind of evidence, such claims remain just that—*claims*.

2   The same applies to other issues in the interpretation field. For example, if a researcher claims that "themes" can or cannot "do" this or that, then you really must ask the researcher to explain what she or he means by *theme*, whether it means a strong theme or a weak theme (and if so, how did she or he determine that?), and whether it means a strong theme that was delivered in an ORE way (and, again, how did she or he determine *that*?). Of course, we also must ask what reason the researcher had in the first place to think that a theme should or ought to be able to do the this or the that. If the researcher doesn't *anticipate* these questions and provide satisfactory answers to them in advance of being asked for them, you can be fairly sure the researcher hasn't done his or her homework and that the conclusions she or he draws from the research are almost certainly flawed or theoretically naive. This is just basic social science.

3   Some of these discussions have been going on in the interpretation blogosphere in recent years.

4   To follow this discussion, you need to recall the rationale behind each of the four qualities we considered in Chapter 2. If you're not yet clear on the rationale, you might want to have another look at Chapter 2.

CHAPTER 5
Making a Difference on Purpose

TORE-quality interpretation has the potential to enrich audience experiences, promote appreciative attitudes, and shape behavior.

Recall from Chapter 4 the three kinds of differences TORE-quality interpretation is supposed to be able to make:

1. Enhance audience experiences (where audiences might be visitors, attendees at an event, web users, consumers of print and broadcast media, and so on).

2. Impact attitudes and promote appreciation (or caring) about a place, thing, or concept.

3. Strengthen protection of important, rare, or fragile resources by influencing how audiences behave with respect to them.

In this chapter, we'll examine each of these claims a little more closely and look for reasons (not just hearsay or conjecture) that would either refute or make each of them plausible. In doing this, we'll search for evidence from research related to each claim, and we'll ask ourselves what, in a practical sense, the research tells interpreters. How might they increase their chances of making such differences with their audiences—not by accident or sheer luck—but on *purpose*, as a matter of professional intent?

Difference 1—Interpretation Can Enhance Experiences

Two lines of reasoning make this a credible claim.[1] I briefly mentioned the first of them at the end of Chapter 3 when I discussed experience as being the same as thinking, and indeed this is generally the way most psychologists see and understand what experience is. Take, for example, two people walking side by side down the same street, under the same blue sky, in the same physical and social environment, yet one of them is having a great time while the other is miserable. Experience, as this example illustrates, is purely a subjective thing. It happens only between the ears of the individual, and it consists only in the thoughts each person thinks. Obviously, to the extent interpretation succeeds in provoking a person to have personal thoughts and to make personal meanings about a place, a thing, a person, or a concept, it helps shape that person's experience. The meanings made are themselves central to the experience the person has. And if the thoughts the person thinks are pleasing or gratifying in some way, her or his experience, by definition, has been enhanced.

The second line of reasoning comes from four published studies that have specifically looked at interpretation's role in tourists' experiences. The first of these was published by Philip Pearce and Gianna Moscardo (1998), who assessed interpretation's influence on visitors' experiences in an Australian rainforest. Their data showed that the interpretive aspects of the visit contributed positively to visitors' overall satisfaction with their experience. In a later study, Hwang, Lee, and Chen (2005) found that visitors' satisfaction with interpretive services contributed in positive ways to their sense of involvement and place attachment in Taiwanese national parks. A third study (Powell & Ham, 2008) explored the specific role of TORE-based interpretation within the experiences of ecotourists in Galapagos National Park. Powell and Ham found highly rated experiences to be largely due to guests' enjoyment of and satisfaction with the interpretive aspects of their trip. Of eight different aspects of visitors' experiences compared by these researchers, "quality of interpretation" and "quality of my guides" were two of the top three associated with high satisfaction ratings.[2] And finally, a study of international tourists in Panama (Ham & Weiler, 2007) found that not only did the interpretive dimensions of tourists' experiences add to their satisfaction, they were the *main* contributors among eleven different criteria examined in the study.[3]

Conclusion about Difference 1:

Based on these two lines of reasoning, it seems plausible that TORE-quality interpretive encounters do indeed have the potential to impact audience experiences in positive ways.

Although we still have a lot to learn about how interpreters can purposefully enhance the experiences of their audiences, claiming that interpretation can make this sort of difference appears to be justifiable.

Interpretation's Role in Memorable Experiences

Since our memory of anything is nothing more than the meanings we've stored in our minds about it, you can think of meaning making as memory making. In this sense, every interpreter who succeeds as a facilitator of meaning making also succeeds in memory making.

In the early 2000s, the Australian state of Tasmania expressed its tourism brand in a single phrase: "Creating Unforgettable Natural Experiences" (Tourism Tasmania, 2003). In this phrase, the Tasmanians captured a relationship between meaningful experience and memory. In fact, many government organizations around the world (including national parks, museums, monuments, and tourism bodies), as well as private tourism enterprises, have singled out memory making as their main business. Obviously, we want people to remember the places they visit and the things they do there, because if those memories are good ones, they can result in even more good things (such as caring, stewardship, repeat visitation, positive word-of-mouth advertising, souvenir and memento buying,[4] and future purchases[5]). Some of these might be the sort of differences you're interested in making.

Probably the best-known source on the business side of experience and memory making is Joseph Pine and James Gilmore's (1999) *The Experience Economy*. In their words:

> While the *work* of the experience stager perishes upon its performance…the *value* of the experience lingers in the memory of any individual who was engaged by the event…to make that shared experience a part of everyday conversation for months, and even years, afterward. While the experience itself lacks tangibility, people greatly value the offering because its value lies within them, where it remains long afterward. (1999: 12-13; emphasis in original)

Pine and Gilmore have described how it probably works for all of us when we have unforgettable experiences. If you think of it as a three-step process, you can see why powerful interpretation might catalyze things:

> *People think; they make meaning; they remember.*

We know from many studies since the 1970s that at least two main kinds of long-term memories are involved. These are our factual memory (usually called "semantic memory")

> Every interpreter who succeeds as a facilitator of meaning making also succeeds in memory making.

and our memory of events in which we ourselves have participated (usually called "episodic memory" or "autobiographical memory").[6] Semantic memory is the one interpreters-as-teachers are usually most interested in (e.g., visitors remembering the name of an animal, how a geologic process works, or historical facts surrounding a particular event). Interpreters-as-provokers, however, often seem more interested in episodic memory (e.g., visitors remembering what it was like to see the animal or view the beauty of the geologic landscape, or imagining what it would have been like to live at the time of the historic event). Recognizing this, Tourism Tasmania (2003) adopted the strategy of developing strong thematic interpretation as the centerpiece of the experiences it offers visitors. As we'll see in Chapters 6 and 7, strong themes presented in appropriate ways provoke audiences to think, and what they think is the sum total of the experience they have and will be capable of remembering and talking about later.

Although researching these sorts of long-term memories is difficult and expensive, the few studies that have been done so far in the interpretation field have shown that visitors are indeed capable of remembering and recounting (sometimes with vivid detail) experiences they've had in national parks and natural settings,[7] with wildlife,[8] and in museums[9], even when they're unable to remember factual information related to interpretive content (semantic memory). In fact, studies by anthropologists Catherine Cameron and John Gatewood (Figure 5-1) have documented the tendency of historic site visitors to *want* to remember their experiences and to be able to project themselves back in time to get a sense or "aura" of how things really were then.[10] It would stand to reason that the more a visitor's imagination was engaged during these "time travels," the more vivid their recollections of them would be. Cameron and Gatewood explained it this way:

> Site designers need to keep in mind that the public's short-term recall of information is poor and long-term recall may simply be a memory of feelings or sensations such as smells, heat, cold, or hunger. The best sites should aim to induce insight, stir curiosity, or fire the imagination. (2003: 69)

Remembering ourselves having experiences—and to use our recollection of them to project ourselves backward in time—is what episodic memory is all about. In the meaning making (interpreter-as-provoker) endgame, interpretation that develops and delivers strong, thought-provoking themes is seen as a key to this sort of memory making.

What Visitors Say They Want from Historic Site Experiences

Cameron and Gatewood (2003) explored what visitors to historic sites *want* from their experience. Their results suggest a role for interpretation that extends beyond its information-giving function. Two studies conducted in the United States, one in a historic town and the other at a national historical park, revealed an interesting impulse in heritage tourists called "numen seeking,"[11] which Cameron and Gatewood described as the quest for "visceral, emotional responses to an earlier event or time." Their findings showed that in both settings more than a quarter of the visitors were "active numen-seekers"—people who said explicitly that they wanted to experience the setting in highly personal ways. Here are a few examples of comments made by these visitors when asked what they wanted to get from their heritage experience:

> "To develop a feel of the experience of the people of that time, what they were thinking, what their reality was."

> "[To develop] a feeling of the times they are showing you. The mindset of the people at that time."

> "[To develop] a feeling of the place, a way to connect with what was."

> "Just to get a feel for that time, something that is memorable. I like to reflect and remember it, to be part of it."

> "To be able to make a connection with the events that took place."

> "I want to feel the aura of the period, gain a sense of connectedness with the way people lived. I want to use my mind to really experience it, not just the externals."

Although it's likely that most of these visitors also wanted to be entertained and to learn, notice the emphasis in their comments on "connecting," "feeling," and "reflecting" as opposed to having fun and gaining knowledge. According to Cameron and Gatewood, the numen-seeking "impulse is not necessarily exclusive of other motives, such as information seeking and entertainment, but it is distinguishable." Because of its focus on reflection and facilitating connections, the interpreter-as-provoker endgame recognizes that there is potentially an active numen-seeker in every visitor, whether the topic being interpreted is historic, scientific, cultural, or natural. It's probably clear, not only from these research findings but also from our own common experience, that our most profound experiences at natural and cultural sites occur when we engage our minds and emotions with what we're seeing and doing, developing a reverence for what's there now or an empathy for what occurred in the past. Reverence, empathy, and caring are among the differences many interpreters want to make.

Figure 5-1. *Examples of historic site visitors' comments about desired experiences. Source: Cameron and Gatewood (2003).*

Difference 2—Interpretation Can Lead to Appreciative Attitudes

Studies do indeed show that TORE-quality interpretation should be able to impact audience **attitudes**.[12] Any communication that succeeds in provoking an audience to think will stand a greater likelihood of impacting attitudes than communication that fails to provoke thinking. And as we've seen, communication that's well endowed with T, O, R, and E is more likely to provoke thinking than communication that's lacking in one or more of these qualities.[13]

> More knowledge does not necessarily mean more "appreciation" or "caring."

But it also can be said that studies done specifically on interpretation have not been so consistent in showing what so many other studies have demonstrated. For example, a fairly typical finding in evaluations of interpretation has been that even when knowledge gains from an interpretive encounter are large, there's little or no attitude impact.[14] Findings like these should remind us that more knowledge does *not* necessarily mean more appreciation will result.[15] Rather, studies show that to impact an attitude, you first have to provoke thinking about the thing you want your audience to have an attitude about—the **attitude object**, as it is called in psychology. So unless the thinking people in an audience do focuses on that *specific* attitude object, there would be no reason to expect their attitude about that object to change.[16] Studies done on interpretation have often assumed that increasing a person's general knowledge about something should alone lead to a change in the person's attitude about it. But this is probably a naïve expectation.

Why else would these studies done in interpretive settings produce results that are different from so many other studies? There are at least a couple of likely reasons. First is that it's unreasonable to expect every interpretive encounter to change the attitudes of its audience. In fact, changing is just one of three possible outcomes, any one of which might be acceptable to an interpreter. Sometimes, for instance, audiences arrive with an already-strong attitude about a topic. If the interpretation presents information that's supportive of what the audience already feels, change in the attitude is probably not going to happen.[17] Reinforcement, however, is likely. Although some believe that reinforcement is nothing more than preaching to the choir,[18] others believe that reinforcement is necessary for maintaining the support of existing constituencies.

Of course, a third possibility is that since interpretation sometimes presents ideas about things an audience has never before considered, a previous attitude might not even have existed, and there was therefore nothing to be changed. In this scenario, interpretation might well lead to a completely new attitude. A lot of interpreters I know consider this their most important job.

Another (and probably more likely) reason interpretation studies haven't always found attitude impacts is that our attitude about something (i.e., an attitude object) is usually based on a very small number of truly pertinent beliefs we have about it. Unless the information an interpreter presents to an audience happens to impact one or more of those truly pertinent beliefs, it's doubtful the audience's attitude will be impacted, even if a lot of other new knowledge is gained.[19] And, of course, the pertinent beliefs will vary from person to person in most audiences.

You can see from this discussion that attitudes are not the same as **beliefs**. Whereas a belief usually describes a person's perception that a given thing has some attribute, characteristic, or quality (e.g., "I think lemons are sour"), an attitude describes that person's evaluation of the thing, whether it's good or bad, desirable or undesirable, positive or negative (e.g., "I like lemons"). Sentiments such as liking, loving, and appreciating are attitudinal. When Tilden said in *Interpreting Our Heritage* that our understanding of something can lead to an appreciation of it, he was saying that our beliefs about a thing give rise to attitudes about it that are consistent with those beliefs. This is well established in psychology, provided we're clear on the thing the beliefs and attitude refer to.

The last sentence above is important, because a concept like appreciation is vague until the object of appreciation is specified (again, the attitude object). In other words, what is it that is being appreciated? For understanding to lead to appreciation—that is, for beliefs to lead to attitudes—the beliefs and attitude must focus on the same thing. So for instance, if we want people in an audience to appreciate a *place*, then it will be their understanding of *that* place that will determine their attitude about *that* place; similarly, if we want them to appreciate a concept such as heritage preservation, then it will be their beliefs about heritage preservation that will determine their attitudes about it. If an interpreter wants to have a *strong and enduring* impact on an audience's attitude about virtually anything, that interpreter *must* first impact the beliefs those people have about that same thing. In psychology, this is called the **principle of compatibility**.[20]

> The principle of compatibility:
>
> to have an *enduring* impact on an audience's attitude about anything, an interpreter must first impact their beliefs about that *same* thing.

Two Paths to Impacting Attitudes

Studies show that interpretation can impact attitudes via two different pathways (see the ELM diagram in Appendix 1). One of them is the **provocation (or strong) path**.[21] When an interpretive encounter causes a person to think *a lot* about the topic being interpreted, strong attitudes can result. These kinds of attitudes are stronger and more enduring than attitudes that don't result from a lot of thinking. According to studies, this not only makes them resilient and resistant to counterarguments, it also suggests they'll be more likely to shape a person's future behavior.[22] We'll return to this point shortly when we consider interpretation's potential role in influencing behavior.

Let's call the other possibility the **quick (or weak) path** to attitude impact.[23] In contrast to the stronger provocation path, the quick path doesn't require an audience to do a lot of thinking. In fact, even a very small amount of thinking can lead to one of these quick impacts. But, as you'd expect, the resulting attitudes are pretty weak compared to the stronger ones that can happen with more thinking. And that often makes them short-lived and not very predictive of behavior except in the immediate or very short time frame.

But what determines which pathway is likely to prevail in a given situation? You might recall from Chapter 2 that two main stars must align for interpretation to succeed in provoking thought. The first of these is that an audience must see the interpretive product as *easy to process* (which largely involves the O for organization and a number of other factors related to the interpreter's language and word choice, sentence structure, use of bridging techniques, and so forth). The second requirement is that the audience must be *motivated* to process the information. Studies show that motivation to process interpretation is affected mainly by its relevance to the audience. When the information being presented connects to what matters to the audience—that is, if it's *relevant* to them (R), they're likely to be motivated to process it.

Laboratory studies have shown that when communication has both of these qualities at a high level (O and R, *not o* and R, or O and r, or o and r), it has a higher likelihood of provoking thought than it would if either of the qualities were missing or deficient.[24] Interpretation, however, doesn't happen in psychology labs, where subjects are instructed to read or listen to a message researchers want to test—which, of course, makes attention paying more or less mandatory. On the contrary, you conduct your interpretation in real-world settings where noncaptive audiences are completely free to ignore the information if they choose. For this reason, the E (for enjoyable or pleasing to process) needs to be added to the O and R. In other words, ORE (which you'll probably recognize as infotainment) is necessary to create the right conditions for provocation to occur. Simply put, when your interpretation is organized, relevant, and enjoyable for your audience, you stand a good chance of provoking them to think. In Chapter 6, we'll see where the T comes into play in terms of influencing what audiences think *about*. But for now, you can assume that the provocation pathway has a greater chance of prevailing when interpretation has all three of these qualities.

However, when one or more of the qualities is missing, you still might have some chance of impacting audience attitudes in a weaker, more modest way through the quick path. Studies have shown this to be easier to do when some sort of "cue" is present that allows people in the audience to ignore most of the details and base their attitude instead on the cue. Common cues for quick-path processing include the credibility and likeability of a speaker, his or her appearance, the trustworthiness of the source, a promise of social approval or conformity (e.g., "people you respect like this," or "most people think this way"), or even the sheer number of points that are made in support of the attitude.

> When your interpretation is organized, relevant, and enjoyable to process, you stand a good chance of provoking thought.

According to a number of studies,[25] even when an interpreter's opportunity to impart a theme is very brief, if the theme is at least relevant enough to attract the audience's attention, and if the interpreter develops the theme in a reasonably compelling way, short-term impacts on visitors' attitudes (and even behavior) are still possible despite the audience's comparatively small investment in thinking. Such a quick-path impact might happen, for example, when your window of communication opportunity is very small (e.g., a five-minute talk or a sixty-word wayside exhibit). Even in such cases, if the audience perceives the information to be very credible and trustworthy, or if they simply like the interpreter's attire, her/his communication style, or the illustration in the wayside exhibit, they might still form a quick but positive attitude about the topic in the short term.

Conclusion about Difference 2:

Interpretation studies that have identified in advance what the pertinent beliefs behind a particular attitude actually are have indeed found that interpretation designed to impact those specific beliefs has resulted in audience attitude impacts.[26] These studies support what research in other fields has shown: When interpretation is specifically targeted to impact the beliefs known to be related to a particular attitude, purposely impacting that attitude is possible. And if the resulting attitude is largely positive and agreeable, then appreciation (as interpreters might prefer to call it) can result. Therefore, the claim that interpretation can lead to appreciative attitudes about things, people, places, and concepts also seems justifiable, provided the interpretation is designed to impact the beliefs that give rise to that particular attitude.[27]

Difference 3—Interpretation Can Shape Behavior

When Tilden claimed that appreciation could lead to "protection," he was making a statement about interpretation's potential to influence how people behave in certain kinds of settings. If you're following this discussion, you probably can see that his words, "through appreciation, protection" were simply saying that having an appreciative attitude about something would lead to certain behaviors. For the most part, he was referring to deterring vandalism and careless actions such as throwing lit cigarettes into dry vegetation:

> He that understands will not willfully deface, for when he truly understands, he knows that it is in some degree a part of himself…If you vandalize a beautiful thing, you vandalize yourself. And this is what true interpretation can inject into the consciousness. (1957: 38)

"Appreciation" to Tilden was a special type of attitude, a *general* one of the kind a parent feels for a child. He reasoned simply that people would not knowingly harm the things they care about. Since he was referring to a general case, he couldn't possibly anticipate every conceivable action a person might or might not carry out. But the point he was trying to make was that if a person is provoked to deep thought about a thing, then that person will make a lot of personal meanings with respect to it. Meaningful things matter to us, and given the opportunity to act one way or another with respect to a meaningful thing, we'll normally choose to behave in a respectful or protective way. Both common sense and research back up this claim.

> People would not knowingly harm things they care about.

Today, however, interpreters are often interested in using interpretation as a management tool aimed at deterring or eliminating *specific* visitor behaviors in fragile settings. My own research over the past few years has dealt with a wide range of problems, including proper food storage by campers in bear country, reducing wildlife feeding, persuading national park visitors to pick up litter left by other visitors, keeping dogs on leashes in protected areas, and convincing tourists to donate to local conservation funds.[28] The behavior of interest in each of these cases is very specific and different from the rest, and the general word *protection* in Tilden's philosophical statement doesn't capture the specificity of each of these behaviors or the differences between them.

And, of course, organizations such as museums, zoos, aquariums, and tourism operators of all kinds are interested in yet another set of behaviors necessary to keep them in business and operating efficiently (e.g., increasing attendance, stimulating sales and future purchases, recruiting volunteers, and so forth). So influencing behavior of one kind or another is something most organizations like these must do at some point.

But is there evidence that interpretation has a viable role to play in influencing behavior? The answer is yes. In fact, since the 1990s, a number of studies have found that strategically designed interpretation can have a strong influence on certain visitor behaviors in protected areas and nature-based tourism settings. The two most successful approaches have been the "normative" approach and the "reasoned action" approach.

The normative approach is often seen as a quick-path to influencing behavior wherein interpretation appeals to an audience's desire to be socially correct and to avoid social ridicule. In other words, normative approaches apply social pressure to encourage appropriate or desirable behavior. As such, normative messages usually stress what most other people "normally" do and/or what important others approve or disapprove of (that is, whether they think the behavior is good or bad).[29] Normative messages have been

> Normative approaches apply social pressure to encourage desirable behavior.

especially effective in reducing littering and deterring off-trail hiking, as well as in influencing other environmentally relevant behaviors such as curbside recycling.[30]

The reasoned action approach comes from studies showing that our behavior is consistent with a small set of truly pertinent beliefs we have about the behavior. According to this approach, to influence people to behave in a given way, you need to influence those people's beliefs about that specific *behavior*.[31] If their beliefs about the consequences of engaging in the behavior are predominantly positive, it will lead them to have a positive attitude about the behavior, which in turn increases the likelihood they'll behave as you want (see the Reasoned Action Model diagram in Appendix 1). Unlike the normative approach, which is often seen as a quick-path to persuasion, the reasoned action approach assumes the stronger provocation path. That is, if you want to impact people's beliefs about a behavior, you must get them to think about that behavior.

> In the reasoned action approach, you must impact people's beliefs about the actual behavior you want to influence.

Many studies have indeed shown that when communication succeeds in impacting an audience's attitude about a behavior in a positive way, the desired behavior is more likely to occur.[32] Studies, however, do not back up the idea that a general attitude about a thing will lead to specific behaviors with respect to the thing.[33] Rather they show that other factors influence our attitudes about a specific behavior that might have little to do with our general attitude. This explains why all environmentalists don't recycle at home, and not all of them donate money to every cause or join every conservation organization. Those behaviors (recycling at home, donating, and joining) are subject to beliefs, not simply about nature and the environment but rather about the spe-

An interactive exhibit aimed at influencing an important behavior—choosing sustainable seafood from a menu or supermarket. *Courtesy Monterey Bay Aquarium, USA.*

cific behavior in question. According to the reasoned action approach, for interpretation to purposefully influence a given behavior it must first succeed in influencing people's beliefs about that specific behavior.[34]

Going back to Tilden's view that appreciation can lead to protection, if we think of *appreciation* as meaning "a generally positive attitude about something" (the attitude object), and if that something is a behavior, then the attitude-behavior link holds up well according to dozens of studies conducted since the 1970s.[35] Therefore, interpretation that provokes the formation of positive beliefs about the outcomes of a given behavior will result in a positive attitude about that behavior. When this occurs, the likelihood that a visitor will engage in the desired behavior (if presented the opportunity) is significantly enhanced. In other words, from understanding (beliefs) to appreciation (attitude) and finally protection (behavior).

The reasoned action approach has been used successfully a number of times in the interpretation field, particularly in influencing behaviors such as tourists donating money to local conservation funds (travelers' philanthropy),[36] deterring bird feeding in national parks,[37] prompting hikers to pick up and carry out other hikers' litter,[38] encouraging national park visitors to use mass transit rather than driving their own cars,[39] and persuading dog walkers to keep their pets on a leash.[40]

Conclusion about Difference 3:

In 2010, the two approaches (normative and reasoned action) were combined into a single, integrated model of human behavior,[41] and research continues to explore new and better ways interpretation can influence behavior, both within this new integrated model and according to other theories.[42] Virtually no study has shown 100 percent success in influencing behavior, but significant increases in preferred behaviors have been documented in so many studies that there seems little reason to question whether interpretation, if it's *purposefully* designed to do it, can make a difference in how audiences behave. Results of a recent nationwide study of face-to-face interpretation in the US National Park Service by Stern, Powell, Martin, and McLean underscore this point about purposeful design (see also Figure 5-5 at the end of this chapter):

> Interpretation can only make a difference in how audiences behave if it's specifically designed to do it.

...programs in which the interpreter explicitly targeted behavior change as an intended outcome were more successful in doing so. (2012:38)

A well-known example of interpretation successfully targeting a behavioral impact is Lindblad Expeditions' travelers' philanthropy programs, which have generated millions of US dollars for conservation around the world. The behavior of interest in these programs is a tourist donating money to a fund earmarked for local conservation. After revamping the interpretive component of its Galapagos Conservation Fund campaign using the TORE approach explained in this book, donations to the fund nearly quadrupled in a single year.[43] See the invited commentary by Sven-Olof Lindblad in Figure 5-2.

The TORE Model

In this chapter and Chapter 4, we've seen that not *all* interpretation is capable of success in enhancing experiences, promoting positive attitudes, or influencing behavior. We concluded that for interpretation to make such differences it needs to be TORE-quality interpretation (which we now know means "high elaboration likelihood"). When interpretation has a high likelihood of provoking thought in its audience, it also stands the greatest chance not only of enhancing experiences but also of impacting attitudes in positive ways. Likewise, we saw that to influence a specific behavior, an interpretive product must successfully target the truly pertinent beliefs audience members have about that behavior. A justifiable conclusion from the research record is that TORE-quality interpretation indeed *can* (and *does*) make the three kinds of differences we've explored.

If interpreters take nothing else from this discussion, I hope it's the recognition that their work can indeed make important differences in the experiences, attitudes, and behaviors of their audiences, and furthermore, that making these sorts of differences requires interpreters to approach their work as provokers of thought rather than as simply teachers or entertainers. Put differently, to the extent they succeed as facilitators of meaning making with their audiences, they stand their greatest chance of making the kinds of differences they want to make.

That's essentially the chain of events shown in Figure 5-3, which depicts the TORE model of thematic communication. As the research record shows, when an interpreter's theme is strong (box a), and she or he delivers it in a way that motivates the audience to focus on it and process it (box b),[44] it provokes the audience to think and make meaning related to what is being presented (box c).[45] With *a lot* of thinking, and depending on how well these meanings fit the person's current thinking, we would expect reinforcement, change, or the creation of new

Interpretation Making a Difference in Galapagos

Travel has become both a boon and a plague, depending on where it occurs and your point of view. It's such a hot-button issue that a few years ago an issue of *Newsweek* magazine devoted 34 pages to the subject with references like "the world's treasures are under siege as never before" but also suggesting that "tourists can be one of the world's greatest forces for preservation."

If you look at the world from the perspective of what's possible, you will acknowledge that tourism, being so powerful as an industry, has all kinds of positive potential; so much so that some day it might be the passion and insistence of the traveler that will save the truly special places on earth. Businesses that operate themselves according to this great potential will always thrive. Simply put, it is what their customers *want* them to do.

Sven-Olof Lindblad
Lindblad Expeditions
www.expeditions.com

But, for that to happen, companies who arrange travel must provide great experiences and, above all, invest in training skilled thematic interpreters and guides. They are not only the lifeblood of business, but the *connectors* between travelers and the places they visit; they are the only ones who can provide the context and the spark that enable a visitor's passion to emerge and have direction. And they are the ones who make it possible for our own guests to make a positive difference in the world. The very product travel companies like mine sell to the world is predicated on the quality of our work—especially the interpretation end of it. This is just plain business sense.

When we created the Galapagos Conservation Fund (GCF), it was clear from the outset that Galapagos presented great geography; but it was equally clear that many pressing conservation needs in the islands could not be filled due to lack of funds. Until then tourism in Galapagos had never really been harnessed in a meaningful way. All we needed to do was facilitate the linkage between our guests and Galapagos through outstanding interpretation, and then allow them to act on their own caring. Our interpretive field staff who lead walks ashore, who snorkel, who chat over drinks and during meals with our guests—they are the connectors. Their skilled delivery of strong, thought-provoking themes ultimately makes them responsible for turning the GCF into one of tourism's most significant contributions to conservation in the world. Without our guides, we would be unable to do what our guests want us to do—which, of course, is to help them make a positive difference in the world. Yes, it's plain business sense.

Figure 5-2. *Making a difference makes business sense.*

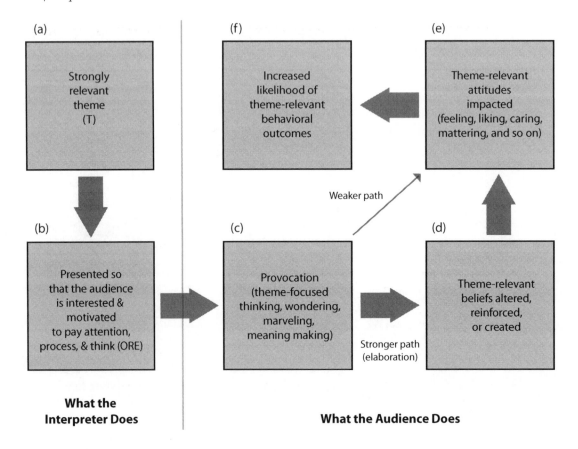

Figure 5-3. *Pathways to making a difference—the TORE model of thematic communication.*

beliefs to result (box d). When beliefs are impacted (reinforced, changed, or created anew), the interpreter can expect an attitude impact related to the theme she or he developed (box e), and if these attitudes are strong enough, they would be expected to give rise to behavioral choices that are consistent with them (box f). These are the events of interest in the stronger (provocation) path depicted in the figure.

As we've already seen, however, studies also show that some types of impacts are possible via a weaker (quick) path, which requires less thinking than the stronger path. Building on our discussion earlier in this chapter, these sorts of impacts are more modest and shorter lived, but they may nevertheless be adequate to bring about certain types of short-term results when interpreters are interested in influencing audience behavior.[46]

Figure 5-3 isn't presented as a causal model of how things will necessarily work every time, but it depicts the main events of interest according to a vast body of research. As the diagram illustrates, the interpreter's theme is the key to starting this process. Because its role on the audience side is to provide a focal point for thinking, it must *matter* to the audience and be presented in a way that makes it *easy* to process.[47] We'll return to the importance of strong themes in Chapter 7, where we'll see that developing themes that are easy to process and loaded with "Vitamin R" (*R* for relevance) is the interpreter's best strategy for making a difference on purpose.

Summary and a Look Ahead

Based on available evidence, it seems reasonable to conclude that TORE-quality interpretation can indeed contribute to making the kinds of differences we've been discussing: enhancing audience experiences, promoting appreciative attitudes, and shaping behavior—at least in the short term (see Figure 5-4). While future research will no doubt sharpen our understanding

Summary about Making a Difference on Purpose		
Can your interpretation purposefully...	**TORE-quality** (likely to provoke thinking)	**Not TORE-quality**
enhance or positively impact a person's experience?	Yes	No
create or reinforce a positive or appreciative attitude about something?	Yes (but only if it's designed to impact that specific attitude)	No
influence a person's short-term behavior?	Yes (but only if it's designed to impact that specific behavior)	No
influence a person's long-term behavior?	Unsure (hasn't been rigorously tested)	No

Figure 5-4. *What research has and has not shown about interpretation's impacts.*

of the pathways and mechanisms through which interpreters can strategically produce such outcomes, claims that the outcomes are achievable seem justified.

In Chapter 6, we'll look at the pivotal role an interpreter's theme can play in this process. There, we'll explore two sides of the theme concept—the interpreter's side and the audience's side. On the interpreter's side, a theme provides an invaluable focus and decision tool in the creative design of an interpretive product. It's on the audience side, however, where we'll see interpretation's potential to make a difference on purpose.

Over the years, I've been intrigued to hear a number of theories about how interpretation can do this or achieve that. Some of these theories originate in the literature on interpretation philosophy, which sometimes paints a picture of a naïve, impressionable audience and describes outcomes in semi-spiritual terms—often invoking references to magic and results that defy logical explanation. Personally, I think this is fine because some of the world's best interpreters are themselves spiritual at heart, and many find energy and purpose in the thought that their work might lead to outcomes that can't be easily described or measured.

Interpretive researchers, however, need to exercise a bit more care when they attempt to adopt such theories to guide their inquiry into the interpretation process. With these readers in mind, I'd like to end this chapter with a playful look at two of the more interesting theories I hear from some interpretive researchers today. I call them Poof theory and Omnipotent Interpreter theory (see Figure 5-5).

Two Myths about Interpretation's Ability to Influence Behavior

Somewhere along the line, two myths about interpretation's ability to influence behavior have taken hold. I hear both often enough in conversations with interpreters (and even in interpretive research blogs) to tell me that the myths are growing "legs" (as they say in journalism). With tongue in cheek, I'll call them "Poof theory" and "Omnipotent Interpreter theory."

Poof theory[48]: Poof theorists believe that "good" behavioral impacts should just sort of "happen" ("poof") because something called "interpretation" has been presented to an audience. That is, virtually every interpretive encounter—regardless of its content or focus— ought to lead audiences to do things that Poof theorists have determined to be "good" (recycle at home, use water wisely, join a conservation group, etc.). When good behaviors like these don't actually materialize in the days, months, or years following an interpretive encounter, Poof theorists conclude that "interpretation can't impact behavior."

The problem with Poof theory: Even if we assume every interpretive encounter is TORE-quality (which means the audience was likely provoked to think), Poof theory fails to recognize that an interpretive encounter must be specifically designed to target a behavior if it really wants its audience to carry out that behavior. But if an interpretive product was never designed to influence any particular behavior, it makes little sense to evaluate it against that measure. For example, if an interpreter presents a truly outstanding TORE-quality program on the history of wildlife conservation, we should *not* expect that even one person in that audience would necessarily join the World Wildlife Fund (also known as the Worldwide Fund for Nature) as a result. That's because the interpreter didn't focus her or his attention on promoting that behavior or target previously known beliefs the audience had about joining the WWF. So when people in the audience don't later become WWF members, it would be erroneous to conclude that the program somehow "failed to impact behavior." As we know, while TORE makes it likely interpretation will accomplish its goal to provoke thinking, unless the thinking the audience does revolves around the truly pertinent beliefs it has about a specific behavior of interest, there's almost *no chance* that behavior (or any other behavior that wasn't similarly targeted) will later occur.[49] "Poof!"

Omnipotent Interpreter theory: Omnipotent Interpreter theorists believe they should necessarily be able to trace the long-term behaviors of normal people to a single interpretive encounter those people had in the past. This is giving interpreters a lot of credit. In fact, it conjures up an image of a communication superpower (the omnipotent interpreter) who can accomplish virtually anything just by speaking or writing in just the right way. It also sets interpreters up for failure because there is no theoretically defensible reason (and certainly no research to suggest) that any single communication event of any kind should *necessarily* be able to achieve such an overwhelmingly powerful influence in a human's life. When researchers criticize "interpretation" for not predictably producing such extraordinary outcomes, they're probably being a little naïve.

The problem with Omnipotent Interpreter theory: Human beings are far more complex than Omnipotent Interpreter theorists recognize. Sure, a lot of *interpreters* will tell you their lives were changed by a single event (and there's truth to the fact that "critical incidents" and "significant childhood events" can influence how some people make major life decisions).[50] But no known theory, no research, and little common experience would suggest that even the best interpretive encounter ought to *regularly* result in such powerful impacts in the lives of most human beings. Their journey in life is subject to many thousands of influences, and a given interpretive encounter is simply one of them. That said, a good, rigorous test of the long-term impacts of interpretive programs has yet to be conducted; however, there is some reason to think that a so-called sleeper effect could, in some situations, result in impacts later in life.[51] However, tracing these impacts to a specific interpretive encounter would prove very difficult or impossible since it has long been known that one of the first things people forget after a communication event is the *source* of communication itself.[52]

Figure 5-5. *Naive theories about what "interpretation" can do.*

Glossary terms: attitude, attitude object, belief, principle of compatibility, provocation (strong) path, quick (weak) path

Additional Thoughts for Chapter 5

1   This idea is about as old as interpretation itself, and a long list of social scientists in the parks and tourism fields have argued in one way or another that good interpretation makes a positive impact on visitor experiences. See, for example, Armstrong and Weiler (2002); Arnould and Price (1993); Beck and Cable (1998); Brochu and Merriman (2012); Cameron and Gatewood (2000); Cohen (1985); Geva and Goldman (1991); Ham (2001, 2002a, 2008, 2009b); Ham, Housego and Weiler (2005); Ham and Weiler (2002); Powell and Ham (2008); Ward and Wilkinson (2006); and Weiler and Ham (2001, 2002).

2   How much visitors enjoyed their experience was also positively correlated with their intentions to donate money to a local conservation fund.

3   The interpretive components of the experience were presentations/exhibits in a visitor center, visitor centers, maps of the area, brochures about the area, and explanations by area staff. The non-interpretive components were the quality of trails, restrooms, fishing areas, parking areas, camping areas, and swimming areas. The interpretive components were found to be roughly twice as important as the non-interpretive components in their positive impact on the overall quality of the visitors' experience.

4   Fennell (2004) makes a case that tourists buy souvenirs as symbolic objects that, in turn, later reinforce their experiences and retrigger meaning making.

5   For example, a study by O'Mahony et al. (2006) was able to link the educational value of winery visits to tourists' purchases and consumption of wine five months later.

6   If you're interested in some of the fascinating research that's being done on the differences and interplay between episodic and semantic memory, some good references are Baars and Franklin (2003, Baddeley (2001); Baddeley, Conway, and Aggleton (2001); Craik and Tulving (1975); Franklin, Baars, Ramamurthy and Ventura (2005); and Tulving (1972, 1983, 2001).

7   See, for example, Arnould and Price (1993); Knapp (2003); Knapp and Benton (2005); and Knapp and Yang (2002).

8   See, for example, DeMares and Kryka (1998); Smith (2004); and Smith, Ham and Weiler (2011).

9   See, for example, McManus (1993); Medved (2000); Medved and Oatley (2000); Spock (2000); Stevenson (1991).

10   See Cameron and Gatewood (2000, 2003) and Gatewood and Cameron (2000).

11 *Numen* is a word from Latin that means a "nod" or beckoning from the gods. Cameron and Gatewood liken it to the deep sense of awe, engagement, and empathy that is awakened when we find ourselves in the presence of something profoundly meaningful.

12 As I've detailed elsewhere (Ham, 2007, 2009a), studies conducted during the past 30 years on the elaboration likelihood model of persuasion (ELM) have produced an impressive record of consistent findings showing that when communication provokes effortful thinking, an impact on attitudes is likely to result. Results of these studies demonstrate that the more thinking an interpretive encounter provokes, the stronger and more enduring the resulting attitudes can be. If you're not so interested in the research end of things, you'll find an engaging overview of basic ELM principles in Griffin (2000). Petty and Cacioppo (1986) is considered the original source, but good summaries of ELM research findings are in Petty, McMichael, and Brannon (1992) and Petty, Rucker, et al. (2004).

13 Recall from Chapter 2 that the two factors necessary for provocation are that the information presented must be easy to process and it must be relevant to the audience. When interpretation is *T*, *O*, *R*, and *E*, both conditions are satisfied and, according to ELM research, provoking the audience to think is likely.

14 Peart (1984), for instance, found that although visitors who viewed an exhibit on wildlife management scored twice as high as other visitors on a knowledge test, there was no impact on their attitudes about wildlife. Two studies by Morgan and Absher revealed a similar pattern. Morgan, Absher, Loudon, and Sutherland (1997) found that although people who attended an interpretive program on insects performed twice as well on a knowledge test than people who didn't attend the program, their attitudes about insects were only modestly impacted. And Morgan, Absher, and Whipple (2003) found that although a guided canoe trip resulted in a 147 percent increase in canoeists' knowledge about the natural and human history of the area, their attitudes about these things were barely impacted at all.

15 Other interpretation studies showing a weak match between knowledge gain and attitude change include Cable, Knudson, Udd and Stewart (1987); Doering, Bickford, Darns and Kindlon (1999); Knapp and Barrie (1998); Lee and Balchin (1995); Orams (1997); Pettus (1976); Tubb (2003); and Wiles and Hall (2005).

16 This is especially important to consider when the attitude object is a behavior. As we'll see later in this chapter, we wouldn't expect an attitude about something general such as "nature" or the "environment" to correlate strongly with any specific environmental or nature-related behavior. To influence people's attitude about a specific behavior, we would need to provoke thinking, not about nature and the environment, but rather about the consequences of the behavior we want them to engage in. See Ajzen (2005) and Fishbein and Ajzen (2010) for explanations of why general attitudes aren't good predictors of specific behaviors. Heberlein (2012) discusses the difficulty of influencing behavior through the path of general attitudes.

17 In research, this is called a "ceiling effect." If a person already has a strong attitude about something, it's unlikely that even a TORE-quality interpretive encounter is going to further strengthen it.

18 See, for example, Beaumont (2001). However, since attitudes can be vulnerable to counter communication, Storksdieck, Ellenbogen, and Heimlich (2005) argue that "preaching to the converted" might serve an underappreciated long-term value by continually reinforcing and affirming previously held attitudes. This opinion is echoed by Bixler (2001). Results of a study on geotourism by Stokes, Cook, and Drew (2003) suggest that the "already converted" may be an impressively large audience in nature- and culture-based tourism settings.

19 These truly pertinent beliefs are called "salient beliefs" or sometimes "accessible beliefs" in communication psychology. Studies show that unless communication impacts a person's salient (accessible) beliefs about a thing, having an enduring impact on the person's attitude toward that thing is unlikely. See, for example, Fishbein and Ajzen (2010) and Ajzen and Fishbein (2005). Ham (2007, 2009a) and Ham and Krumpe (1996) present examples related specifically to interpretation.

20 The evidence supporting the "principle of compatibility" is so strong that it is has been nominated as a law of human psychology (Ajzen, 2005). Ham (2009a) and St. John, Edwards-Jones, and Jones (2010) discuss the principle in the context of interpretation and conservation education.

21 You might recall our earlier discussion about the ELM (elaboration likelihood model). In the ELM, this is called the "central route to persuasion." It's also sometimes called "systematic processing." See Chaiken (1980) and Petty and Cacioppo (1986). Elaboration and systematic processing are psychological terms for effortful thought (pondering, contemplating, deliberating, wondering, and so on). In interpretation, we call it meaning making. When Tilden said "provocation," he meant what psychologists today would call "high elaboration likelihood" (see Rand, 2010).

22 According to research by Holland, Verplanken, and Knippenberg (2002), a strong attitude about a behavior can guide that behavior, but a weak attitude wouldn't have much influence. Based on elaboration likelihood studies, we can expect interpretation that provokes a lot of thinking to also stand a better chance of influencing a behavior because it's likely to result in a strong attitude about the behavior—at least if the thinking the audience does has to do with that behavior. See, for example, Petty, Rucker, Bizer, and Cacioppo (2004) and Petty, Cacioppo and Schumann (1983).

23 In the ELM, this is called the "peripheral route to persuasion" (Petty & Cacioppo, 1986). In the Heuristic-Systematic Processing Model, it's called "heuristic processing" (Chaiken, 1980). Both involve minimal thinking by the audience.

24 In Chapter 7, we'll define interpretation possessing both qualities (i.e., easy to process and relevant) as having high "provocation likelihood."

25 In ELM research, see Petty and Cacioppo (1986) and Petty, McMichael, and Brannon (1992). Norms have often been used as a quick-path to persuasion. See, for example, Cialdini, Kallgren,

and Reno (1991); Hall and Roggenbuck (2002), Reno, Cialdini, and Kallgren (1993), and Starkey (2009). See also Ham, Weiler, Hughes, Brown, Curtis, and Poll (2008) for examples involving protected areas and nature-based tourism settings.

26   Examples include Brown, Ham, and Hughes (2010); Ham, Weiler, et al. (2008); and Hughes, Ham, and Brown (2009).

27   I explain these ideas in more detail in Ham (2007) and (Ham 2009a).

28   On proper food storage in bear country, see Lackey and Ham (2003, 2004); on deterring wildlife feeding and persuading national park visitors to carry out litter left by other visitors, see Brown, Ham, and Hughes (2010); Ham, Weiler, Hughes, Brown, Curtis, and Poll (2008); and Hughes, Ham, and Brown (2009); on convincing tourists to donate to local conservation funds, see Ham (2004); Ham and Ham (2010); and Powell and Ham (2008).

29   The normative approach has been championed by Robert Cialdini. See especially Cialdini (1996) and Cialdini, Kallgren, and Reno (1991). These two types of norms are respectively called "descriptive norms" (which appeal to a person's sense of what most people "normally" do), and "injunctive norms" (which appeal to the person's sense of what is socially desirable or socially approved). In the reasoned-action approach, both types of norms are combined as "perceived norm" (Fishbein & Ajzen, 2010).

30   Heberlein (2012) offers a good summary of the potential of normative messages to influence environmental behaviors. Studies have reported success in using both injunctive and descriptive norms to reduce (in some cases, dramatically) littering in public places. See Cialdini (1996); Cialdini, Kallgren, and Reno (1991); and Reno, Cialdini, and Kallgren (1993). See also Winter (2006) who found that negatively worded normative messages worked effectively when the desired behavior could occur in a short time-frame following communication of the message, and Starkey (2009) who found that an injunctive normative message was effective in reducing litter left by campers in a national forest campground.

31   This means that interpreters cannot simply intuit or guess about the beliefs and then hope to be successful in influencing a behavior by targeting them (on this point, see Ajzen, 1992; and Curtis, Ham, and Weiler, 2010). Rather, the beliefs need to be identified through a fairly simple research process such as the one described in Fishbein and Ajzen (2010). Ham, et al. (2009) provide instructions for carrying out this research specifically in protected areas and nature-based tourism settings. Fishbein and Ajzen (2010) is the most up-to-date presentation of the reasoned action approach. See also Ajzen (2005); Ajzen and Fishbein (2005); Fishbein and Manfredo (1992); Fishbein and Yzer (2003).

32 Fishbein and Ajzen (2010) provide a comprehensive summary of this research.

33 You'll find explanations of why this occurs in Ajzen (2005); Ajzen and Fishbein (2005); Bamberg (2003); Fazio (1986); Fishbein and Ajzen (1974, 2010); Weigel (1983); and Weigel and Newman (1976).

34 You'll probably recognize this as the "principle of compatibility" at work again (see note 20). Since the reasoned action approach assumes persuasion will occur through the provocation path (more thinking), we can assume that the impacts made via this approach have the potential to be stronger and more enduring than would be possible if the audience followed the quick path (less thinking). Recall the research by Holland, Verplanken, and Knippenberg (2002) showing that strong attitudes can shape human behavior, whereas weak attitudes don't.

35 This research track record is presented in detail both in Fishbein and Ajzen (2010) and Ajzen and Fishbein (2005).

36 Ham (2004) designed an interpretive philanthropy campaign that targeted previously identified beliefs tourists had about donating to the Galapagos Conservation Fund (GCF). The resulting campaign nearly quadrupled donations. See also Ham and Ham (2010) who used a similar process to design one of National Geographic's ocean awareness campaigns and Powell and Ham (2008) who explored possible connections between TORE-quality interpretation and intentions to donate to the GCF.

37 See Ham et al. (2008) and Hughes, Ham, and Brown (2009). Interpretive signs in a national park picnic area targeted previously identified beliefs about not feeding birds. One of the messages virtually eliminated bird feeding by first-time visitors to the park.

38 See Brown, Ham, and Hughes (2010) and Ham et al. (2008). This study identified hikers' beliefs about picking up litter they encountered on a high-use trail. Two interpretive sign messages targeting these beliefs were tested for their ability to persuade more hikers to pick up litter. Both signs proved effective in significantly increasing litter pickup.

39 Curtis (2008) identified and targeted visitors' beliefs about using a national park shuttle bus (in lieu of driving their own cars) and succeeded in influencing visitors' use of the bus service. He found that more than half of visitors who arrived intending to drive their own cars were persuaded by one of his experimental signs to take the bus instead.

40 See Hughes, Ham, and Brown (2009). This study used a sign message targeting a key belief dog walkers in a regional park had about keeping their pets on a leash. When the message was in effect, nearly 80 percent of dog walkers kept their dogs on a leash, compared to about 60 percent that did so when the sign was absent.

41 Fishbein and Ajzen (2010) relied largely on Cialdini's work and research by Rivis and Sheeran (2003) in extending the reasoned-action model to include an additional type of normative influence ("descriptive norms") that it lacked previously. See Fishbein and Ajzen (2010) for details and Ham and Ham (2010) for a practical example related to interpretation and nature-based tourism.

42 Simply for brevity, I've not presented details on the work of several others who have looked at interpretation's role in influencing various kinds of behavior. A small sample of these would include Bass, Manfredo, Lee and Allen (1989); Bitgood, Patterson and Benefield (1988); Goulding (2001); Gramann (2000); Hockett and Hall (2007); Schulhof (1990); Stevens and Hall (1997); Vander Stoep and Gramann (1987); Widner and Roggenbuck (2001, 2003). Additional studies are presented in Ham and Weiler (2006).

43 In 1997, the campaign's inaugural year, Lindblad's guests contributed USD $81,000 to the GCF. In 1998, the author was asked to redesign the interpretive component of the campaign incorporating the TORE principles presented in this book. In the ensuing twelve months, the TORE campaign led to donations of USD $300,000 (an increase of about 270 percent). At this writing, donations now total around USD $6 million.

44 As we'll see throughout the rest of this book, the interpreter's choice of methods must be well matched to the situation and the audience in order to be successful. An interpreter's potentially relevant theme will be rendered irrelevant if it's presented in a way that misses the audience's interests or violates their preferred ways of acquiring information in that setting. Studies on the ELM (e.g., Petty & Cacioppo, 1986) demonstrate convincingly that both motivation and ability to process a message are required for this sort of provocation to occur.

45 Box c (provocation) is where interpretation's oft-cited role in enhancing visitor experience mainly occurs. See, for example, Ham (2002a); Pearce and Moscardo (1998); and Tourism Tasmania (2003).

46 These so-called peripheral (or heuristic) effects are well documented in studies. Some psychologists (e.g., Griffin, 2000; Kahneman, 2011) believe that most of our attitudes are based on comparatively little information and little thought.

47 One could make the argument that any assemblage of interesting facts could provoke thinking, whether or not they were chosen and developed with a theme in mind. And this is probably correct. However, the interpreter's theme provides an essential focal point for provocation. Without this focus, the meanings an audience makes from an interpretive encounter would otherwise be scattered or even random. To impact an audience's attitude about a place, thing, or concept, the place,

thing, or concept itself needs to be the focus of their thinking (Ajzen & Fishbein, 2005; Petty & Cacioppo, 1986). When an interpreter's theme is strong and it's presented in accordance with the audience's tastes and interests, it provides this focus.

48 Yes, I'm aware that "poof" has taken on a derogatory meaning in recent years targeting certain people's sexual orientation. But I certainly do not intend that connotation here. Poof is a word commonly used when something suddenly or magically appears or disappears. It carries a sense of surprise or astonishment similar to the French *voilà*. These are the meanings I intend in describing Poof theory. It insists that interpretation should regularly be able to produce semi-magical outcomes that defy logical explanation.

49 Unless, of course, the interpreter achieved some sort of quick-path persuasion with some members of the audience. But even this would require the interpreter to design her or his communication ahead of time to focus on the *behavior* (and not simply a topic peripherally related to it). Furthermore, even if a quick-path result was achieved, it wouldn't last very long and would almost certainly have faded by the time people in the audience are back at home. So for all intents and purposes, to impact an audience's behavior in the *long term*, interpretation must specifically target the beliefs that are known to underlie that behavior, and the interpreter's communication must also succeed in provoking the audience to give effortful thought to those same beliefs.

50 Shuman and Ham (1997) found that environmental educators sometimes are able to isolate an important event earlier in their lives that influenced their later professional decision to teach environmental education. Smith, Ham, and Weiler (2011) found that having a profound experience with wildlife sometimes can influence the choices people make later in life. And similar findings were reported by DeMares and Kryka (1998). As studies such as these suggest, to have such an enduring impact requires a truly extraordinary encounter. Clearly, not all wildlife encounters are so powerful for normal people. Yet, Omnipotent Interpreter theorists assume all interpretive encounters are supposed to be powerfully meaningful and emotional events in the lives of *all* participants. Although this will sound quite odd to most analysts, a particular researcher has criticized (even to the point of calling for the elimination of) many traditional forms of interpretation because they don't produce long-term behavioral impacts. This should strike you as a curious recommendation at the very least. Although interpretive encounters might have the potential to be significant emotional events for some of the people in their audiences, the encounters are usually so brief that achieving that level of visceral intensity is unlikely. Therefore, to indict any interpretive encounter for its inability to consistently produce long-term behavioral impacts is probably a little naive. To reiterate, no known theory exists that would explain why interpretation (even TORE-quality

interpretation) should necessarily result in long-term impacts on audience behavior, and as of this writing, no study has addressed this relationship in a rigorous way, despite occasional claims to the contrary (see Figure 5-5 at the end of this chapter).

51 Although it might seem backwards, the "sleeper effect" in persuasive communication is the tendency of communication from a *low-credibility* source to *increase* in its persuasiveness over time as the source becomes vaguer in the audience's mind. Ironically, studies show that if a communication event is initially seen by the audience as highly credible, it's likely that its biggest persuasive impact will happen immediately and then decay over time (unless there is future reinforcement). If you're interested in learning more about the sleeper effect, you'll find a good review of studies in Kumkale and Albarracín (2004).

52 Source forgetting was one of the most consistent findings in the earliest studies on persuasive communication published more than a half century ago by Hovland, Janis, and Kelley (1953) and Hovland and Weiss (1951).

CHAPTER 6
Two Sides of Theme and Sentences in the Head

The idea of thematic communication is to develop a strong theme in an ORE way. When you do this well, provoking thought is likely.

It might surprise some to hear me say that I've never really liked the word *theme*—not because there's anything inherently wrong with it, but because it sometimes leads to a lot of unnecessary mind bending. Rarely have I encountered such an elegant idea that has required so much explanation and qualification. Only the word interpretation itself demands as much effort to explain to an outsider.[1]

I marvel sometimes at the number of writers who would make so much more of the idea than I ever foresaw or intended. Among these are the "thematic taxonomists" who seem to have invented a whole vocabulary of theme-related notions (e.g., metathemes, megathemes, macrothemes, minithemes, and microthemes).[2] Discussions in the late 1990s about the qualitative differences between a theme and a thesis, and whether the latter was different or better, also fall into this category.[3] The theme idea is really much simpler, as Larry Beck and Ted Cable suggest with their invited commentary in Figure 6-1.

Thanks to Bill Lewis, one of my early mentors, the word *theme* is probably here to stay. When he first introduced the idea to me in 1979, it was innocent and pure in its implications. He called it "your message," in the sense that if an interpreter could give advance thought to the central idea she or he wanted to get across to an audience, it would be easier to make decisions about the presentation's content and delivery. Although today the advantage of having an organizing idea in mind before you start seems plainly obvious, this simply wasn't the way most people thought about interpretation in those early days. More prevalent were the teaching and infotainment views of interpretation we discussed in Chapter 3, and interpreters everywhere seemed driven by their passion and Tilden's principles but without a communication strategy to guide them. Lewis's notion of a theme provided a starting point from which such a strategy could grow.

According to Lewis, a theme should always be expressed in a complete declarative sentence that answers the question "so what?" with respect to the thing being interpreted. A year later, Bill put this advice in writing in *Interpreting for Park Visitors*:

> Development of a theme provides both organizational structure and clarity of understanding. Once the theme of a presentation has been chosen, everything else tends to fall into place.
>
> The use of a theme can steer you away from such things as: mere ticking off of dates, giving lists of happenings, making identifications with no reference to context. By wording a theme, you narrow and refine your topic. (1980: 38)

More than three decades later, I've found no reason to question Lewis's advice. His original advancement of the idea arguably contributed to a paradigm shift in this field. Today, the words *theme* and *thematic interpretation* are recognized and used by interpreters all over the world.[4]

It's important for us to recognize that Lewis's explanation of themes was mainly from the point of view of the communicator in the interpretive exchange (the **interpreter's side of theme**) as opposed to its potential impact on an audience (the **results side of theme**).[5] The sound advice he gave had mainly to do with how an *interpreter* could use a theme to make good decisions about what to include in a presentation and what kinds of things should be emphasized in order to flesh out and develop the theme. He saw the theme as a conceptual tool interpreters could use to make better judgments as they worked through the creative planning process of a face-to-face interpretive activity. This was his main purpose at the time, and it stands today as one of the great contributions to the interpretation field.

But to fully understand the importance of Lewis's advice to interpreters, we also need to see themes from the audience's (result side) point of view. In *Environmental Interpretation* (Ham,

Theme or Thesis?

The term "theme" has, in effect, taken hold in the interpretation profession. But are there other possibilities? Is there not a better word than "theme" to describe the central point interpreters are trying to convey? Why not "proposition"? Why not "topic" or "subject"? How about "thesis"?

Ann Lundberg (1997) put forward an eloquent case suggesting that themes don't go far enough and that the intent of an interpretive program should be a "thesis." According to her, a thesis goes beyond subject matter content to challenge peoples' perspectives.

Larry Beck and Ted Cable
Authors of *Interpretation for the 21st Century* (1998)
and *The Gifts of Interpretation* (2011)

Since it is an expression of an opinion that someone might agree or disagree with, a thesis, in Lundberg's thinking, can *provoke* a person, but a "theme" does not.

Our view is that this argument over themes and theses is rooted in semantics. As readers of this book will see, a key to any message is that it connects to something relevant and important to the audience. Strong themes do this, whether they are very brief or more elaborate. So another word just isn't needed.

A theme encompasses the nuances of a thesis, and more. An interpretive program, driven by a theme, may be provocative by arguing a point of view (like a thesis), or it may be provocative by enlightening people to see something in a new way *without* introducing an overriding opinion. Or the program may present *multiple* points of view. All of these possibilities fall under the broad category of *themes*. A thesis, then, is a narrower category than theme and doesn't capture the full range of possibilities in interpretive programs.

To paraphrase Freeman Tilden's comment about the use of the word "interpretation," we have not been able to find a word more aptly descriptive of the key message of an interpretive program than "theme." A theme encompasses the vast array of possibilities for defining the central message an interpreter hopes to convey through an interpretive program. For the sake of consistency, simplicity and historicity, we believe that "theme" is the proper term.

Figure 6-1. *Does "thesis" really bring anything new to interpretive practice?*

1992), I attempted to provide interpreters a *rationale* for thematic interpretation grounded in cognitive and social psychology, while keeping my presentation of the concept as simple and practical as possible for the applied reader. This proved a challenge not only then but also now, since the body of theory and research pertinent to thematic interpretation is enormous. Were there space in this book and interest from more readers, it would be possible to fill many pages with descriptions of studies that demonstrate, from an audience (result side) perspective, why approaching interpretation as Lewis advised is a very good thing to do.[6]

With this bit of background, the remainder of this chapter attempts to thicken the plot on the theme concept by addressing some common questions and presenting a two-sided view of thematic interpretation. What words can we use to describe what a theme is? How would we know if we've done thematic interpretation well or poorly? Should an audience be able to say exactly what the theme was after being exposed to a thematic interpretive product? And should we expect them to say there was just one theme?

How Do You Describe What a Theme Is?—Intention versus Result

Because *theme* has so often been used synonymously with *topic*, one of the real challenges for anyone who teaches thematic interpretation is to find ways to explain it. We can teach conceptually that it's not a mere topic, but rather an important statement about that topic. We can teach it grammatically (a theme is a complete declarative sentence, which means it has a subject, a verb, and a period or full stop at the end). We can teach it structurally by completing a lead-in sentence such as, "I think it's absolutely critical for my audience to really understand that _____." We can teach that it's a statement linking the tangible meanings of places and things to their intangible meanings. And there are other ways, some of which consistently produce strong themes and some of which don't.[7]

One of the most useful ways I've found to get interpreters to develop strong, really compelling themes is to help them understand the psychological foundation underlying the idea itself. Once they have these underpinnings fairly well thought out, I find they're able to grasp thematic thinking, essentially harnessing the concept and making it their own.

To do this, they must have a notion of what a theme would look like inside a person's head, how it gets there, and how it functions once inside. My experience over many years has been that the most accomplished communicators in any field (whether interpreters, playwrights, lawyers, teachers, or marketers) not only know how to think thematically, but they understand why it works as it does and can *explain* the pathways and mechanisms through which they might achieve their own impact on an audience.[8]

Throughout the applied communication literatures on interpretation, free-choice learning, storytelling, playwriting, screenwriting, and oration, as well as the more esoteric research literatures in communication psychology, psycholinguistics, persuasion, and marketing—and in *many* conversations with interpreters around the world—I've encountered a number of euphemisms for *theme*. Whether they're synonyms or just look-alikes I'll leave to the semanticists and philosophers among you. But to a psychologist they are one in the same (or should I say, to the human mind they're one in the same?). These include the words and phrases shown in Figure 6-2.

Words and Phrases That Have Been Used in Place of *Theme*	
What the interpreter wants to communicate (*intention*)	What the audience takes away (*result*)
Answer to the question "so what?" (or "big deal?")	Belief(s) formed
Big or key idea	Central idea(s) gotten
Big picture	Conclusion(s) drawn
Central idea	Emotional connection(s) made
Controlling idea	Implication(s) drawn
Idea to cohesively develop	Impression(s) formed
Idea to explore	Inference(s) made
Main message	Key idea(s) taken
Main point	Lesson(s) learned
Moral of the story (to develop)	Meaning(s) made
Overarching meaning	Message(s) taken
Plot structure	Moral(s) of the story extracted[9]
Premise	Personal theme(s)
Proposition	Proposition(s) formed
Thesis	Relationship(s) understood
	Thought(s) stimulated

Figure 6-2. *Euphemisms for theme as intention and result.*

A few things may leap out at you from the two lists of phrases. First is that your sense of what constitutes a theme will vary depending on whether you're thinking about what the interpreter is trying to do (intention) or how the audience is impacted by it (result). As we've seen, on the **intention side** we have interpreters making decisions about the content and delivery of

> Your sense of "theme" will depend on whether you're thinking about what an interpreter is trying to do or how the audience is impacted by it.

some face-to-face or nonpersonal interpretive product. Here, their sense of the overarching meaning, idea to explore, or main idea they want to develop will guide them to include this and exclude that, to make this connection and not that one, to relate this anecdote and not that one, to emphasize this point or fact over others, and so forth. To the interpreter, the theme brings a powerful decision rule. As we saw in Chapter 2, without one, interpretation too easily reverts to infotainment and presentations become ad hoc collections of "cool facts" and interesting linkages aimed mainly at entertaining the audience for an allotted time.

On the **results side**, however, an interpreter's theme serves a different function and takes on a different form. Larsen aptly saw a theme as an idea that

> provides a platform for the audience to consider, react to, build upon, appropriate, and transform. (2003: 193)

The verbs he invokes (*consider, react, build upon, appropriate,* and *transform*), imply mental activity. Here on the audience side of thematic interpretation we see the results of the interpreter's work if it's well done—audiences are thinking, pondering, wondering, contemplating, questioning, agreeing, disagreeing, drawing conclusions, changing, reinforcing or adding new beliefs, forming impressions, developing ideas, extracting personal morals of story, and, at least for the moment, internalizing them. As I mentioned in Chapter 5, a theme's main purpose on the audience side is to provide the focal point for provocation—a "platform" for mental activity, as Larsen put it.

You might be thinking that a conclusion we can draw from this is that *people who interpret must have the audience side firmly in mind* in order to harness the organizational benefit of having a theme in the preparation stage. And you're right; the two must go hand in hand. When we're thinking thematically, we're merging the two sides of theme, even if we don't consciously recognize it.

Sentences in the Head—One Theme Can Give Rise to Many

A second thing you might observe from the list in Figure 6-2 is that all of the phrases on the audience side are potentially plural. This shouldn't be too surprising when you consider your own experience as a member of the audience, whether at an interpretive program, watching a good movie, or reading the autobiography of a famous person. Imagine that someone walks up to you right as you finish the last page of the autobiography and asks, "So what did you get from that story? What are you thinking now that you've finished the book?"[10] Initially, you might reply by commenting on how much you liked or disliked the book. But if the interviewer pressed you for the meaning you took away from the story, is it likely you'd have just one sentence in your reply, or many? Obviously, if the autobiography were especially moving or thought provoking, you might talk for several minutes before you felt you had exhausted yourself of all the "meanings" the book had created in your mind. Beck posed and answered a related question after a trip to New York to see a Broadway play with his son:

> What did I gain, what meanings struck a resonant chord…? Far more than can be conveyed in this short essay. (2005: 17)

In their analysis of more than 3,300 visitor comments about an exhibition at the Ontario Science Centre, Livingstone, Pedretti, and Soren (2002) found that the meanings their respondents took away with them were both diverse and revealing in terms of what the exhibition was stimulating them to think. In the authors' words:

> Within this majority of comments is evidence of a broad range of questions raised, conceptual associations made, and philosophical orientations on the part of the sample of visitors. (2002: 362)

Although an interpreter will usually have a single theme in mind in crafting an interpretive product,[11] if she or he does a good job of developing and delivering it, that same theme might result in any number of themes in the audience's mind. I call these "sentences in the head." In fact, when the main purpose of interpretation is to provoke audiences to think, it's easy to reason that the more "sentences" an interpretive product generates in a person's mind, the better and more effective the product is.[12]

> **An interpreter's well-developed theme can result in many sentences in another person's head.**

There is no evidence from research to suggest that people in an audience should (or even can) extract only a single theme from an interpretive product, despite the fact that the interpreter was trying to develop just one. To the extent we hold an interpretive product accountable for producing just a single unifying thought in a person's mind, we're possibly dooming the product to failure or mediocrity, at least if the idea of it all was to provoke audiences to think as much as possible. In *The Passionate Fact*, internationally acclaimed storyteller Susan Strauss put it this way:

> A teller should always begin by choosing a story whose message seems good and important to the teller, but should remain fully open to the idea that a story can have many messages. (1996: 44)

A study by Dave Bucy (2005) helps to illustrate how an interpreter's single theme can give rise to a number of themes in another person's mind. Bucy alternated different versions of interpretive signs at a recreational lake in Oregon, United States, in order to test hypotheses about what people were learning from the signs and the personal themes they were extracting from them. One of his experiments involved asking visitors to list the thoughts they were having as a result of reading the signs. Figure 6-3 shows the thoughts listed by eleven different visitors after viewing a sign about a historic ranger station ("guard station") whose location

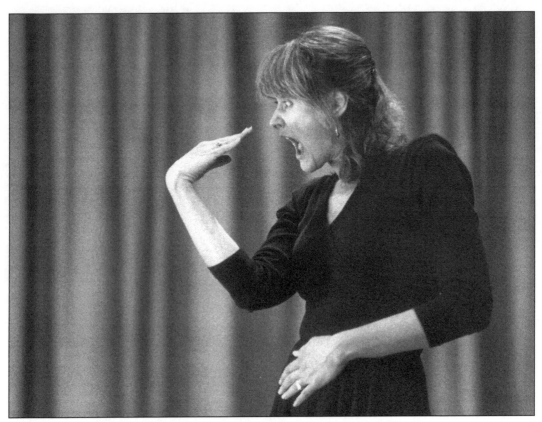

A well-told story can have many messages. *Courtesy of Susan Strauss Storyteller, USA.*

Thoughts Generated by an Interpretive Sign about a Historic Ranger Station

Interpreter's theme: "While the guard station's location may seem odd today, it was the key to everything its first occupants had to accomplish—from their work to sheer survival."

Visitor 1: "Location is important! Long history of USFS at this site. Water is nearby. Fuel is nearby."

Visitor 2: "It was good to picture the original setting and how people lived and survived with so little and yet they had all they needed."

Visitor 3: "The type of social development? They who lived here learned. How did people adapt to climate? Did the people trade with the neighboring tribes? Where did they relocate to? Were there diseases? Was there a doctor? How was hunting - good or bad? Did they hold their own justice?"

Visitor 4: "Must have been an exciting time in 1933. A lot of hard work went into this place. I like the idea of having the food and refrigeration close by! Having to work right outside your front door is good!"

Visitor 5: "Surprised at age of the station. Interested in learning more."

Visitor 6: "Of course they didn't have electricity, it was 1906. The buildings don't look as old as they apparently are. What building was attached to the chimney? The sign doesn't mention a fire. Is it really so good to live so close to work? What a beautiful place to work! Hard work!"

Visitor 7: "Surprised guard station built in the first place. Even more surprised it has lasted nearly 100 years. Glad it has been renovated. Leaves me wanting more information, like an invite to enter the ranger station. Need more exhibits and info on what forest service employees do here in a typical day."

Visitor 8: "They worked hard. Thankful (to have this today). Learned about location importance. Glad all preserved still."

Visitor 9: "Thoughts about early rangering. How fish to eat was a bonus. Where/why ranger stations were located. Proximity to water. How remote early stations were."

Visitor 10: "Very remote. Horses very important. They need pastures. Wish I was a ranger 50 years ago."

Visitor 11: "Old time logging. How people made it years ago. Shows how important water was. Shows how important place for horses to eat was."

Figure 6-3. *Multiple themes generated from a single interpretive sign (adapted with permission from Dave Bucy).*

Location! Location! Location!

From this site, a crew could step out the door of the bunkhouse and be at work.

Why live here?

Imagine arriving here for work in 1906. What would be different? For starters, you have no electricity, running water or telephone and you have ridden for most of a day on horseback from the nearest town. A long commute!

The stream in the meadow to your right provided water to drink and fish for dinner.

Look around you!

A meadow on your right for pasture;
A stream in the meadow for water and refrigerating food;
Wood for building material and fuel;
The main access road at your front door,
. . . and your work all around.

A perfect place to live! So the US Forest Service built a cabin and barn here in 1906. In 1933 they expanded the station, building the office in front of you, the ranger's residence across the road, and a bunkhouse, barn, mess hall and other buildings in the trees behind the office – everything for a crew to live and work here, and all in a perfect location . . . in the 1930s.

The meadow to your right was important as pasture for horses, the key means of transport in 1906.

Figure 6-4. *Thematic panel interpreting a historic guard station (with permission from Dave Bucy).*

was strategically important to the jobs US Forest Service rangers had to do in the early 1900s. The writer-designer's theme for the interpretive sign was: "While the guard station's location might seem odd today, it was the key to everything its first occupants had to accomplish— from their work to sheer survival" (Figure 6-4).

What do you notice about the personal meanings these eleven visitors took from the sign? First is probably the sheer diversity in what they were provoked to think about. Not surprisingly, their minds were going in all kinds of directions. Most focused on the story of the station, some on their reaction (surprise) at what they saw. Some were provoked to think about broader aspects of how life there was, and still others related thoughts about the sign itself. Obviously, the interpreter's input theme generated a wide diversity of themes in the visitors' minds.

You probably also noticed that only a few of the visitors had thoughts that more or less para-phrased the interpreter's intended theme.[13] Visitors 1, 2, 8, and 9 probably came closest by expressing thoughts about the importance of the station's location. Nonetheless, most of the visitors listed thoughts that are in some way consistent with, or a personal extension of, this theme. Note that visitors 4 and 6 disagreed in their thinking about whether having one's home so close to work is a good idea. Of course, it didn't matter to the interpreter who was "right." It mattered only that both visitors were provoked to think about it, even though the sign itself didn't specifically prompt them to do so.

Finally, you probably noticed that most of the visitors' thoughts are expressed in the form of declarative sentences, either explicit ("Location is important!") or implicit ("[I was] Surprised at [the] age of the station."). Recalling that themes are whole ideas expressed in sentences, you can see that these are, in fact, the themes each visitor is taking away from the interpretation.

Did you notice how many of the visitors expressed their thoughts in the form of speculation—things they are now *wondering* about as a result of viewing the sign? Visitor 3 wonders how it might have been to live in the location back then; Visitor 4 speculates that things must have been exciting; Visitor 6 makes an unprompted connection to the fact that there wouldn't have been electricity in 1906; Visitors 9 and 11 wonder about the lifestyle of old-time rangers and loggers; and Visitor 10 fantasizes about being one. You probably can see that these are *new* meanings created—not by Bucy's sign but by the eleven visitors themselves.

You might also have noticed that several of these same visitors were provoked to pose questions as a result of reading the panel. Technically, these aren't themes (since themes answer questions rather than pose them), but each will potentially produce its own themes as the visitors' thinking continues and they arrive at their own conclusions and answers to the questions—potentially producing yet more sentences in their heads.

Here we can see in the visitors' own thoughts the impact of a well-developed theme. In this case, the sign hasn't simply "communicated its theme" or "gotten its theme across," it has provoked visitors to make their own meanings and to wonder about and entertain new possibilities related to the story. To suggest the sign was successful only with the four visitors whose thoughts came closest to expressing the interpreter's theme would be illogical if one accepts that the purpose of the sign was to provoke visitors to make their *own* connections. Therefore, to ask which of the themes listed by the visitors matches "the" theme of the sign seems an

> When interpretation makes us think, our thoughts can generate a lot of sentences in our heads—not just the one an interpreter was trying to generate.

Provoking sentences in the head at Hawai'i Volcanoes National Park, USA. An interpreter helps visitors connect a rock sample to the magma being erupted from an active volcano. *Photo by Arthur Wierzchos.*

irrelevant question in this case. Indeed, from the standpoint of the provocation endgame, it's often the wrong question. As we'll see in Chapter 8, there are times when you'll most definitely want an audience to take away "the" message, but even then we might be naive to think it's the only message they'll get. Indeed, when something makes us think, our thoughts can generate a lot of sentences in our heads—not just the one an interpreter was intending to generate.

This is how it goes between our ears. When something makes us think, it causes us to make meanings that explain it and put it in personal perspective.[14] Metaphorically, you might say that thinking makes the sound of meaning making. If we had very good ears or highly sensitive listening devices, we might be able to evaluate interpretive products by listening for the sound of the "wheels spinning" between a person's ears. When something makes us think *a lot*—when it profoundly impacts our point of view—it generates many thoughts in our minds which in turn produce a lot of meanings. Therefore, when something is meaningful to us, it's because it has caused us to make a lot of connections related to it. That's why it's easy to talk for hours on end about something you really care about. You have a lot to say about it because you have lots of sentences in your head that relate to it.

This idea that a well-developed interpretive theme can provoke a listener or reader to think and make personal meanings isn't as new or as revolutionary as some might think. If you're familiar with the writings of Freeman Tilden, you'll recall he advanced a very similar view:

> the purpose of interpretation is to stimulate the reader or hearer…to gain an understanding of the greater truths that lie behind any statements of fact. (1957: 33)

> to search out meanings for himself…(1957: 36)

A half century later, we now know from dozens of studies that a single relevant message can stimulate people in an audience to think their own thoughts and make personal meanings about the topic.[15] That is, one well-developed theme can give rise to many.

Where to from Here

In Chapter 7, we'll turn our attention to the practical task of writing themes. We'll see what themes look like (their structure), and we'll compare different themes and decide which ones are "better" and why that is. In doing this, we'll see that not all themes are equally capable of provoking thought in an audience. Here we'll contrast the qualities of weak themes and strong ones and see that their difference lies not in the fanciness of the language used to write a theme but rather in the power of the idea it expresses. Not surprisingly, this will lead us back to the *R* in TORE.

Glossary terms: intention (interpreter) side of theme, results (audience) side of theme

Additional Thoughts for Chapter 6

1   In fact, one writer, (Lonie (1998: 33), concluded that finding a universal definition of *interpretation* to please all stakeholders might be impossible.

2   It certainly might be useful in interpretive master planning to think about a hierarchy of themes, but claims that this same hierarchy ends up in an audience member's mind are unfounded.

3   I won't distinguish between these terms. In the provocation endgame, they refer to the same thing. A theme is a *meaning*, regardless of whether it's small, big, restrictive, or inclusive. As long as the theme is strongly relevant for an audience, it really doesn't matter what you call it.

4   A short list would include Argentina, Australia, Belize, Brazil, Canada, Chile, China, Costa Rica, Denmark, Dominican Republic, Ecuador, Egypt, El Salvador, Finland, Germany, Guatemala, Honduras, Indonesia, Japan, Latvia, Malaysia, Mexico, The Netherlands, New Zealand, Nicaragua,

Norway, Panama, Papa New Guinea, Singapore, Spain, Sweden, Taiwan, United Kingdom, Uruguay, United States, Venezuela, and Vietnam.

5   These two sides of theme (the interpreter's and the audience's) were introduced in Chapter 5. See Figure 5-3.

6   I presented some of these studies with the provocation endgame in Chapter 3. Interested readers can find earlier discussions in Ham (1983, 2002b) as well as in Tarlton and Ward (2006).

7   Some good sources on the "intention side" of themes are Brochu (2012); Brochu and Merriman (2012); Field and Lente (2000); Gross and Zimmerman (2002); Ham (1992); Kohl (2004); Larsen (2003); Moscardo (1999b); Moscardo, Ballantyne, and Hughes (2007); Pastorelli (2003); Regnier, Gross, and Zimmerman (1994); and Ward and Wilkinson (2006).

8   These pathways were depicted in Figure 5-3.

9   Although an esoteric interpretation of "moral of the story" is that it implies some judgment about "right and wrong" or "good versus bad," I'm using the term here in the popular sense of "a lesson learned," "conclusion drawn," "principle extracted," or "implication."

10 In Chapter 8 ("The Zone of Tolerance") you'll recognize this sort of conversation as the "thought listing" method of evaluating an interpretive product's success in provoking thought.

11 But not necessarily. See Chapter 9, where we consider some creative alternatives to the "one-theme" rule.

12 In later chapters, we'll use the term *personal themes* to refer to these "sentences." Provoking a lot of personal themes is usually a good sign, as long as they don't clash with what the interpreter was trying to say—that is, when the interpretation leads people to factually incorrect ideas or when they draw conclusions that are somehow in moral conflict with the interpreter's intended theme. In some cases, however, an interpreter might even be happy provoking incorrect or morally objection-able thoughts. It depends on the interpreter's subjective "zone of tolerance," an important concept we'll consider in Chapter 8.

13 You'll find another detailed example of this in Chapter 10 and Appendix 3. If your theme is strong and well presented, you'll usually find it provokes thoughts that hover somewhere around the one you're trying to develop. Remember, your goal was never to "teach" an audience your theme; rather it was to provoke them to think their own thoughts with respect to your theme.

14 An interesting article by Klaus Manhart (2005) maintains that humans create myths and stories mainly because of our brain's biological need to explain the things around us and to bring order to our world.

15 Tilden appears to have seen these relationships at least three decades before they were revealed by studies on elaboration and information processing. See "Two Paths to Impacting Attitudes" in Chapter 5 and Ham (2009a). See also "personal themes" in Chapter 8 ("The Zone of Tolerance").

CHAPTER 7
Not All Themes Are Equal

When you begin with a strong, thought-provoking theme, you're already close to success.

With every sip of this wine, the toil and blood of our ancestors become part of you.

So went the theme of a very astute participant in a course I taught in Spain a few years ago. The young man was expressing a theme about a Basque grape (*tempranillo*) that has been grown in the Rioja region of northern Spain for at least 1,500 years.[1]

Most would agree that his words make you think. If he uttered the phrase just as you raised a glass to your lips at a Rioja wine-tasting bar, you might pause before swallowing. If he blurted it out one day in a Spanish history course you were taking from him, you might beg him to give you more detail. In both cases, his theme is successful because it provokes thinking—*it makes you want to know what lies behind it.* This is a quality all strong themes have.[2]

From this single example, we can take away two principles of thematic interpretation. First, like all things in communication, the strength of a theme is audience dependent—a theme that impacts a particular group in a particular way in a given place or context won't necessarily have the same result when the group or the context is changed. The second principle is that strong themes are relevant—they make connections to things that matter to people in the audience.

In this chapter, we'll see that not all themes are equal. We'll contrast strong and weak themes and look for the qualities that make them different. This will lead us to several practical guidelines that can help an interpreter strengthen a theme. The chapter concludes with some tips and a creative decision framework for adding interest to difficult themes.[3]

How Do You Know if a Theme Is Strong?

One of the perplexing disconnects in persuasive communication is that studies tell us a message is strong when it *results* in the audience thinking agreeable thoughts about it.[4] The trouble with this notion of strong is that a communicator can't know until *after* the act of communication whether she or he actually had a strong message. Most interpreters, of course, would consider this a little late. They want to know ahead of time how to craft a strong message.

A strong theme makes you want to know what lies behind it.

The same problem exists with interpretive themes. We know that a strong theme (1) provokes its audience to think, (2) attracts attention and creates curiosity, and (3) begs for additional detail and development because of the intrigue it creates—people simply want to know more about a strong theme. Obviously, if you were walking down a city street and happened to overhear someone utter a phrase that was especially relevant to you in that particular place and at that particular moment, you'd probably stop, hoping to hear more, or you'd at least slow down a bit as you tuned your ear into the speaker's voice. Wouldn't you?

But as much as the example above gives three good explanations of what a strong theme does, it doesn't tell an interpreter much about how to craft the theme ahead of time, and it doesn't offer any practical insight into what the qualities of a strong theme might be. This is what the rest of the chapter attempts to do. Let's start by considering the main ingredients strong themes possess.

Theme Tip

The idea is that if you start with a theme that's already thought provoking, imagine how much more likely it is that your finished interpretive product will be successful. Remember from Chapter 2 that TORE means you have a strong theme that's communicated in an ORE way. So once you have a strong theme (the *T*), you're just ORE away from success.

Ingredients of a Strong Theme

Imagine you have to give a five-second talk—which, of course, leaves you only enough time to state your theme. Recalling that the purpose of thematic interpretation is to provoke thinking, how would you decide what to say in your five seconds? What few words would you express that would capture the essence of your message and leave your audience thinking?

There's no single best answer to this question, of course, but most would probably hone in on the need to say something simple and that matters to the audience—in other words, something they'll easily understand and that connects to their main interests and experience at the time. "Simple" is important because noncaptive audiences won't invest a lot of effort trying to follow something they don't understand. And, of course, "mattering" (relevance) is important because it motivates the audience to engage with your words and think about them.

Going back to our wine example, imagine your talk was about the *tempranillo* grape. What theme would you express in your five seconds? You most likely wouldn't simply state a straight fact such as:

This grape has a long tradition among people in this part of the world.

Although the theme is simple enough, a lot of people wouldn't find it especially thought provoking. Instead, you might think of ways to connect the fact to something your audience would care more about—maybe something like:

With every sip of this wine, the toil and blood of our ancestors become part of you.

Most people would probably agree that the second theme is stronger. But *why* is it stronger? Both themes are accurate from a historical perspective, but the second one expresses the idea in a more thought-provoking way, doesn't it? By definition, that makes it stronger than the first theme.

Thought-Provoking Themes Have Two Essential Features

We've seen in several previous chapters that interpretation needs two main qualities in order to stand a good chance of provoking thought: (1) it must *motivate* the audience to process it by connecting to things that matter to them—that is, it must be relevant to them, and (2) it must be perceived by the audience to be *easy to* understand and process.[5] As we've seen throughout this book, when interpretation possesses both qualities it's more likely to provoke thought than interpretation lacking either or both of the qualities. That is, it has higher **provocation likelihood**.

And the same can be said for individual themes. When a theme is *relevant* to its audience and *easy to process*, it's likely to provoke thought. Since provoking thought is the hallmark of a **strong theme**, let's consider what you might do to ensure your themes have these two essential ingredients for high provocation likelihood (relevance and ease of processing).

A Strong Theme Has High Provocation Likelihood

When a theme is both easy to process and relevant to its audience (that is, when it's both *O* and *R*), it stands a better chance of provoking thought than a theme lacking in either of these qualities. Because such themes are more likely to provoke thought, you can say they have "high provocation likelihood." By definition, a *strong* theme is a theme with high provocation likelihood.

As we saw in Chapter 5, when a whole interpretive product has both qualities, it too has high provocation likelihood. In fact, TORE is just a short way of saying that an interpretive product is built around a thought-provoking (OR) theme, which is in turn, presented in a thought-provoking and enjoyable (ORE) way.

Some Ways to Strengthen a Theme

Following are seven ways you can increase a theme's provocation likelihood, either by adding relevance or by making it easier to process. These are not the only ways to do it, but they are tried and proven by some of the world's most accomplished interpreters.

Add a Dose of Vitamin R

1. Themes that invoke universal concepts are loaded with "Vitamin R"

The first thing you might notice about our example wine theme is its use of universal concepts to heighten relevance. Recall from Chapter 2 that universal concepts are intangible or symbolic connections to things that (as far as we know) have always been important to human beings. They include extreme emotions such as love, hate, fear, loneliness, elation, and sorrow; biological imperatives such as death, suffering, hunger, and thirst; and human fascinations with uncertainty, the cosmos, and mystery, among many other connections.[6]

You probably can see that notions such as "toil," "blood," and "our ancestors" are also universal concepts. When you wrap a theme around an appropriate universal concept(s), you give it power it wouldn't otherwise have. This is why so many of the truly great plays, screenplays, novels, poems, and song lyrics revolve around universal concepts. It loads them with built-in relevance—"Vitamin R," as I like to call it.

With every sip of this wine, the toil and blood of our ancestors beome part of you. *Photo by Barbara Ham.*

2. A well-placed metaphor or simile can add relevance to a theme

Another reason the second theme in our example is stronger is that it expresses the idea in metaphorical terms (obviously, ancestral toil and blood aren't tangible things that can actually be sipped and incorporated into a human body). Using a metaphor or simile, as we've already seen, is one of many ways to strengthen a theme's relevance because it causes an audience to make connections to things they know and understand. You might recall from Chapter 2 the example theme that used a metaphor describing Chuck Berry as the "architect" of rock and roll.[7] Chuck Berry, of course, was a brilliant guitarist and composer, but he wasn't an architect. And yet, metaphorically, his creations helped establish a sort of design or "blueprint" for rock-

and-roll music—which is something architects in fact do. Describing Berry as an architect of rock and roll adds interest because the word *architect* isn't usually used in that way, yet it makes (metaphorical) sense in the context of our theme.

3. Building personal language into a theme increases its relevance

> **When you insert the personal word *you* into a theme, you start a conversation with your audience.**

Another thing you'll notice about the *tempranillo* theme is that it's personal; it speaks directly to its audience (you). Such themes are usually high in relevance because most people's favorite topic is themselves. When you insert the personal word *you* into a theme, it seems instantly to start a conversation with your audience as opposed to making a third-party statement.[8] That is, it puts the audience directly into the story.

Compare these two themes about ancient Maya civilization. Which do you think is stronger?

If you were an ancient Maya, being clever was often more important than being strong, especially if you wanted to stay alive.

In ancient Maya culture, being clever was often more important to daily survival than being strong.

Human sacrifice was an integral part of ancient Maya culture. Copán Ruins World Heritage Site, Honduras. *Photo by Ron Force.*

You might find both themes equally interesting, as a lot of people are fascinated by ancient Maya civilization. But one could argue that the first theme gives you more to think about because you yourself are now center stage in the story. If this is true, the first is the stronger of the two themes since it provokes more thought. This is what you attempt to do by adding the word *you*—engage the audience's imagination by putting them into the theme itself.[9]

Make it Easier to Process

4. Analogies make connections easier to see

A theme's strength comes not only from its relevance but also from being easy to process. Sometimes an appropriate analogy is the key to ease of processing. Consider, for example, an interpreter who wants to explain how the internal plumbing of an active volcano works. An entirely factual (but weak) theme might be:

> Active volcanoes contain both heat and gas pressure.

After a little thought, the same interpreter might build an analogy into the theme, reasoning that pressure cookers create heat pressure, and gas pressure is what happens when you shake a bottle of soda or champagne:

> The internal plumbing system of an active volcano works just like a pressure cooker and an agitated bottle of champagne.

5. Short themes are easier to process than long ones

An obvious way to make processing a theme easy is to keep it short. But what does *short* mean? I like the advice offered by the Smithsonian Institution's Lothar Witteborg, which is to limit a sentence to roughly fifteen to twenty words.[10] If more words are needed, you might need two sentences. As I explain shortly, although it's good practice to keep a theme to one sentence, the most important thing is to capture a single (and relevant) *idea* in your theme. So when themes involve ideas that are more complicated than one fifteen-to-twenty-word sentence can express, a second (rarely a third) sentence might be helpful.[11]

> It's good practice to limit a theme to one sentence when you can, but the most important thing is to capture a single relevant idea.

6. Breaking a theme into two sentences can make it work—an exception to the one-sentence rule

For many years I followed the advice that themes should always be expressed in a single sentence. And indeed, most themes probably require just one.[12] But as I mentioned in Chapter 2, interpreters sometimes want to communicate ideas that are too complex to be expressed in a single *thought-provoking* sentence. Perhaps the theme is simple but multifaceted; perhaps it must allude to an essential chain of events that requires many more than Witteborg's recommended fifteen to twenty words. For whatever reason, there are times when limiting yourself to the **one-sentence rule** will lead you to write a long (run-on) sentence that will simply sound silly to the ear and has no hope of provoking thought. In these situations, adding a second sentence might make the essential difference between a strong theme and a weak one.[13]

Consider, for example, the interpreter who wants her audience to think about the plight of nocturnal birds in her area. She's concerned that the birds' secret lives in the dark have led to widespread and dangerous misconceptions about them. And she wants to motivate her audience to get involved in nocturnal bird education programs.

She first tries to express her theme in a very long single sentence:

> Most people rarely have a chance to see nocturnal birds, which has made them the subject of many superstitions, and sometimes these misconceptions are potentially threatening, but all of us can do something to protect them.

She quickly realizes, however, that although it captures the whole idea she wants to develop, her run-on sentence is so long that both she and her audience get lost in the words. The result is that it fails to motivate processing.

With a little editing, and breaking the theme into two short but related sentences, she ends up with a theme that says what she wants to say and yet is more motivating for her audience:

> Because we rarely see them, nocturnal birds around here are the subject of local superstitions and potentially threatening misconceptions. Fortunately, there's something all of us can do to correct the situation.

7. Themes that use the everyday conversational language of the audience are easier to process

Another way of making a theme seem easy to process is to use the conversational language of your audience as you express it. Remember that the effectiveness of a theme depends on the tastes and preferences of the audience it's intended to impact. So when I say to use conversational language, I'm really saying that you should try to express your theme using the informal language your *audience* would typically use to express the same idea.

Because many interpreters are highly trained and conversant in one or more technical fields, it's quite understandable that they get used to using the esoteric vocabulary and sentence structure that specialists in that field use when they talk to each other. However, when those same interpreters are talking to nonspecialists, a different vocabulary and tone are often required. This is not to say that interpreters need to "dumb down" their themes for nontechni-

Another Theme Tip

Start by stating your theme using words and sentence structure that inspire and motivate *you*. Then play with it and edit it until you transform it into an expression that you think will have the same effect on your audience.

cal audiences. Rather they should simply adopt a different way of expressing them. The great interpreters of science—for example, John Muir, Albert Einstein, Isaac Asimov, Carl Sagan, Aldo Leopold, Steve Irwin, and David Attenborough—are renowned for their ability to use common everyday language to talk about complicated subjects.

Imagine you're a well-known expert in Iron Age history. One day during a neighborhood barbecue, one of your neighbors innocently asks whether anything other than the metal itself was important during the Iron Age. Which of the following themes do you think would make the better answer? (Hint: If you think the first one is better, you need to attend more neighborhood barbecues.)

> During the Iron Age, the widespread adoption of iron for making tools and weapons coincided with other changes in society, including differing agricultural practices, religious beliefs, and artistic styles.

> People in the Iron Age not only discovered a far better material for making their tools and weapons, they also found new ways to farm and worship, and to express themselves in art.

Beginning interpreters sometimes assume that expressing a strong theme requires a lot of frilly, flowery language. Some even think they're unable to express strong themes because they're not "good" writers. Both assumptions are patently untrue—first because normal people rarely use flowery language in everyday conversation, and second because too many "decorations" can spoil a perfectly good sentence.

In fact, my experience has been that flowery language (i.e., lots of adjectives, adverbs, prepositional phrases, and dependent clauses) usually *ruins* a theme. Any accomplished thematic interpreter will tell you it's the power of the idea a theme expresses—not the fanciness of the words it uses—

It's the power of the idea a theme expresses—not the fanciness of the words it uses—that makes a theme strong.

that distinguishes a strong theme from a weak one. Common, everyday plain language is usually a faster path to strong themes than fancy prose.

A Way to Add Interest to Difficult Themes

The main reason strong themes attract people's attention is that they make statements about things that interest their audiences. As we've seen, themes loaded with "Vitamin R" have this feature because they connect to things that matter to people. Put simply, this makes them interesting. A lot of attention has been given to the general idea of "interestingness" in recent years,[14] and some of the lessons learned can be applied by interpreters in search of strong themes.

A basic principle of interestingness is that our attention is called to things that somehow stand out from the ordinary—they're unusual (e.g., the tallest mountain or the first person to accomplish something); sometimes we notice things because doing so might keep us safe (e.g., dangerous things, moving things, and loud noises); at times we're fascinated by things because they surprise us or fly in the face of conventional wisdom (e.g., a man biting a dog, a powerful clam); or we're drawn to things because they present uncertainty or intrigue (e.g., a mystery or legend). And we're almost always interested in things we can empathize with or relate to firsthand (e.g., a story about other people that we project ourselves into).

Interpreters must remember that most of the time our audiences are different from us in terms of their interests. Oh sure, we share some interests with virtually everyone, but the depth and range of our interest in the topics we interpret are not widely shared by other people. This is why we need to find ways to show connections between the things we interpret and what our audiences care about most.[15]

Just as universal concepts are thought to be important to all people, there are other things in life that are thought to have high inherent (built-in) interest for most people. Two paragraphs above, I listed a few of them: other human beings, dangerous things, moving things, unusual things, facts that surprise us, and so forth. So it makes sense that an interpreter might try to work one of these inherently interesting connections into a theme.

Sometimes this is almost mandatory—such as when a theme must focus on something that isn't so inherently interesting to everyday people. Among these less inherently interesting topics are ordinary ("unspecial") things, safe things, things that don't move, nonliving things, and so forth. A challenge most interpreters will face from time to time is needing to develop themes about something that is truly significant and important to the overall story but low in inherent interest. That's where **Knockan theory** might help.

Knockan Theory for Exploring Creative Connections

I coined Knockan theory[16] in 2002 when I was at Knockan Crag near the village of Ullapool in the Scottish Highlands. Knockan Crag is one of Scotland's most important geological interpretive sites, and the place where nineteenth-century geologists first discovered that land masses could thrust sideways, uplift, and fold over—so that what was once on the bottom ends up on top.

Two things impressed me most about the interpretation at Knockan Crag: (1) the approach was highly successful (and I'm not a person who's innately interested in such things as geologic thrusting and uplifting), and (2) the story was about rocks—yes, plain old, nonliving, motionless rocks—which was brought to life by telling visitors not so much about the rocks but rather about the two geologists who made the discovery (Ben Peach and John Horne).[17]

Like other geologists doing research at Knockan Crag, Peach and Horne noticed they were finding older rock on top of younger rock, which of course was the opposite of what geology then would expect. The question no one could answer at the time was "why?" But Peach and Horne did provide an answer (thrusting, uplift, and folding), and their explanation remains today one of the great contributions to our understanding of how the earth works.

At the time of my visit, interpretation in the small visitor center put visitors in the place of Peach and Horne, explaining the dilemma they were faced with and engaging readers in the uncertainty and excitement of scientific inquiry. As the story of the discovery reached its conclusion, visitors came to share the geologists' joy of being able to explain their observations with a new theory that forever changed geological science. According to an evaluation of the visitor center,[18] visitors leave the site both with a concrete idea of the geologic phenomenon and recognition that the discovery was important. And yet the story was at least as much about the two human beings who made the discovery as it was about the rocks they studied.

The lesson we can take from Knockan Crag is that one way to strengthen a theme about something we think has low inherent interest (like rocks, perhaps) is to connect it to something of higher inherent interest (like human beings). The theme at Knockan Crag could have been a relatively weak theme:

> Early geologists' discovery of older material on top of younger material at this site presented a dilemma that was resolved by the theory of thrusting, uplifting, and folding.

Instead, by applying the principle of connecting less interesting things to more interesting things, a stronger theme resulted:

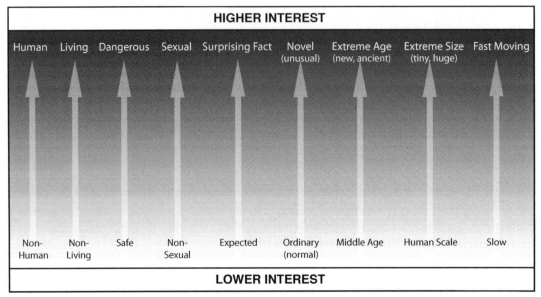

Figure 7-1. *Knockan theory—a tool for exploring creative connections in theme development.*

The discovery made here by geologists Ben Peach and John Horne was a journey marked by intrigue, mystery, and ultimately triumph. Thanks to them, science could finally explain how older layers of earth can end up on top of younger layers.

Of course, this is just one example of how Knockan theory can work.[19] In Figure 7-1, you might be able to see a number of other possibilities. Each upward pointing arrow represents some quality or dimension that ranges from lower inherent interest (at the bottom) to higher inherent interest (at the top).[20] If you're faced with the challenge of developing a theme about a topic you believe has low inherent interest, look to the upper part of each dimension to see if it suggests any creative linkages with your topic. At Knockan Crag, the interpreters connected the bottom part of the second dimension (i.e., rocks are nonliving) to the upper part of the first dimension (human). Moving around to the other dimensions, however, what additional possibilities do you see?[21] For example, where would your mind take you if you connected rocks to the "dangerous" column? Do you see any potential connections to the "novel" column, "surprising fact" column, or "extreme size" column?[22]

> One way to strengthen a theme of low inherent interest is to connect it to something of higher inherent interest.

Applying Knockan Theory

Knockan theory helps you explore ways to enhance the interest level of something that isn't inherently appealing to an audience. The theory says simply that one way to make something more interesting is to *connect it to something else that has higher inherent interest*. Figure 7-1 shows what some of these connections might be.

Notice that the chart displays nine different scales (you can call them "Knockan scales"). Each Knockan scale represents a dimension or quality that a topic might have, and each ranges from low inherent interest (at the bottom) to high inherent interest (at the top). The idea of Knockan theory is to somehow make a connection between your topic and the *upper part* of one or more of the scales.

To use Knockan theory, start with a topic (for example, ceramic plates and cups in a historic home).

Since the topic of ceramic plates and cups probably isn't inherently fascinating to a lot of people, you might scan the upper portion of the nine Knockan scales and look for creative possibilities. That is, you can ask yourself in each case if making a connection to that dimension might enhance the topic's appeal to your audience.

For example, glancing at the human-nonhuman scale, you might instantly think, "Sure, I could emphasize the people who actually used these plates and cups—who they were, their names and ages. Are there any anecdotes to tell? Were there any interesting, funny, or sad occasions for which the cups and plates were used?

Of course, your creative thinking might go in an altogether different direction when you get to the dangerous-safe Knockan scale. How were these ceramics made? Was danger involved in the sculpting and firing of the raw material? Were there any household accidents involving these cups or plates? Did Mrs. X ever throw any of the plates at Mr. X?

Moving to the sexual-nonsexual scale, was there a romantic connection or steamy encounter associated with the cups or plates?

Were they shipped from China or another faraway place? Back in those days, how unlikely was it the plates and cups would even arrive on the boat (surprising fact-expected scale)?

Are these ceramics unique or unusual in any respect? Where were they made, and by whom? Is there anything in the history of these particular plates and cups that sets them apart from other ceramics (novel-ordinary scale)?

You get the idea. Try substituting your own topic and see where the Knockan scales take your creative thinking.

Tips for Strengthening a First-Draft Theme

Look at the themes listed in Figure 7-2. If these were your first drafts, chances are you wouldn't be completely satisfied with any of them just yet. Although they're all factually correct and written in complete sentences, they probably don't provoke as much thought as you'd like. In most cases, it's because they're still not strongly relevant for most nonspecialist audiences. And in a couple of cases, they might not be as easy to process as they could be. So for one or both of these reasons, all the draft themes could use some strengthening. But where do you begin?

Step 1: Focus first on relevance and ease of processing.

As a first step, you might consider applying some of the methods we discussed at the beginning of this chapter:

1. wrapping the theme around a universal concept

2. adding a metaphor or simile

3. incorporating personal language

4. using an analogy

5. shortening the theme to fifteen to twenty words

6. breaking the theme into multiple sentences

7. using the conversational language of your audience

As we've seen, each of these methods provides a way either to increase the relevance of a theme or make it easier to process. Because none of the themes seem excessively long (all contain fewer than twenty words), method 5 (shortening) and method 6 (using multiple sentences) probably wouldn't be especially helpful in our example. But the other five methods might well be worth considering.

For example, the fourth theme about Alberta's flora might be easier to process if technical words like *vascular* and *bryophytes* were either eliminated or substituted with plainer language. Although you might have a good reason for wanting your audience to know that vascular plants have special features that allow fluids to pass through them (which allows the plants to grow larger than non-vascular plants), you probably don't need to make that small detail a centerpiece of your theme. And, of course, *mosses* would probably be a better word to use than *bryophytes*. Remember, using the everyday plain language of your audience is important in strengthening a theme.

Carl Linnaeus was the father of modern taxonomy.

The American Civil War was a very difficult period for most people at the time.

Bedouin lifestyles in Abu Dhabi have changed rapidly during the past thirty years.

Alberta, Canada, has some 1800 species of vascular plants and over 1000 species of bryophytes and lichens.

A lot of Maori served in World War II.

Making cheese is difficult but worth the effort.

Fifty percent of Galapagos birds are endemic.

People have been living in Australia for a very long time.

Figure 7-2. *Draft themes you could strengthen.*

Of course, there are other ways to strengthen this theme beyond simplifying the language. What might you do, for instance, to increase its relevance for a non-specialist audience? Do you see possibilities for using a metaphor? For example, can Alberta be likened to an elaborate garden? Or incorporating a universal concept, like what secrets do Alberta's plants harbor? Do they hold answers to questions that humans are incapable of even asking yet?

The more you practice thinking this way (i.e., writing a first-draft theme and then looking for creative ways to strengthen it), the easier theme writing is going to be for you. As I mentioned previously, the seven methods we considered in this chapter aren't the only ways to strengthen a theme, but each of them gives you a different perspective for evaluating a draft theme and ultimately improving its potential to provoke thought.

Step 2: Edit with special attention to the verb(s) in your theme.

Another thing you can do to strengthen a draft theme is simply edit it. Most skilled writers will tell you that a crucial factor in well-written language is the use of verbs. And since *all* themes have a verb (remember, themes are complete sentences), your editing might pay special attention to the verbs you use.

In their natural form, verbs are "doing" or "action" words. Good writers know that the most engaging verbs are ones that accentuate their action quality. In addition, the most interesting verbs are often those that describe actions a human being can readily "see" in the mind's eye. That is, the best verbs to use are those that create mental imagery. Drawing on these characteristics, here are three tips for improving the verbs in your themes:

Try to avoid passive voice sentences

As we saw in Chapter 2, a verb expressed in active voice is more interesting than the same verb expressed in passive voice.[23] In the active voice, the subject of a sentence performs the verb's action. That is, a person or a thing *does* something. For example:

Active voice: "The boy threw the ball."

Passive voice: "The ball was thrown by the boy."

To see how using the active voice helps a theme, consider the Iron Age theme we looked at earlier:

> *People* in the Iron Age not only *discovered* a far better material for making their tools and weapons; *they* also *found* new ways to farm and worship, and to express themselves in art.

The words in italic highlight two active voice parts of the theme. In the first part, *people discovered* a far better material, and in the second part, *they found* new ways. In both cases, the subject of the sentence (people and they) is doing the action.

If we converted both parts of the theme to passive voice, it would look something like this:

> Not only was a far better material for making tools and weapons discovered by people in the Iron Age, new ways to farm, worship, and express themselves in art were also found.

Your eye, your ear, and common sense should tell you that the first (active voice) version is more engaging than the passive voice version. In part, this is because the active voice in the first theme accentuates the actions of discovering and finding, whereas the passive voice (in the second theme) softens the sense of action. In addition, it's almost always easier for people to envision an action expressed in active voice compared to passive voice. For example, you can probably construct a mental image of people "discovering" and "finding" things in the active voice version. But in the passive voice version, how easy is it for your mind to construct a concrete image of things "having been discovered" and "having been found?" This leads us to a second verb tip.

Use verbs you can "see"

That is, build theme statements around verbs that describe a concrete action—something everyday people can easily visualize ("visual verbs"). To understand what makes a verb visual, close your eyes while you use the verb in an active voice sentence, and judge for yourself whether you think you can easily "see" it happening. Below are two lists of verbs. Which list (A or B) has verbs that are easier for you to see in your mind's eye?

A	B
understood	nodded
moved (suddenly)	lurched
left (secretly)	slithered (out)
left (angrily)	stormed (out)
cried	wailed
said (loudly)	screamed
signed	inked
swallowed (quickly)	gulped
ran	sprinted
released	unleashed

You probably noticed that each verb in column B is simply a more visual form of the same verb in column A. If you close your eyes and say each of the verb pairs (A then B), you'll probably agree that the second one always conjures up a more concrete mental image of the action. Although every theme is different, if your theme uses a verb in column B instead of its counterpart in column A, it will probably be stronger as a result. To make things easier, I've compiled around 2,500 verbs in Appendix 2. If you're in search of an active, visual verb, you might find what you're looking for there.

> The most interesting verbs are those that describe actions a human being can readily "see" in the mind's eye.

When possible, avoid the verb *to be* or use another verb in its place

Although the verb *to be* is one of the most versatile and commonly used verbs in any language, it's not a particularly interesting verb.[24] Unlike most verbs, *to be* doesn't describe any sort of action or movement. Rather it describes a status or condition (*is, was, were, will be, would have been*, and so on). For this reason, you might sometimes want to substitute another more visual verb in its place when you're editing a theme. This usually requires only very minor tweaking.

For example, instead of saying, "This castle *is* five centuries old," you might say, "This castle *tells* a 500-year story." In this case, not only have you replaced the verb *to be* with a more active verb (*to tell*), you've also made the castle do the talking (see "Use personification" in Figure 2-8).

What Themes Are *Not*—Four FAQs

Sometimes interpreters confuse themes with "theme-like" ideas that don't serve the same function a theme itself serves. Among these look-alikes are titles, taglines, imperatives, and questions.

FAQ 1: Is a title a theme?

Short Answer: Not usually.

As we all know, themes are complete sentences. So unless a title expresses an entire sentence, it can't be a theme. Many (probably most) titles are sentence fragments. For example, the title of the movie *How the West was Won* is not a sentence, and therefore not a theme either. Yes, it tells what the movie is about, and it promises what you'll learn about if you actually invest the time to watch the movie—which is to say that it describes the topic of the movie—but it doesn't express the theme of the movie.

A theme, however, expresses *not* merely the topic but rather the moral or overarching conclusion you hope people will think about if they actually engage with an interpretive product.

> Unless a title expresses an entire sentence, it isn't a theme.

When a title states the *entire* theme in a *complete* sentence, you can indeed see the theme and title as being one and the same. Much more common, though, are titles that convey either just the essence of a theme (what I've called "theme titles") or only the topic ("topic titles").[25] In both of these cases, you need to see the title and theme as different things because in neither case does the title actually state the theme.

Compare, for example, these three possible titles for an exhibit whose theme is that the power of the ocean masks its fragility:

Title 1 (title = theme):   The Power of the Ocean Masks Its Fragility.

Title 2 (theme title):   The Ocean—Powerful yet Fragile

Title 3 (topic title):   The Power of the Ocean

You can see that only in Title 1 are the theme and the title actually the same thing. Although Title 2 (the theme title) is effective in communicating the *essence* of the exhibit's theme, it does it in two sentence fragments and leaves out a key detail ("masking"). So obviously, it doesn't state the theme. Title 3, of course, simply tells a prospective viewer only what the exhibit is about (its topic).

In some cases, a theme title might even use just a single word placed next to a graphic or illustration to convey the essence of the theme. For example, the one-word exhibit title "Endangered!" (placed to the left of a large illustration of a gray wolf) conveys in only a second or two the theme that the gray wolf is in danger. But again, notice that although the title is effective in conveying the *essence* of the exhibit's theme, it doesn't *state* the theme itself. The theme of this exhibit was actually:

Our persecution of wolves is driving them to extinction.

FAQ 2: Is a tagline a theme?

Short Answer: Again, not usually.

Beginning theme writers often struggle with the difference between a tagline (or slogan) and a theme. Their confusion is understandable because some taglines *are*, in fact, themes. Take, for instance, De Beers Jewelers's well-known tagline, "A diamond is forever." This tagline is indeed a theme. It's a complete declarative sentence and expresses a whole idea about diamonds. Likewise, the tagline of the United Negro College Fund in the United States is a theme: "A mind is a terrible thing to waste." It, too, is a complete sentence.

However, another well-known tagline, "The real thing," is not a theme. It's not a complete sentence, and without additional words (i.e., "Coke is") it conveys only part of an idea. And Nokia's tagline "Connecting people" is, for the same reason, not a theme.

> Some taglines are themes, but many are not.

FAQ 3: Can a theme be expressed as an imperative (command)?

Short Answer: No.

An imperative is a special kind of sentence that tells someone (the audience) to do something. A theme, however, is a declarative sentence (what screenplay guru Robert McKee[26] calls the "controlling idea," and playwright scholar Lajos Egri[27] calls the "premise"). The famous author of fables, Aesop, called it "the moral of the story."[28] In poetry and prose, the same concept invoked by McKee, Egri, and Aesop has traditionally been called a "theme." This is probably what led Lewis (1980) to adapt the word *theme* for use in the interpretation field. In all of these usages, a theme (controlling idea, premise, or moral) needs to be expressed in the form of a declarative sentence—not as an imperative.

As we've seen throughout this chapter, *the* key defining characteristic of a theme is that it makes a *statement* about something. Another way to say this is that a theme expresses a belief or a stance on something. It makes an inference, *not* a demand. It articulates the overarching conclusion an interpreter hopes an audience will draw from an interpretive product and think about (recall here our discussion in Chapter 6 about the audience side of theme and "sentences in the head"). But imperatives don't draw inferences or conclusions; rather, they order people to do things.

For example, "Let's all fight for the future of the polar bear" is a provocative statement that will no doubt motivate some audiences. But it's not a theme; it's an imperative. It motivates the audience—as commands often do—because it's a personal statement (i.e., the implied subject of every imperative is the personal word *you* or in this case, *we*)—and also because the statement is wrapped around the universal concepts of fight and survival (which is implicit in the phrase "the future of the bear").

So yes, issuing such a command to an audience is something a skilled interpreter might do to motivate them, but doing so is a theme development technique, not the theme itself. The actual theme of such a presentation would probably be something like "All of us need to join forces to fight for the future of the polar bear" or "If we fight together, we can save the polar bear from extinction." And in an effort to provoke an audience to think thoughts around this theme, an interpreter might make a savvy decision to issue the command: "Let's all fight for the future of the polar bear."

> Using an imperative is good communication technique, but an imperative doesn't express a theme.

Another way to see that imperatives aren't themes is to use the old familiar complete-the-sentence format for theme writing:

> I think it's very important for people in my audience to realize (appreciate, think, understand, accept, know, etc.) *that*[29] _____.
> (Complete the sentence with your theme.)

Obviously, you could complete this sentence with "all of us need to join forces to fight for the polar bear's future," and it would sound fine to the ear. In other words:

> I think it's very important for people in my audience to realize (appreciate, think, understand, accept, know, etc.) that *all of us need to join forces to fight for the polar bear's future.*

But if you try completing the sentence with the imperative "let's fight for the polar bear's future," the result is quite different:

> I think it's very important for people in my audience to realize (appreciate, think, understand, accept, know, etc.) that *let's all fight for the future of the polar bear.*

The second completion of the sentence doesn't work because the part you filled in doesn't express a declarative sentence—rather it expresses an imperative. And although saying that imperative to an audience is a good technique to use in *developing* the theme, the imperative isn't the theme itself.

FAQ 4: Can a theme take the form of a question?

Short Answer: No.

There are three main types of sentences: declarative sentences (which make statements), imperatives (which issue commands or orders), and interrogatives (which ask questions).[30] As we've seen repeatedly, themes always take the form of a declarative sentence.

Again we must recognize there's a big difference between *crafting* a theme (in order to guide your creative planning of an interpretive product) and actually *developing* and *presenting* that theme to an audience. As in the case of using imperatives, asking well-phrased questions is a valuable method for developing and presenting a theme. But the theme and a technique for developing that theme (such as asking a question) are two different things.

If you're confused about this difference, it might help to ask yourself why it even occurred to you to ask the question. Chances are you have some overall point you hope asking the question

> Asking a question is a good communication technique, but a question doesn't express a theme.

will help you make. That point, if you say it to yourself in a complete sentence, would probably be your theme. Following on from our polar bear example, if you're planning to ask your audience a question such as "Do you think the polar bear is worth fighting for?" it's probably because you think doing so will provoke your audience to have an answer, such as "Yes, this amazing creature is definitely worth fighting for!" or "Of course it's worth fighting for—I would be so sad if the polar bear were gone forever!"

Your anticipation of these kinds of responses probably originated somewhere in your mind with a theme—that is, an overarching idea that led you to ask the question at all. It might have been something like:

> It's going to take all of us, fighting together, to save the polar bear from extinction—but it's a battle well worth having.

The most accomplished interpreters intuitively think in terms of questions because their experience tells them that asking an audience a thought-provoking question is an effective way to *develop* a theme. But bear in mind that how you craft and express a theme for yourself during the creative planning process can be very different from how you decide to present and develop that theme for an audience. These are two separate tasks—the first one leading to the second one. At the moment of presentation, that declarative sentence you drafted, played with, edited, and finally committed to paper (or simply to your mind) as you planned and prepared an interpretive product might be expressed in the form of a question you now hope will provoke thinking related to it.

You might recall Socrates, the Greek instructor who became famous for teaching his students primarily through asking them thought-provoking questions. Today, of course, we call his technique the Socratic method. Socrates asked his students questions to provoke them to think thoughts that would lead them to draw certain conclusions.[31] This is something skilled interpreters frequently do because they know that asking a good question automatically provokes thinking—which is the whole purpose of doing interpretation at all. So, as we saw in the case of imperatives, a question is an important and useful technique an interpreter might use in presenting and developing a theme, but it's *not* the theme itself.

Another way to convince yourself of the difference between a theme statement and a question is to use the same complete-the-sentence format we used above. If you try to complete the sentence with a theme in the form of a question, you'll find it doesn't make sense grammatically.

Finally, recall that a well-crafted theme *answers* a question. That question is "so what?" And, of course, you can't answer any question with another question. In Chapter 6 ("Two Sides of Theme and Sentences in the Head"), we saw that if an interpreter does a good job of developing a theme (perhaps by using tried and proven techniques such as imperatives and asking good questions), she or he stands a pretty good chance of provoking people in the audience to think thoughts that hover somewhere around that theme.[32] This, of course, is both the premise and promise of thematic interpretation if it's well done, and it's an idea we'll return to in much more detail in Chapter 8.

Summary and Where to from Here

Throughout this book I've stressed that the ultimate purpose of interpretation is to provoke audiences to think and draw their own conclusions and morals of the story—in essence, extracting their own personal themes from an interpretive encounter. In Chapter 5, we saw that an interpretive product designed around a strong theme (T) and presented in an ORE way stands a good chance of provoking this kind of thinking. And in this chapter, we've seen that themes that are both easy to process and relevant to an audience will have higher provocation likelihood than themes lacking either of these qualities. We therefore saw that a strong theme, by definition, is a theme with high provocation likelihood.

You might recall from Chapter 6 that a single well-developed theme can give rise in an audience member's mind to many personal themes (see Figure 6-3)[33]. The more interpretation provokes a person to think, the more of these themes will be generated in the person's mind. So obviously, interpreters who begin with a strong theme as they design a new interpretive product will make their jobs as provokers-of-thought much easier than interpreters who begin with only a weak theme.

However, is provoking just *any* kind of thought sufficient, or are some kinds of thoughts more important? This is the question we'll take up in Chapter 8. There, we'll consider a dilemma about how much latitude you should allow when comparing the personal theme(s) people take away from an interpretive encounter with the theme you were actually trying to develop. That is, how closely should the themes audiences extract from your interpretation match the one you had in mind when you designed it? Understanding this dilemma will lead us to examine both our philosophy of interpretation and our purposes for doing it at all.

Glossary terms: Knockan theory, one-sentence rule, provocation likelihood, strong theme

Additional Thoughts for Chapter 7

1   By incorporating "toil" and "blood" into his theme, the young interpreter was making reference to the persecution of Basque people during the thirty-six-year dictatorship of Francisco Franco (1939–1975). The grape is pronounced "tem prah NEE yo" (not "tem prah NIL o"). *Tempranillo* means "early one" due to the fact that it ripens several weeks before other grapes in the region. Owing to the exceptionally high-quality wines it produces, *tempranillo* is known as the "Noble Grape" of Spain.

2   Another quality is that they're *accurate* according to current knowledge. One of interpretation's most important ethical foundations is intellectual integrity, and interpreters must never knowingly fabricate or stretch the facts in order to spice up a story. Fortunately, however, they rarely have to choose between the two. A skilled interpreter can make even the most esoteric truisms about science, nature, and humanity thought provoking.

3   Jon Kohl (2004) offers a very good review of different approaches to theme writing.

4   This is a basic principle of the elaboration likelihood model of persuasion (ELM). In ELM studies, a strong message is one that generates a preponderance of agreeable (pro-argument) thoughts, whereas a weak message is one that generates mainly disagreement with the message. That is, the strength of the message is determined by its results and therefore can't be known until *after* it's been communicated to an audience. But this doesn't help a communicator know ahead of time whether she or he has a strong message. See Petty and Cacioppo (1986) and Petty, McMichael, and Brannon (1992).

5   As I explained in Chapter 2, studies show that ease of processing and message relevance are the two stars that must align for interpretation to stand the greatest chance of provoking an audience to think. Simply put, when interpretation is easy to digest and makes connections to things that matter to its audience, it stands a much better chance of provoking thought than interpretation that is deficient in either of these qualities. Likewise, when a theme possesses both qualities, it has high provocation likelihood.

6   You'll find several examples of universal concepts in Figure 2-4. Notice that "blood" is already on the list. You probably could add "toil" and "ancestors" as well. You might also want to read the invited commentary by master interpreter, Shelton Johnson, in Figure 2-5. Shelton's interpretation of Yosemite "Buffalo Soldiers" is an outstanding example of the power an interpreter can harness using universal concepts.

7   See Figure 2-1.

8   I'm often asked whether the inclusive *we* is also a way of making a theme more personal. I don't think so. This doesn't mean using *we* in a theme isn't sometimes a good idea; it just means that doing so doesn't make the theme more personal. That's because *we* usually doesn't start the same kind of personal "conversation" with an audience that I'm talking about here. It's been my observation that interpreters sometimes substitute *we* for *you* because of its political correctness (especially if some undesirable human trait is being discussed). That is, saying "we" means all of us, including "me" the interpreter; and so it sounds more polite and not indicting of the audience. But *you* is a very special word in any language because it communicates specifically to the individual. In fact, in many languages there are multiple forms of *you*—each one more or less informal than the others—and using one that isn't appropriate for the person you're talking to, or the setting you're in, can even offend that person and others who might be listening. Likewise, communication is never as personal as it is when *you* is used in combination with eye contact. So yes, *we* is perfectly acceptable if the situation calls for it, but *you* is the more personal of the two.

9   Recall from Chapter 2 our discussions about shadowing experiments, self-referencing, and labels. When interpretation refers directly to us (by name or a personal description of some kind), we often cannot resist paying attention to it—even when other things are vying for our attention.

10   See Witteborg (1981). Although Witteborg's main focus was on developing exhibit texts, I think his advice makes good sense for all kinds of writing—including theme writing.

11   Note that I'm not saying twenty words is some sort of absolute maximum. Rather I'm saying it's a reasonable goal for the maximum length of a sentence in a theme statement. I've seen thirty-to-forty-word sentences that work just fine, but I think it's much more common to find strong, thought-provoking themes expressed in shorter sentences.

12   The first to recommend the one sentence rule was Bill Lewis (Lewis, 1980). I considered it good advice then (see Ham, 1992), and I still do today. However, in the ensuing three decades, I've worked with many budding theme writers who struggled unnecessarily trying to make a strong, provocative idea fit into a single sentence. In so many of these cases, the sentence became the end in itself, and the interpreter's challenge became one of grammar and punctuation rather than worrying about how to bring out the power of the idea she or he had started with. A frequent result was that a perfectly good theme was transformed into boring gobbledygook. But when I told the interpreter to try saying the theme in two related sentences (with a much-needed breath in between), the strength of the theme often suddenly emerged. The difference was obvious. So my recommendation is still to try first to state your theme in a single sentence (an "irreducible idea," as screenplay guru Robert McKee puts it). But when complying with the one-sentence rule seems to rob the theme of its power, you should feel free to break the phrase into multiple sentences and determine for yourself if a stronger theme results.

13   Some interpreters prefer to use a semicolon between the sentences as a way to show they're related. But however you decide to write and punctuate your theme, remember it should express just one whole idea even if it takes a couple of sentences (or more) to say it.

14   If you're interested in research into the "interestingness" concept, two (dare I say, "interesting") studies are those by Schank (1979) and Frick (1992).

15   Tilden (1957) called this the "visitor's chief interest." He summarized the idea in his first principle of interpretation: "Any interpretation that does not somehow relate what is being displayed or described to something within the personality or experience of the visitor will be sterile" (p. 11).

16   In case you're wondering, yes, I'm aware of the double meaning of *knockan* in the street vernacular of some countries. But Knockan Crag is indeed the name of the amazing place where these ideas first occurred to me, and so the theory rightly deserves to bear its name. Many thanks to James Carter who not only helped develop the interpretation concept at Knockan Crag—he also served as my visual aid when I first unveiled Knockan theory at Scotland's First National Conference on Interpretation (Ham, 2002a).

17   If you're interested in learning more about the story of Knockan Crag and how Peach and Horne's discovery changed geological science, a good place to start is http://en.wikipedia.org/wiki/Knockan_Crag.

18   See the evaluation report by Julie Forrest (2006).

19   Moscardo, Ballantyne, and Hughes (2007) showed how Knockan theory can be applied to designing interpretive signs.

20   On rare occasion, an interpreter will disagree with one or more of these scales. And that's to be expected. I invented the scales subjectively based on my own observations of ordinary people over many years. But they could not possibly capture 100 percent of reality. Some people, for example, might think slow things are more fascinating than fast things, and some people are repulsed or embarrassed by any mention of sex. So like all things in interpretation, the scales presented here could be more accurate for some audiences than for others. The idea of Knockan theory isn't to dictate what's interesting to all people. Rather, I offer it only as a tool for interpreters who have to develop themes for difficult topics and who know their audiences well. So if you're compelled to change any of the scales, make sure your changes are based on what you know about your *audiences'* interests, and not simply on what you personally find interesting. Remember, your deepest interests and those of your audiences are likely to be different.

21   If you're interested in learning about other ways to jump-start creative thinking, you might enjoy von Oech's (1990) classic, *A Whack on the Side of the Head—How You Can Be More Creative*. A very readable book on the origin and function of creativity is Csikszentmihalyi's (1996) *Creativity—Flow and the Psychology of Discovery and Invention*.

22   Discerning readers will notice that I've not tried to suggest a connection between rocks and sex, but that doesn't mean such a connection might not be plausible somewhere. Of course, the same is true of the novel-ordinary, extreme age, and fast-moving dimensions.

23 This is a very old and accepted idea. Rudolf Flesch first advanced it in 1949 in his classic text, *The Art of Readable Writing*. If you use Microsoft Word, you know that one of the grammar-checking features is a measure of how many sentences are constructed in passive voice. The higher the percentage of passive voice sentences in your document, the more boring it is. Fortunately, this chapter is just 7 percent passive.

24 In fact, many (if not most) first-draft themes contain some form of the verb *to be*. This is not necessarily a bad thing, because sometimes it's the best verb for the sentence. But *to be* often ends up in the first draft simply because it came easily to the interpreter's mind. With a little thought, the same interpreter is frequently able to replace it with a more active, visual verb.

25 In Chapter 10 (Nonsequential Theme Development), we'll look at theme titles and topic titles in a lot more detail.

26 See McKee's (1997), *Story: Substance, Structure, Style, and the Principles of Screenwriting*.

27 See Egri,'s (1946) classic text on stage play development, *The Art of Dramatic Writing: Its Basis in the Creative Interpretation of Human Motives*.

28 Aesop (who lived roughly 620–564 BC) was, of course, the author of dozens of fables that became famous for the themes they developed—that is, the morals of the stories and lessons they taught. Themes such as "a bird in the hand is worth two in the bush," "a man is known by the company he keeps," and "one man's meat is another man's poison" are among the most memorable morals of Aesop's fables.

29 Notice the word *that* is emphasized. I do this to make clear that the lead-in to the sentence *must* end with the word *that*. This is because ending the lead-in this way requires you to complete the sentence with an independent clause—which in grammar is a phrase that itself contains a subject and a verb and can therefore stand alone as a complete declarative sentence. If you leave out *that*, you'll probably end up writing a topic rather than a theme. Themes, of course, are always expressed as complete declarative sentences. For this reason, I often say that writing a theme is as easy as *that*.

30 Some grammar experts add a fourth type of sentence, "exclamatory" sentences, which end in an exclamation point. But exclamatory sentences are really just emphatic variations of the other three types of sentences. For example, "The ship sunk!" is an exclamatory declarative sentence; while "Get out of here now!" is an exclamatory imperative sentence, and "Why in the world would you think that?!" is an exclamatory interrogative sentence.

31 Arguably, Socrates's method was the origin of what today would be called "constructivist" teaching—the idea that fact-bearing teachers don't "put" knowledge into their students' heads. Rather, the students "construct" their own knowledge through the process of thinking and self-discovery. If this reminds you of Tilden's (1957) claim that "interpretation isn't instruction, but rather provocation," you've made an important connection. As I pointed out in Chapter 3, Tilden was indeed

thinking like a constructivist when he wrote *Interpreting Our Heritage*, but Socrates was probably the first constructivist teacher. In Chapter 3, we also saw that the provocation endgame of interpretation is based on the idea that interpretation serves its most fundamental purpose when the audience is provoked to do its own thinking and make its own meanings about things. Sometimes, asking a good, thought-provoking question is the best way to achieve this outcome.

32   In fact, the value of asking good questions to provoke thinking around a theme has been documented in a number of studies. Two relevant sources for interpreters are articles by Fosnot (2005), "Constructivism Revisited" and Petty, Cacioppo, and Heesacker (1981), "The Use of Rhetorical Questions in Persuasion." Of course, Socrates knew about the value of asking good questions two millennia before anyone got around to researching it.

33   In Chapter 8, we'll formally define "personal themes" as the subjective meanings an individual takes from an interpretive encounter.

CHAPTER 8
The Zone of Tolerance

Provoking people to think their own theme-related thoughts is your main job. But how would you know if you've done it well?

Imagine you and three friends are discussing the theme of William Shakespeare's *Romeo and Juliet*. Further imagine that Shakespeare has somehow managed to go forward in time and is now eavesdropping on your discussion (the proverbial fly on the wall). You can bet that four centuries after writing his historic play he'd be very interested to hear what all of you are saying. "What meanings are these strange people from the future extracting from my play? How are they interpreting what I was trying to say with my story about those two kids?"

From time to time, all of us should try being the fly on the wall—listening to what audiences say about our interpretive products. Oh sure, we'll want to know if they liked the thing or not, if they thought it was easy to follow, interesting, or funny or moving. But beyond these basic reactions, we might also be interested to know something about the internal "conversations"[1] they were having about it in their minds—what messages they took away, what impressions they formed with respect to the content of the presentation, what conclusions they drew, what morals they extracted, what meanings they made from it inside their own heads—that is, the **personal themes** each individual subjectively took from it.[2]

What personal themes did you take from my story about those two kids?

The eavesdropping Shakespeare applying his zone of tolerance.

It would be unrealistic to think that everyone ought to extract the same personal themes or to evaluate a presentation's success according to the proportion of people that could paraphrase what the interpreter's theme was. As we've seen, any human being faced with an assemblage of information will draw conclusions about what it all means, but that doesn't mean they'll arrive at the same conclusions. Indeed, two scientists may examine the same raw data and come to different opinions about what they mean. World leaders today look at identical situations and form dramatically different impressions about the status quo and what needs to be done to improve things. Although interpreters are well served to follow a thematic approach in developing their programs, whether audiences will take home with them that *exact* same theme is a different issue.

The personal themes people take away from interpretation are subjective meanings they themselves ascribe to the whole of the presentation. Some may "get" it just as the interpreter intended, whereas others may get the gist of it, and still others might extract new and perfectly acceptable meanings that the interpreter never even considered. In the worst scenario, some people might get wrong ideas or even ideas that are in moral conflict with anything the interpreter intended to say. Such is human communication in whatever form it occurs.

Any human being faced with an assemblage of information will draw conclusions about what it all means.

The master teacher of playwrights, Lajos Egri (1946), tells us that Shakespeare's theme in *Romeo and Juliet* is that "great love defies even death." So we shouldn't be surprised if the eavesdropping William cringes just a little when one of the men in your discussion group claims that the message he took from the play is that "men should stay away from women. They'll just get you killed." Likewise, he would frown when one of the women counters with the theme, "Love just isn't worth all the trouble it takes to find and keep it." But why is he frowning? Is it simply because none of the participants got the "right" theme (that great love defies even death)? Or is he displeased because the two themes offered so far are simply unacceptable to him? In his mind, they're just not in the realm of what he intended to say—not even close. The important word here is *close*.

What if the third person in your group offered, "True love is important in human society?" Would Shakespeare have been more tolerant of this offering than of the previous two, even though it wasn't exactly the message he intended? Probably so. At least your friend is on the right track by concluding that Shakespeare was making a positive statement about love. How about if you yourself suggested the theme was that "people who are really in love are willing to do almost anything to have it and protect it?" Your words might well bring a smile to Shakespeare's face. Why do you suppose that is? None of the four of you could articulate exactly the theme he had in mind when he wrote what is arguably the world's most famous play, yet two of you offered personal themes that were quite acceptable to him. William is smiling because the latter two themes were within his **zone of tolerance**. The first two were outside the zone.

> Although an interpreter might develop a specific theme, whether audiences take home with them that exact same theme is a different issue.

Of course, we'll never know what Shakespeare's reaction to this conversation really would have been—but he probably would want to do a little better than two out of four. Fortunately for him, the broad theme of *Romeo and Juliet* has stood the test of time. About sixteen generations of readers and playgoers have gotten his message about the power that love can have over human beings, so he can give himself a well-justified pat on the back. Were this not the case, however, he might want to keep working on his play until he's more satisfied with the proportion of people taking away personal themes that fall within his zone of tolerance. In doing so, he would need to entertain two possibilities. One is that despite his best efforts to leave his audience feeling something about the power of love, they're simply drawing the only conclusions they're capable of drawing: their own. So he agrees to disagree, thereby widening his zone a bit. The other possibility is that he simply missed the mark in how he developed the story, and that if he modified this or tweaked that, more readers would get his message. As we'll see when we discuss the widths of a zone of tolerance, this is both a practical and philosophical issue.

You might be wondering what accounts for the fact that different people attending to the same interpretive activity or device can extract different personal themes. Recall that every person in an audience brings a different schema to the interpretive setting. Their schemas consist largely of what they're thinking at the time, what's important to them at the moment, all of their background and knowledge about the topic and the place, and their personal experiences in similar situations. We know from a lot of research that their schemas will be all determining in terms of what each of them pays attention to or ignores in the presentation, what is relevant and worthy of their focus, what is interesting and what is boring, what is useful or useless, and so forth.[3] Because everyone brings a different schema to the encounter, we can expect that different people in the audience will find different parts of the interpretation most relevant and worthy of their attention. Consequently, not everyone pays equal attention to the same things, and this alone, of course, would lead to differences in the personal themes they take away.[4]

However, as we saw from Bucy's (2005) study in Chapter 6 (see Figure 6-3), if you anticipate schema differences in your audiences and develop your theme cohesively, you'll usually find that even people who paid attention to different things will draw conclusions lying somewhere within your zone of tolerance. If you fail to develop your theme cohesively, you may find that the personal themes people extract from your programs vary more widely than you'd like. But if you allow your theme to guide your choice of content and the emphasis you give each part of your presentation, some of the conclusions they draw will tend to hover somewhere around the one you intended. When this happens, you can be fairly sure they're making meanings that are, at some level, consistent or agreeable with the theme that guided your development of the interpretive product, regardless of whether they can say it exactly the way you would.

How Wide Should a Zone of Tolerance Be?

Like answers to all complicated questions, the answer to this one is "it depends." Specifically, it depends on what your interpretive product is trying to achieve. As we've already seen, for interpretation to accomplish anything, it at least has to provoke the audience to think. Provocation is always a first and *necessary* outcome before you can hope to achieve anything else through your interpretation, at least with any degree of predictability. Beyond this, the size of your zone of tolerance will be based on your own sense (and sometimes your agency's or organization's sense) of the kinds of personal themes you're happy for people in your audience to take away from your interpretation. You can think of your zone of tolerance as your thematic "comfort zone" or "happy zone." Depending on what you're trying to accomplish with any particular interpretive product, your zone of tolerance probably falls into one of three possibilities: the unrestricted zone, the wide zone, or the narrow zone (Figure 8-1).

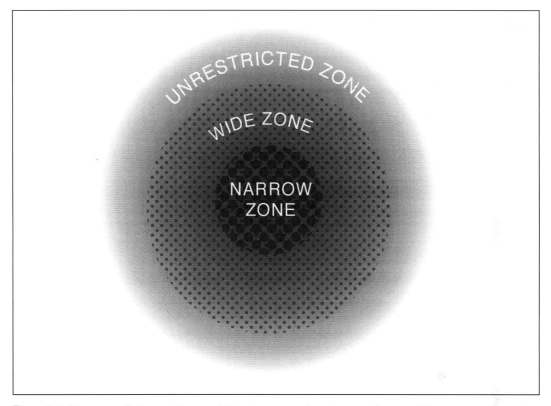

Figure 8-1. *Three zones of tolerance. How much latitude can you tolerate between the personal themes your audience takes away and the theme you tried to develop?*

Unrestricted Zone

In some cases, your zone of tolerance might be unrestricted. You may reason that the important thing is to get people thinking, making meaning, and arriving at whatever conclusions and implications suit them. Exploring unknown possibilities in science, grappling with the subjective meaning of historic fact, or examining difficult social issues are examples of the kinds of purposes that might drive interpretation in this zone. Toward this end, you might be happy with any amount of disagreement in the personal themes people draw from your interpretation.

An interpreter's theme in the unrestricted zone usually captures a sense of the diversity in opinion that is expected or desired. So instead of expressing a particular point of view about a topic (as a lot of themes do), unrestricted zone themes would express the importance of each of us having our *own* opinions, however conflicting or contrasting they might be.[5] For instance,

Unrestricted zone of tolerance: you allow unlimited latitude in the personal themes individuals take away.

rather than promoting reverence or an appreciative point of view about something (as interpretation of nature or culture often does), an unrestricted zone theme might encourage polar extremes in emotions or views, possibly even those that are socially taboo or so-called dark ones. These decisions, of course, depend entirely on the interpreter's purpose.

In the provocation endgame (see Chapter 3), the first and most important outcome of interpretation is that audiences are provoked to think and to find personal relevance in the places, things, and concepts we interpret. In the unrestricted zone, the individual connections they make and the conclusions they draw are of little concern to us. We just want to leave them full of personal thought. A guiding principle is that the interpreter's job isn't to cover the topic, but to *uncover* it. In this philosophy of interpretation, an ultra-wide zone of tolerance is the default and interpreters give little thought to it. Indeed, the size of the zone is not simply unpremeditated—for many interpreters, it's irrelevant.

For example, in *Meaningful Interpretation*, Larsen describes a view of interpretation in which expanding audiences' comprehension of the range of possible meanings is a central purpose:

> Interpretation also facilitates democracy. It allows for and stimulates a conversation of multiple meanings and points of view. Interpretation encourages audiences to find themselves in the resource as well as engage, comprehend, and appreciate the perspectives of others. (2003: 73)

Whether interpretation falls into the unrestricted zone depends entirely on your motive and purpose for doing it. An example is storytelling. Although sometimes a teller might want to weave together some type of overarching meaning, often the idea is just to have fun with a good story and not to make anything more of it. Rejecting the idea that every story ought to result in some "message" or "moral," storytelling scholar Susan Strauss observed in *The Passionate Fact* that:

> most stories, and especially fairy tales and myths, can be butchered by people who think the point of the story is to give a single message…They [fairy tales and myths] show things, such as images and consequences, but they don't moralize. (1996: 48)

In fact, there may be times when you explicitly design your interpretation to produce as much diversity as possible in what an audience concludes—for instance, when you want to stimulate people to form their own opinions and to show the sheer range of possible viewpoints. It's as though the theme of this sort of interpretation is:

> This is an important issue in our society. What any of us personally thinks about it is unimportant. What matters is that we are thinking about it at all.

Sometimes, you might even want to create disagreement as a means of encouraging debate or introspection. Such are often the themes of programs on controversial issues—what Roy Ballantyne and David Uzzell have coined "hot interpretation."[6] Fallon and Kriwoken commented on the opportunity that such forms of emotion-laden interpretation bring for stimulating visitor center audiences to question and challenge what they already think they know:

> [Creating] cognitive conflict presents visitors with new knowledge, attitudes, values or behaviors that are incompatible with their present understandings. (2003: 48)

Storytellers and museum theater experts often tout the special opportunities these forms of interpretation bring for provoking audiences to think more deeply about difficult social and

Museum theater and storytelling often have an unrestricted zone of tolerance. *Courtesy of Sovereign Hill Museums Association, Australia* and *Susan Strauss Storyteller, USA.*

moral issues, both past and present.[7] Observes Tessa Bridal in *Exploring Museum Theatre*:

> Theatre thrives on conflict and inquiry and is invaluable in inspiring people, challenging them, and making them less fearful of encountering ideas, especially those foreign or new to them. Theatrical characters can embody what we most love and most fear; couched in a theatrical performance, issues can be discussed and examined in a non-threatening way, and we can be invited to laugh and to cry about ourselves and others. (2004: 7)

In the unrestricted zone of tolerance, the limits we place on the acceptability of themes an audience might extract from interpretation are so far "out there" that, if they exist at all, we don't see them. And a hallmark of this zone is that diverse emotional extremes are sometimes an outcome of interest precisely because they provoke thought that in turn intensifies meaning. Although other forms of interpretation also strive for emotional response, it's the sheer range of acceptable meanings we "allow" (indeed encourage) audiences to make that sets this zone apart from the wide zone of tolerance.

> In the unrestricted zone, the limits we place on the acceptability of personal themes are so far "out there" that we don't see them at all.

Wide Zone

Most times, however, there are subtle limits in our zone of tolerance, even if we don't always recognize them. For example, the main purpose of a lot of interpretation is bonding people to places or connecting them profoundly to some concept or feature—"icons," as some have aptly called them.[8] Here the desired response from audiences is, by definition, positive. Although we're happy for them to make their own individual meanings, we're even happier if those meanings hover around an appreciative point of view. As we saw in Chapters 4 and 5, interpretation's role in "making a difference" is frequently predicated on audiences appreciating, valuing, and caring about the things we interpret. So most heritage interpretation probably falls in this zone of tolerance.

Following the provocation endgame, the main purpose of this kind of interpretation is to provoke the audience to wonder or marvel in the presence of the extraordinary, and to find in it personal meaning or truth. In many ways, this was Freeman Tilden's (1957) purpose in writing *Interpreting Our Heritage*. He wanted us to understand that interpretation's most important outcome wasn't in "teaching" anything to any-body but rather in provoking them to marvel at the special places they visited. I personally consider this interpretation's best and highest purpose when tour-ists and travelers are the main audience, and a view of meaning-making interpretation as being central to visitor experience is certainly widespread today.[9]

In Chapters 4, 6, and 7, we considered the role of strong themes in this process, and we discussed prov-ocation as the first and foremost outcome of interest. Getting visitors to marvel is a worthy goal in and of itself. The thinking and wondering they do are what make the meanings between their ears, and these meanings themselves constitute the connections they

Wide zone of tolerance: you're happy for audiences to take away almost any personal theme, as long as it's philosophi-cally and factually consistent with your intended theme.

make to the place or thing or icon. We're aware also that meaningful things matter to people, and so the constituency for special places potentially grows each time a visitor to one of them makes meaning.[10] And finally, we know that visitors' experiences will be enriched and deep-ened by the thinking we provoke them to do.[11] In this view of interpretation, we usually give ourselves wide latitude in the meanings we hope will transpire in people's minds. As long as they're making meaning in an *appreciative* way, we're happy.

It's often the case, however, that even though we're thrilled when our audiences are provoked to think and are drawing their own conclusions, we (like Shakespeare in our example) would be happier if they *didn't* draw certain kinds of conclusions from our interpretation. Although those of us who live in free, pluralistic societies justifiably pride ourselves in freedom of thought and expression, we interpreters sometimes overlook the hint of manipulation in our well-in-tentioned motives. As I've written elsewhere, as long as we're convinced that what we're doing is in the best interests of the audience or the place, we may not see (or accept) that much of our interpretation is aimed at producing a narrower range of acceptable meanings than we realize:

> We may want people to think or know certain things so that they will have a rich experience; we often want them to value what we value; and we almost always want them to behave in certain ways (and not in others) when they are in the midst of the places and things we interpret. (Ham & Weiler, 2003: 1)

Most heritage tourism interpretation probably has a wide but subtly restricted zone of tolerance. Lindblad-National Geographic Expeditions guide in Galapagos, Ecuador. *Photo by Barbara Ham.* Heritage interpreter at Fort George National Historic Site, Canada. *Photo by Benoît Aquin. Courtesy of Parks Canada.*

Commenting on interpretation's meaning-making role, Dave Larsen reminded us that although the range of meanings we're happy with may be very wide, it's usually bound by a value orientation an interpreter or organization espouses:

> Interpretation provokes the discovery of personal meaning, connection, and care about the resource. (2003: 73)

Added Cable, Knudson and Theobald:

> Although some interpreters may use an objective approach to communication of facts, stories, and analogies, with no apparent attempt to color the information, their basic purpose is to persuade the visitor at least to consider the facts as perceived by the interpreter. (1986: 14)

Often in interpretation, we promote the idea that we're happy for our audiences to think whatever they want, as long as we succeed in provoking them to think at all. And there is value in reasoning this way. But even when we tell ourselves that we're open to a wide range of interpretations, we may unconsciously be applying a zone of tolerance in our thinking. We assume that if we do our job well, there would be no reason to fear what our audiences might go away thinking—that we can accept anything. But it's doubtful that most of us—or the organizations we work for—are always as open to the *full* range of possibilities as we'd like to think we are.

Figure 8-2 presents some examples of thematic interpretation in which the themes that certain visitors extracted were almost certainly inconsistent with the kinds of conclusions the interpreter would have wanted them to draw. I've taken these examples from personal experiences in Spain, Australia, and the United States, but they could have occurred anywhere. In fact, you probably could add your own experiences to the list. Although I intuited the interpreter's objective and theme in one of the examples, the comments from audience members in the last column (i.e., the personal themes they took from the interpretation) are actual outcomes. It's doubtful that the people responsible for the interpretation in each case would be satisfied with the conclusions these individuals were drawing. Although the interpreters might have had a fairly wide zone of tolerance, these particular themes probably fell outside the boundaries.

The examples, of course, are just isolated cases, and most people in each audience probably took away themes that were more "acceptable." But the point remains that usually there are limits to what we would be comfortable with, even if we haven't consciously considered what they might be. In fact, some interpreters are so good at their craft that they don't even entertain the notion that people might misconstrue, reject, or morally object to their themes. But even these gifted few may have a zone of tolerance, however subconscious it might be.

Interpreter's Objective	Theme that Guided Program Development	Themes Extracted by People in the Audience
To convince park visitors that they should be extra careful in how they store their food while camping in black bear country.	A lot of us may not realize that we are unwitting signatories on the death sentence for the bears that live in this park.	When you think about it, once the bears are gone, we'll be a lot safer. Camping here would be better if we didn't have to worry about using those stupid food storage lockers.
To provoke visitors to marvel at the brilliance of the museum idea.	The idea that there should be places dedicated to nothing but preserving our story was born of pure genius.	Museums are mainly for old people.
To leave the audience appreciative of the value of indigenous wisdom in contemporary society.	Indigenous people reason in ways that evolved over centuries with their view of the land and the cosmos; their wisdom often leads them to see things differently from the ethnic majority.	It's about time those people entered the twenty-first century.

Figure 8-2. *Examples of themes that might fall outside an interpreter's zone of tolerance.*

Narrow Zone

We've seen that when the purposes of interpretation are to stimulate diverse opinion, discussion, or debate, an unrestricted zone of tolerance is the norm. When the goal is to facilitate appreciative personal connections, or when the acceptable range of meanings is defined by a value orientation or organizational mission, a wide but subtly restricted zone of tolerance may prevail. But are there situations in which you'd want very little variation between your theme and the ones audiences take away—that is, when you'd want them to get the "right message?" The answer is "possibly."

> Are there times when you'd want audiences to take away a specific "best" personal theme? The answer is "possibly."

When interpretation merges with education (as it often does, for example, in museums, science centers, and environmental education centers that have specific educational missions or that offer programs to complement formal school curricula), the question of audiences getting the "right" message becomes intertwined with the educational objectives that guided the interpretive design and development process. Often such interpretive programs have clear and specific learning outcomes in mind, and sometimes they're focused explicitly on countering audiences' misconceptions about a topic. Wrote Ross Loomis about a study that revealed museum visitors' misunderstanding of how gravity works:

> Naive ideas about scientific principles and concepts can be countered with effective interpretation. (1996: 42)

While the providers of narrow-zone interpretive services may also value broad critical thinking, there are times when they're primarily interested in getting specific intended messages across to their audiences.[12] Free-choice learning theorist John Falk, for example, tested an approach to museum exhibition design in the California Museum of Science and Industry (CMSI) by comparing the "big ideas" visitors said they extracted from the exhibition to the ones museum scientists said they *wanted* visitors to get:

> Scoring of responses was based on comparing visitor responses to a range of acceptable answers provided CMSI scientists. (1997: 681-682)

Interpretive programs designed with the hope that audiences will take away "correct" or "acceptable" ideas (whether facts or feelings) are widespread, including not only in museums but also in nature centers and outdoor tourism settings such as parks and nature reserves.[13] Although interpreters more accustomed to wider zones of tolerance may have trouble accepting the idea that certain meanings are the "right" meanings, the fact remains that interpretation often seems interested in producing narrowly defined learning outcomes over and beyond the more general meaning-making outcomes one might want to achieve. As we've seen repeatedly, the two kinds of outcomes aren't at all mutually exclusive, and the choice between them usually isn't about one or the other—it's about both. As Rennie and Johnston describe:

Narrow zone of tolerance: for any number of reasons, you consider personal themes that are very close to your intended theme to be better and more desirable.

> The educational leadership in a museum may create a *teaching* curriculum of learning opportunities intended to help the visitors ("newcomers") participate in the museum's agenda, but from the perspective of the visitors, who come with their own agenda, the *learning* curriculum is dominant and their involvement in it is their choice. Thus, visitors will each construct his or her own learning curriculum and each will have a unique, personal learning experience… Meaning is made from that experience. (2004: S6)

When interpretation intersects with the formal school curriculum, a narrow zone of tolerance is often called for. *Courtesy of California Academy of Sciences, USA.*

So a hallmark of the narrow zone of tolerance is that often there's a mission or curriculum of some sort in the background that dictates a comparatively narrow range of meanings considered to be most appropriate or acceptable. The zone, although narrow, doesn't necessarily negate the value of visitors making other meanings; it just sees some meanings as more important or essential.

Another example of the narrow zone of tolerance comes into play whenever it's necessary to influence how audiences behave in a particular setting. As I've argued elsewhere:

> We invoke a variety of euphemisms to justify our need to manipulate our audiences (e.g., "use of interpretation as a management tool," "managing visitor behaviour," etc.), but there is little doubt that we are squarely in the manipulation business. (Ham & Weiler, 2003: 1)

Much is made in the interpretation literature about influencing protected area visitors to behave in ways that are consistent with management objectives.[14] Going back as far as the 1960s–1980s, use of interpretation as a management tool became, to some, a claim for the legitimacy of interpretation, especially in public land management agencies that lacked a clear mandate for interpretation.[15]

Although much of interpretation's promise in influencing audience behavior is based on anecdotal accounts that "interpretation" has "done this" or can "accomplish that," at times there is truth to the claim. As we saw in Chapter 5, success usually results from a strategic approach based on behavioral psychology that links communication input to behavioral output—in other words, theoretically meaningful approaches based on established (not assumed or generalized) relationships between persuasive communication and audience behavior.[16] A premise of interpretation's role in management is that visitors can be persuaded via well-crafted messages to behave in certain ways, at least in the short term. As we saw in Chapter 5, research on persuasive communication shows that these messages need to influence some of the beliefs that visitors have about the behavior we want to bring about.[17] While interpretation might provoke them to think about a lot of different things, for persuasion to occur at least some of their thoughts must be consistent with and supportive of the behavior-related themes we intended to communicate to them.[18] This means that our zone of tolerance is tighter than it would be if we had some other objective in mind.

> Although you might provoke a lot of different thoughts, for persuasion to occur at least some of them must be consistent with and supportive of the behavior-related themes you intended to communicate.

A final example of narrow zone interpretation sometimes comes into play when highly sensitive or controversial subjects are interpreted. Especially touchy is interpreting events that have involved a lot of human suffering, and about which individuals and different organizations harbor extreme opinions as to which themes are "right" or "correct" for audiences to take away.

As we've seen, sometimes interpreters approach this sort of problem with a wider zone of tolerance, where the intent is not to dictate any particular message but rather to stimulate people to draw their own conclusions.

Many times, however, the social pain or guilt of certain events is still so recent that balanced interpretation of opposing views is seen as risky or unwise, at least in public settings. Decades, generations, or even centuries often must pass before a given society is ready to accept or embrace disagreement.[19] In these situations factions evolve, each defending its own narrow zone of tolerance. When the zones of tolerance meet head on, censorship, job terminations, loss of political office, lawsuits, strong public outcry, and even bloodshed can result. For example, controversy abounds today over which themes people should accept with respect to such topics as Auschwitz, September 11, the atomic bomb, slavery, South African Apartheid, Princess Diana's death, the US Civil War, the Crusades, Australia's Stolen Generation, Adolph Hitler, and the war in Iraq.[20] Because historians, religious leaders, heads of state, and common citizens hold extreme views about the morals of such stories, their zones of tolerance are, by definition, very narrow.[21]

Ethics in the Narrow Zone of Tolerance

Adopting any zone of tolerance requires an ethical stance. Even when the zone is completely unrestricted, an ethic of democracy and a belief in the sovereignty of the individual are present. As we've seen, a lot of interpretation is based on a zone that is very wide and forgiving but nonetheless is bounded somewhere or another by an obvious or implicit value orientation (i.e., "any meanings the audience makes are OK as long as they result in 'caring for the resource' or 'valuing their heritage,' etc."). If audiences concluded the *opposite*, for example, most of us would change our programs in a hurry. So an interpreter's sheer choice of themes, and how she or he chooses to develop them, are themselves the reflection of an ethic.

> Interpreters' sheer choice of themes—and how they choose to develop them—are themselves the reflection of an ethic.

As the zone of tolerance narrows, a different type of ethic emerges. Interpreters everywhere have to realize that they're being a bit Machiavellian whenever they claim to know the "truth" or attempt to influence the attitudes or behavior of their audiences simply because they know it's the "right" thing to do.[22] We have to be confident that the best interests of the audience and/or the place or object we're interpreting are honestly served by attempting to persuade people to think, feel, or act in a particular way. This is truly a subjective call, and disagreement is almost inevitable.

Confronting your ethics may sometimes lead you to ask difficult questions—questions that force you to choose between personal values and those that your own organization embraces. Some interpreters find themselves in a terrible bind because they disagree philosophically with the values their employer or bosses represent, or with the mission of the organization they work for. However, because they're being paid or otherwise enabled by that body to represent that mission or point of view—whether it relates to how a particular resource should be managed or to a curriculum that dictates which facts and meanings are most important to advance—it's their ethical obligation to do so, and to do it as well as they can. As distasteful as the individual might find it, to the organization the interpreter is simply an arm or instrument for advocating that point of view. Any of us who have been on either side of this bind can empathize.

I've been a confidant to many interpreters over the years who've expressed deep unresolvable disagreement with the values they're expected to represent to the public. It's as though their own sovereignty as free individuals and their obligations as paid employees have collided head on. When asked what they can or should do about this conflict, my reply is empathetic, but clear: "If you can't honestly and passionately represent the values of your organization in the interpretive work you do, you should search for a different job as soon as possible. Both you and your organization will be better off for it." None of us wants to feel that we're somebody else's instrument for propaganda, especially when we think the message is ethically wrong.

But what if we ourselves are the propagandizers? As we saw in Chapter 2, it's easy for interpretation to slide into propaganda, particularly when a theme emanates from our own sense of right and wrong. "Interpreganda" as Larsen (2003) called it, falls by definition in the narrow zone because it advocates a single point of view about something. Driven by their deep convictions about what's best and right—especially when it comes to things natural and historic—interpreters sometimes are a little too zealous in telling their audiences what to think, and occasionally they even proselytize. This rarely results in anything good. In the worst case, interpreters are so blinded by their own beliefs that they underestimate how intelligent and discerning their audiences are. A result is that the theme the audience hears is not necessarily the one the interpreter intended:

> There's something wrong with you, and we'll all be better off when you think more like I do.

Even granting the rare instance when this might be true, I can see little benefit in saying it to an audience. In fact, according to studies on persuasive communication, a likely outcome is a "boomerang effect" in which the audience further entrenches itself in a point of view *opposite* to the one advocated by the interpreter.[23] Even when dealing with biased audiences, interpreters following the provocation endgame recognize that they'd be better off encouraging their audiences to make their own connections to things. These connections, as far flung as they might seem, are themselves the *only* source of whatever sense of stewardship those people are capable of feeling. This is tantamount to saying that a wider zone of tolerance is probably called for. Figure 8-3 presents two points of view—one from the interpreter's side and one from an audience perspective—about the kinds of sensitivities we need to be mindful of when the Machiavelli in us begins to emerge.

An interpreter's view:

I'm wary of propaganda disguising itself as interpretation. I readily admit that interpreters and agencies have a choice. They can cleverly or obviously use interpretive themes to try to persuade audiences to take action or come to specific viewpoints or beliefs. There are moments and circumstances where this is appropriate—such as communicating rules like "Don't feed the bears," or perhaps when a resource is immediately threatened. And certainly all interpretation attempts to persuade the audience that the resource is worth caring about and caring for. However, the risk of using a theme to persuade or influence an audience as to the validity of a particular idea, perspective, or ideology, is that our audiences usually know when they're being told how to think, and they don't like it. It simply is not the interpreter's role to tell anyone how they should think. We will achieve far more if we can succeed in getting them to think at all.

—David Larsen, US National Park Service (personal communication, 2005)

An audience view:

I believe in reading books because others dislike them or find them dangerous. I believe in choosing the hardest book imaginable. I believe in reading up on what others have to say about this difficult book, and then making up my own mind…I believe there is not now and never will be an authority who can tell me how to interpret, how to read, how to find the pearl of literary meaning in all cases…In just this way, I believe in the freedom to see literature, history, truth, unfolding ahead of me like a book whose spine has just now been cracked.

—Rick Moody, *The Joy and Enthusiasm of Reading* (2005)

Figure 8-3. *Ethical issues in the narrow zone of tolerance.*

Was Your Interpretation Successful?—Your Zone of Tolerance Tells You

You might recall that this was the question we considered in Chapter 3 ("The Endgame of Interpretation"). Although interpretation can certainly result in teaching and entertainment, its goal to provoke thinking emerged as its most fundamental endgame. This, as we saw in Chapter 5, is because the kinds of differences interpreters usually want to make (e.g., in audiences' experiences, attitudes, and behaviors) are going to be far more likely if people in their audiences are first provoked to think their own thoughts. Therefore, those same thoughts—whatever they might be—must somehow figure into the success or failure of an interpretive product.

> If your main purpose is to provoke thinking, it would be instructive to know what kinds of thoughts you're actually provoking.

Put another way, it simply makes sense that if your main purpose is to provoke thinking, it would be instructive to know what kinds of thoughts you're actually provoking. If you were eavesdropping on a group of people who had just viewed your exhibit, watched your performance, or participated in your guided tour, what kinds of thoughts would you be hoping to hear? Imagine an evaluator engaged them in a discussion and asked each person to write a response to the question, "So what did you get out of that? What are you thinking now?" How would you like them to respond? In listening to or reading their words, you would discover for yourself the boundaries of your own zone of tolerance.

A good way to evaluate a communication product is to ask such questions to real audience members and then listen carefully to their replies (a method usually called "**thought listing**"). If you do this, and then find yourself smiling more than not smiling as you listen,[24] it will be because what they're saying is largely within your zone of tolerance. But if the opposite happens, you'd be well served to reexamine your approach and ask yourself what you might do or say differently next time. It's as simple as that. In this way, applying your zone of tolerance tells you something not only about how much success you're having, but equally important, what you might do to improve.[25] I've listed some simple instructions for conducting a thought-listing procedure in Figure 8-4. In addition, you'll find a detailed example of how a one might work in Chapter 10 (and Appendix 3).

Thought Listing—
A Quick Way to Know How Well You're Doing as a Thought Provoker

The thought listing method is best done in a simple interview in which you ask people to tell you (orally or in writing) what they're thinking with respect to the topic or content of an interpretive product they've just heard or seen. Although analysis of people's thoughts can be complicated depending on your purpose, if your reason for eliciting their thoughts is simply to determine whether those thoughts make you "smile," the analysis can be pretty straightforward.

Since you can count and classify people's thoughts, the method I'm suggesting here could tell you two things: (1) the *number* of thoughts people are thinking (i.e., amount of provocation) and (2) what they're thinking *about* (i.e., the kinds of thoughts the people are having and whether they fall into your zone of tolerance).

Of course, to do this sort of assessment would require you to have some rule for counting thoughts—that is, what constitutes a thought, and when does one thought end and a new one start? In formal interpretive research, this can be quite complicated.[26] But in an informal evaluation aimed mainly at getting immediate feedback on program performance, you could simply let your reactions to what you're hearing (or reading) define a thought.

For example, when something someone says makes you smile, simply write (in a complete sentence) what you think the person is saying and count it as *within* your zone of tolerance.

Similarly, when something *doesn't* make you smile, do the same and count it as *outside* your zone of tolerance.

Then, in each case, just continue reading or listening until something else makes you react with a smile or nonsmile.

You'll probably find that some audience members can talk for quite a while about their thoughts. In these cases, you'll have whole paragraphs containing many thoughts that aren't organized neatly in individual sentences. In formal research, this complicates counting. But if you use the more "organic" method suggested here (i.e., counting the number of times you smile and don't smile), you'll gain a pretty good sense not only of the number of thoughts your interpretation provoked but also whether they're within your zone of tolerance. Although a research journal probably wouldn't publish it, such an evaluation might well lead to important improvements in your interpretation.

Figure 8-4. *Instructions for conducting a simple thought-listing procedure.*

Summary and a Look Ahead

We've seen in this chapter that the practical implications of the zone of tolerance concept extend not only to interpretive design and development, but also to evaluation and judgments about whether an interpretive product is succeeding or failing. Depending on your purposes at the time, the width of your zone of tolerance might be unrestricted; in other cases, it might be very wide but with subtle limits on the kinds of thoughts you're happy to be provoking; and in some cases, it might be more narrowly defined (and possibly more ethically sensitive).

Whichever of the three zones of tolerance applies in a given situation, you'll always be able to know whether you're achieving interpretation's most basic form of success—provoking thought. You (or a helper) simply need a forum in which to hear from people what they're thinking as a result of your interpretation. As you listen to (or read from a transcript) each thought, you'll instinctively apply your zone of tolerance. If a given thought makes you smile, well done; chalk it up as falling within your zone of tolerance. If the thought doesn't make you smile, count it as outside your zone of tolerance.

In the next two chapters, we'll consider the important task of "developing" a theme for two main kinds of interpretive products—sequential and nonsequential. Chapter 9 looks at theme development strategies for situations in which the *interpreter* controls the sequence of information an audience receives. In Chapter 10, we consider how the strategy might change when it's the *audience* (and not the interpreter) who determines the sequence of things. As you'd expect, our focus in both cases will be on how to flesh out and present a strong theme so that the thoughts it provokes find their way to an interpreter's zone of tolerance.

Glossary terms: personal theme, thought listing, zone of tolerance

Additional Thoughts for Chapter 8

1   Celebrated psychologist George Meade (1934) was the first to characterize "thinking" as nothing more than a conversation you have with yourself inside your own head.

2   Recall from Chapter 6 that one well-developed theme can give rise to many personal themes inside a person's head.

3   See, for example, Anderson and Pitchert (1978); Crocker (1984); Fiske and Taylor (1991); Kardash, Royer and Greene (1988); Lampinen, Copeland, and Neuschatz (2001); Smith-Jackson and Hall (2002); Tuckey and Brewer (2003); and Werner, Rhodes, and Partain (1998).

4 In his discussion of cecity (or "blindness"), Doug Capra (2006) reminds interpreters that they, too, are affected by their *own* schemas.

5 Don't think that allowing such wide latitude somehow negates the value of an interpreter having a theme at all. On the contrary, the interpreter would still need a theme to guide her or his choice of content and emphasis and to give the audience a focal point for provocation. But themes in this zone might be very different from themes in the wide and narrow zones because they don't themselves express an attitude or value-laden conclusion about the topic. For example, instead of having a theme such as, "We're all lucky that X lived when he did; he was the perfect man for the critical role he played at that time in our history," an interpreter in the unrestricted zone might have a theme such as "X's life made an indelible mark on all of us; whether you revere him or loathe him for what he did, we have to recognize the magnitude of his impact for better or worse." You can probably see in each case that the choice of theme itself reflects the width of the zone of tolerance.

6 See Ballantyne and Uzzell (1999); Uzzell and Ballantyne (1998).

7 See, for example, Bridal (2004); Hughes (1998); and Strauss (1996).

8 The "icon" idea was first introduced by Goldman, Chen, and Larsen (2001). See also Larsen (2003).

9 This premise is implicit in Pine and Gilmore's (1999) *The Experience Economy* and is found extensively in the interpretation literature. See, for example, Carter (1997); Ham (2002a); Ham, Housego, and Weiler (2005); Larsen (2003); Moscardo (1999b); Moscardo, Ballantyne, and Hughes (2007); Tourism Tasmania (2003); Ward and Wilkinson (2006), and Woods and Moscardo (2003).

10 This philosophy underpins not only interpretation in public places such as national parks and historic sites, but it can be found in the way certain forward-thinking travel companies conduct their business. For example, New York-based Lindblad Expeditions espouses part of its corporate mission this way: "Ultimately, it will be the passion and insistence of the traveler that will save the special places on earth." See http://www.expeditions.com.

11 In Australia, Tourism Tasmania (2003) has adopted this thinking as a standard operating procedure. See http://www.tourismtasmania.com.au/__data/assets/pdf_file/0017/35108/experience_strategy.pdf.

12 See, for example, Falk and Storksdieck (2005) and Savage and James (2001).

13 See, for example, Hughes and Morrison-Saunders (2002); Knapp and Barrie (1998); Morgan, Absher, Loudon, and Sutherland (1997).

14 See Absher and Bright (2004), Gramann (2000), Knudson, Cable, and Beck (1995), and Roggenbuck (1992) for detailed discussions.

15 See, for example, Brown and Hunt (1969); Cable, et al. (1986); Griest (1981); Hooper and Weiss (1991); Marler (1972); Oliver, Roggenbuck, and Watson (1985); Sharpe and Gensler (1978); and Roggenbuck and Ham (1986).

16 See Manfredo (1992) for a survey of some of these approaches.

17 The idea that beliefs about a behavior figure prominently in people's decision to perform or not perform the behavior is well established and widely applied both in psychology and in the interpretation field. See, for example, Absher and Bright (2004); Ajzen (1991); Ajzen and Driver (1992); Ajzen and Fishbein (1980, 2005); Ballantyne and Packer (2005); Cable, Knudson, and Theobald (1986); Curtis, et al. (2006); Fishbein and Ajzen (1975); Fishbein and Manfredo (1992); Hall and Roggenbuck (2002); Ham and Krumpe (1996); Lackey and Ham (2003); Manning (2003); Roggenbuck (1992); Vander Stoep and Gramann (1987); and Ward and Roggenbuck (2003).

18 Themes express beliefs. See Ham and Krumpe (1996).

19 Examples of these sensitivities abound. Ballantyne and Uzzell (1999), Batten (2005), and Frost (2005) offer thoughtful discussions on the challenges of interpreting Aboriginal and Chinese history in Australia and New Zealand. Blizzard and Ellis (2006) discuss the still-recent pain of slavery in the United States and the importance of interpreting it accurately. Blackburn (2004) analyzes the potential for meanings to clash, using as an example heated controversy over how to interpret the first atomic bomb. Simon (2003) and Reidy and Riley (2002) attempt answers to questions about *who* should interpret indigenous cultures and sacred places, and how they should be interpreted.

20 Examples include Alvord (2000), "Auschwitz Disco Draws Outrage"; Harwit (1996), *An Exhibit Denied: Lobbying the History of the Enola Gay*; Curry (2002), "The Better Angels: Why We Are Still Fighting over Who Was Right and Who Was Wrong in the Civil War"; and Roxborough (2004), "*Downfall* Breaks Taboo, Portrays Hitler's Human Side."

21 Christina Goulding (2000, 2001) has written widely about the ethics of manipulating, distorting, and selling heritage in the tourism industry. Goulding and Domic (2008) analyzed the serious ethical challenges of presenting just one heritage in a multiethnic society such as Croatia.

22 Niccoló Machiavelli, you might recall, was the Italian philosopher who is often (but inaccurately) credited as advocating the belief that you should do whatever it takes, as long as you know you're *right* (the end justifies the means). In common usage today, a "Machiavellian" person is someone who would knowingly manipulate others to achieve something of personal importance.

23 See, for example, Griffin (2000); Hovland, Janis, and Kelley (1953); Petty, Cacioppo, and Goldman (1981).

24 Notice that I say "not-smiling" as opposed to "cringing" or "frowning." I don't want to imply that thoughts outside your zone of tolerance are necessarily offensive or objectionable. It's just that you

don't feel they're consistent with the kinds of thoughts you were hoping to provoke. Sometimes such thoughts might cause you to frown or cringe, but other times you might simply be ambivalent or roll your eyes and wonder "how in the world did she take that idea from my talk?" Whatever your reaction to a given thought, if it's not a smile, the thought falls outside your zone of tolerance. Again, the key to your assessment of each thought is simply whether you're happy with it (or not). A fruitful project for future research would be developing a user-friendly procedure for interpreters who want to reliably classify and categorize thoughts expressed by their audiences.

25 I'm suggesting here that a fundamental measure of "success" or "effectiveness" of an interpretive product is the proportion of thoughts it provokes within your (and/or your employer's) zone of tolerance. What the minimum proportion should be is a subjective decision that extends all the way to your philosophy of interpretation and your purpose for doing it at all. However, the basic decision rule would be something like: "The higher the proportion of thoughts that fall into your zone of tolerance, the better (more 'successful,' more 'effective') the interpretation is." Depending on a researcher's purpose, a formal systematic evaluation might combine this fundamental measure with others (for example, measures of enjoyment, attention paying, or knowledge gain) in order to explore a bigger picture of "success." But to the everyday practicing interpreter, applying the simple thought-listing method described here (i.e., smiling versus not smiling) will likely be both instructive and insightful as decisions are made about improving real-world interpretive products.

26 If a researcher wants to do more sophisticated analyses of the thoughts, she or he can use specially-designed computer software such as NVivo for this purpose. See, for example, Bazeley (2007); Bucy (2005); and Rand (2010).

CHAPTER 9
Sequential Theme Development

When you control the order of things, you have a lot of creative options for developing your theme.

In communication, when we say "**develop**" a theme, we mean to flesh it out, give it substance, and put meat on its bones. In other words, in developing a theme, interpreters now bring to the *forefront* carefully selected facts, points of interest, universal concepts, tangible-intangible connections, anecdotes, analogies, examples, metaphors, and other forms of "color" to make the theme resonate for the audience.[1]

It's important to remember that the sole purpose of developing a theme is to provoke the audience to think thoughts that will hover somewhere around the theme you developed. That's why we've stressed the importance of strong themes (*T*) over weak ones (*t*), and it's why an interpreter's presentation of the theme must be easy to follow (*O*), relevant to the audience (*R*), and enjoyable for them to process (*E*). Of course, this is just another way of saying that TORE is a model for interpretation with high provocation likelihood.

In Chapter 8, we saw that the more interpretation provokes thoughts that fall into your zone of tolerance, the more successful and effective your interpretation is. In some cases, these might be thoughts you were hoping and trying to provoke. And in other cases, they might be surprises—thoughts you never expected or anticipated. But if the surprises are pleasant (that is, if you're happy with the unexpected thoughts), they, too, fall within your zone of tolerance. This chapter considers some practical ways to develop a theme so that more thoughts find their way to your zone of tolerance.

An example of a sequential interpretive product, Grand Teton National Park, USA. *Courtesy of Becky Wiles, US National Park Service.*

Sequential Theme Development

Thematic interpreters face two main kinds of communication problems, each of which requires a different approach to theme development. I call them sequential and nonsequential. **Sequential communication** occurs whenever you (the interpreter) control the order in which your audience receives information. Almost any kind of face-to-face interpretive encounter is sequential because audiences usually don't hear or see anything until you decide it's time to say or show it. That is, *you* control the sequence of things.[2] In **nonsequential communication** (which includes most forms of nonpersonal interpretation such as exhibits, websites, and signs), people in the audience determine the sequence of information they pay attention to.[3] Although thought-provoking themes can be developed in both categories, having sequential control gives you several creative options that aren't available in nonsequential communication. These will be our focus in this chapter.

The Structure of Sequential Communication

In sequential communication, you have the great advantage of using the three-part strategy of an introduction, body, and conclusion.[4] I've often said that "good talks and good tours have good parts." By that I mean each part plays a different role in developing the theme, and when all the parts do their jobs well, the theme will be better developed. In Figure 9-1, I've summarized the main purposes of the introduction, body, and conclusion in theme development.

The Introduction

Although all three parts of a sequential presentation are equally important, the introduction is usually the most complicated of the three. That's simply because it has a bigger job. Besides the very necessary task of creating interest and attracting the attention of a noncaptive audience, your introduction needs to do three other things. First is to orient your audience (at least generally, if not specifically) to the theme.[5] In other words, you want your audience to start thinking in theme-related ways from the very beginning.

What You're Trying to Do	
Introduction	Attract interest and create curiosity in what follows. Orient your audience both to your theme and organization. Set the stage for your conclusion. That is, prepare your audience in advance for a thought-provoking ending.
Body	Flesh out your theme. Add the facts, figures, stories, personal anecdotes, analogies, examples, and so forth that help to bring out the essential aspects of your theme. That is, you need to substantiate (in an ORE way) the point your theme makes.
Conclusion	Reinforce your theme and provoke theme-related thoughts. You might summarize (recapitulate) the key points you made in the body, you might suggest what the theme means in the bigger scheme of things (e.g., where to from here, or what does this mean for all of us when we return to our homes?), or you might use the conclusion to plant a seed for later reinforcement.

Figure 9-1. *The structure of a sequential thematic presentation.*

You also want to give your audience some sense of how your presentation will be organized so they can follow along without a lot of effort. For instance, you could offer a general phrasing of your theme in a way that suggests the organization:

> Among the many talents polar bears possess, they've honed two particular skills to a high level of perfection—these are loving and killing.

Or you could reveal your organization in a more detailed way:

> On our walk today, we'll start off at A, and then we'll walk up to look at B where we'll have a chance to witness for ourselves the amazing…

Regardless of how you do it, the important thing is that your introduction offers a sort of mental road map of where your presentation is going. Doing so greatly facilitates attention paying because the audience knows in advance more or less how things are going to unfold. This makes following your train of thought easier (recall our discussion of *O* in Chapter 2).

Finally, one of the most important things an introduction can accomplish in a thematic presentation is setting the stage for a thought-provoking conclusion. That is, even while presenting the beginning you have the ending firmly in mind. As we'll see, this usually involves saying, doing, or showing something in the introduction that you return to in some way in the conclusion. For example, you might issue some key phrase or memorable sentence in your introduction and repeat it with emphasis in the conclusion, you might begin a story in the introduction and then finish it in the conclusion, or you could show a particularly memorable image in the introduction and show it again in the conclusion (so-called flashback slides). And if your theme statement is strong (i.e., if it has high provocation likelihood), stating it in your introduction and again in the conclusion is another way for the two parts of your presentation to work in tandem.[6] We'll see shortly how this might work.

The Body

The body of a sequential presentation has just one, albeit important, purpose. That's to flesh out (some might say "hammer home") the theme. Here's where most of the "color" is revealed: the facts, universal concepts, examples, analogies, metaphors, anecdotes, and so forth that you've carefully selected because they substantiate and give life to your theme.[7] Because the body is usually the biggest part of a sequential presentation, it has a lot of influence on whether you achieve your goal of provoking thought.

It's often in developing the body of a presentation that your skill as a communicator will face its biggest test. That's because you need to present the *tangible* facts behind your theme, but you must do it in ways that ignite curiosity and provoke thinking in your audience. Many authors[8] have offered good advice on how to approach this two-part task—most of whom follow the lead of David Larsen (2003), who pioneered the method of *linking tangible things to intangible meanings*. Although the body of a presentation certainly isn't the only place for making tangible-intangible connections,[9] doing so in the body is almost inevitable in a good interpretive talk or guided tour.

Tangible-Intangible Connections

According to Larsen, all things embody at least two kinds of meanings—tangible and intangible. **Tangible meanings** come to us through our physical senses (i.e., things we can see, hear, touch, smell, and taste). For example, using your eyes, you can verify the shape and size of a mountain; using your ears, you can verify that a certain piece of music is jazz or classical; using your fingers, you can verify if the texture of a rock is rough or smooth; and using your taste buds, you can verify whether you're eating fish or an apple. The tangible meanings interpreters impart usually have to do with the scientific, cultural, or historic significance of something they're interpreting (i.e., the reason the thing is special and worthy of attention).[10] You can consider these sorts of meanings to be objective meanings in that audiences can use their senses to objectively assess the truth of what you're saying (e.g., this rock is basalt; Picasso painted that canvas; a great battle happened here; that's a maple tree, not a eucalypt).

When you enter the world of **intangible meanings**, however, everything changes. First, there's nothing objective about intangible meanings. They're personal, they're fuzzy, and they rely more on metaphor and subjective association than logic. They refer to things that can't be detected with any known sensory receptor. That is, you cannot objectively assess their validity—they're imagined and created subjectively in the human mind. This is precisely what makes them so powerful in interpretation.

Consider three visitors to a historic battlefield. One of them feels remorse, the second feels pride, and the third feels anger. Emotions (remorse, pride, anger) are *intangibles*. And yet to each of the people, they constitute the meaning they will forever associate with that place. Similarly, a visitor to a forest might associate the verdant aroma with intangibles such as clean, serene, and pure, whereas another might liken

> Intangible meanings are personal, they're fuzzy, and they rely on metaphor and subjective associations.

Intangible meanings are about *symbolism*—what something *represents* to an audience.

it to the bouquet of fine red wine, and yet another is moved by the beauty of the place and feels a sudden urgency to protect it—all intangibles.

As you can see from these examples, intangible meanings are about *symbolism*—what something being interpreted *represents* to an audience. For this reason, they often readily connect with emotions along with other universal concepts—such as those I listed in Figure 2-4 (e.g., evil, good, pain, empathy, love, hate, fear, joy, and so on).[11] When you make a connection between a tangible thing and an intangible meaning, you're suggesting to the audience what the tangible thing can represent, what it can symbolize—what it can mean not only to science or history, but also to the human spirit and to humanity itself.[12] For this reason, when you successfully make a tangible-intangible connection, provocation usually follows.

In Larsen's words:

> Resources are made up of tangible objects, places, people, and events as well as the intangible meanings to which each is linked. To neglect one is to squander the power of both.
>
> All successful interpretation can be described as linking a tangible resource to its intangible meanings. Effective interpretation is about connecting one to the other—tangibles and intangibles exist together. (2003: 92)

Add Brochu and Merriman:

> Interpretation weaves these threads of the tangible into the threads of the intangible. The fabric that results is a story that your audience can touch and feel. It becomes real because life is not just a litany of facts. It is a blend of facts, ideas, meanings and universal feelings—tangibles and intangibles. (2008: 48)

Take, for example, the Alaskan interpreter who developed this theme in the body of her talk on climate change:

> If the world is actually warming, sooner or later people everywhere will have to change the way they're living—probably dramatically. But it doesn't have to be that way.

The interpreter used the technique of a contrived situation (as discussed in Figure 2-8). The scenario she created looked 100 years into the future and revolved around a conversation one warm winter day in an Eskimo family's household (the Chilkoots, she named them).[13] In developing the Chilkoot family's dialogue, the interpreter presented a scientific explanation for the now-warm climate (a tangible) along with their reactions to the new challenges they faced in finding game, warding off insects, and the father's recent diagnosis with skin cancer. What these hardships meant to that family—their fears, anger, and frustrations—became the intangibles. In a similar manner, she concluded her talk by linking the intangibles of hope, victory, and joy to the tangible impacts world governments could have if they chose to halt greenhouse contamination of the atmosphere.

Likewise, I've seen the Liberty Bell in the United States interpreted as a symbol of defiance, the Berlin Wall as a physical manifestation of tyranny, and a flock of birds in flight as a metaphor for happiness. Tangible-intangible connections such as these will not only add interest to a sequential presentation, they're likely to achieve your ultimate purpose of provoking thought.

The Conclusion

The conclusion of a sequential presentation also has just one main purpose—reinforcing the theme. Some consider it the "crown jewel" of a talk or guided tour in the sense that it's the final deciding touch that makes everything preceding it resonate. As we'll see shortly, interpreters have a lot to consider in designing a conclusion.

Although a conclusion can take many forms, what it's trying to accomplish is always the same—leaving the audience thinking theme-related thoughts. You usually know when you've delivered an effective conclusion because audiences

For Americans, universal concepts such as defiance and freedom are embodied in the iconic Liberty Bell. Independence National Historical Park, USA. *Photo by R. Miller, Courtesy of US National Park Service.*

will show their appreciation with spontaneous applause, by asking many questions, and by staying afterward to talk more. And if you work in a tipping culture, you might well be rewarded monetarily for a thought-provoking conclusion.

Earlier we noted that it's a good idea to design an introduction to prepare the audience for a more powerful conclusion. Several methods for doing this were discussed, including the reiteration of key phrases in both parts of the presentation, the use of "flashback" slides, leaving a half-finished story or anecdote for the conclusion, and so forth. We saw also that a *strong* theme stated twice—once in the introduction and again in the conclusion—is a way for the conclusion to capitalize on the content of the introduction.

The reason audiences seem to respond well to this kind of design—that is, talks and guided tours that have interrelated introductions and conclusions—has to do with an idea some psychologists[14] call **prägnanz**. Prägnanz is a German word that means roughly "wholeness," "completeness," or "unity." Psychologists believe that people like completeness in their world because it gives them order and predictability. In a sequential presentation, completeness occurs when the audience senses that everything has come full circle—or when there's **closure,** as educational psychologists call it. When you introduce a memorable idea or scenario early in a presentation, and then come back to it again at the end, it seems to bring everything you've been talking about back to the beginning; it gives the talk a quality of being complete and whole, rather than only partly finished; and it reassures the audience that it now has the whole story and that there

> When you introduce a memorable idea early in a presentation and then return to it at the end, it seems to bring everything back to the beginning.

are no loose ends. Audiences who've just listened to a good talk or concluded a good guided tour usually feel this sense of closure or prägnanz, just as they feel it at the end of a good book, movie, or play.

In the big picture of thematic communication strategy, the main reason you need to do a good job with your introduction and body is that they give your conclusion its best chance to finish the job they simply *started*. I've seen many talks and have been on numerous guided tours in which the interpreter masterfully introduced the theme, artfully developed it in the body—all the while engaging the audience and priming it for something more—and then for some reason just seemed to stop, ending abruptly and awkwardly, without even attempting any sort of conclusion that pulled things together. This is frustrating for an audience. It's as though the interpreter has simply run out of steam or just doesn't know what to make of everything she or he said in leading up to that moment. Whatever the reason, the audience feels nothing short of cheated. They sensed they were on the cusp of a thought-provoking conclusion, but it never came.

A conclusion doesn't have to be long or detailed. In fact, some might require only several seconds to a couple of minutes. But they *do need to be delivered* in order to complete the task of provoking thought. Recall from Chapter 2 our discussion of themeless (ORE) interpretation, which we equated with infotainment. When a sequential presentation ends without the theme reinforcement that a conclusion provides, the result is likewise infotainment, and a golden opportunity to reinforce the important idea of the whole is squandered.

Although the purpose of any conclusion is to reinforce the theme, there are a lot of ways to do it. The following discussion highlights three of the most successful forms: recapitulating, extrapolating, and planting a suggestion for later reinforcement.

Recapitulation

In a **recapitulation**, you begin your conclusion by reminding your audience of the key points you developed in the body—that is, you summarize the main things you now want your audience to consider simultaneously. In doing so, you hope they'll be provoked to think further about the collective meaning of your whole presentation. For example, after a guided snorkeling tour on Australia's Great Barrier Reef, an interpreter might remind her audience of the different ways the animals they observed have evolved to protect themselves from danger:[15]

> We saw fish that protect themselves through camouflage or by traveling in large numbers, we saw others that have conspicuous false eyespots near their tails to confuse would-be predators, and we saw animals with spines and others with hard shells.

On the heels of this recapitulation, the interpreter might then connect everything to her theme:

> So it's easy to see that coral reef wildlife have evolved all kinds of fascinating and effective ways to keep themselves alive.

Extrapolation

A conclusion in the form of an **extrapolation** attempts to provoke thinking beyond the theme itself. That is, it asks the question, "What might this mean in the bigger scheme of things?" Or it might ask, "Where to from here?" For example, our Great Barrier Reef interpreter might extrapolate her theme about coral reef wildlife by asking her audience to:

> look around your own gardens when you return home. You'll almost certainly find that the same battle for survival is going on right in front of you every day. Birds, mammals, insects, spiders, and all kinds of things are out there making a living and trying to protect themselves from other animals (including humans) in all kinds of ingenious ways. When we take the time to notice that nature occurs everywhere—not just in famous places like the Great Barrier Reef—we're reminded that even the most ordinary places are both fascinating and important in our world.

Planting a Suggestion

Planting a **suggestion** is another form a conclusion can take.[16] Your purpose with this sort of conclusion is to trigger later reinforcement of your theme by linking it to something people in your audience are likely to encounter or experience within a day or two following your presentation. That is, you plant a seed for reinforcement by suggesting to them that the next time they see, hear, or do a certain thing (i.e., something you know is very probable within twenty-four to forty-eight hours or so),[17] they should—at that moment—recall some aspect of your theme. If you do it well, the suggestion method can lead to strong reinforcement of your theme at a time when audience members are back in their everyday environment. Of course, reconnecting with your theme in such a familiar setting opens the door for other forms of reinforcement that otherwise might not have been feasible.

Two things are required for the suggestion method to work well. First, you need to use common sense in deciding on the type of suggestion to issue; it needs to involve something you can realistically relate to your theme. For example, if you're giving a talk about the famous battle at Culloden, Scotland, in 1746 and you want your audience to remember the tragedy of fathers, sons, brothers, and cousins fighting on opposite sides, you might plant a fairly visceral suggestion:

> Your purpose in planting a suggestion is to trigger later reinforcement of your theme by linking it to something your audience is likely to experience in the near future.

The next time you sit down for dinner with your family, look across the table and imagine yourself in mortal battle with that person. Then look at everyone else around the table and imagine them watching.

Similarly, if your talk stresses the importance of reducing electricity use, you might connect your theme to the "next time you open your refrigerator door." Or if you're concluding a guided tour of a winery, your suggestion could have something to do with grapes. Bear in mind, however, that the effectiveness of a suggestion will depend not simply on how well it matches your topic but even more so on the extent to which it connects in a memorable way to your *theme*.

The second requirement for a suggestion to work well is that you *must* have your audience ready and primed for it. This means they must already be provoked to thought before you issue the suggestion. If they aren't already engaged and focused on theme-related thoughts, your suggestion will probably sound trite, and they'll be unlikely to remember it later when they're supposed to.

However, if you've succeeded in provoking focused thought around your theme, and if your suggestion is meaningfully associated with your theme, the results can be impressive. One of the most skillful uses of the suggestion method I've seen was in the conclusion of a talk about Abraham Lincoln at Ford's Theatre in Washington, DC (Figure 9-2).

The Lincoln Memorial, National Capital Parks, USA. *Photo by Paul Caputo.*

Sequential Communication Techniques

Because you control the order of things in sequential theme development, you can take advantage of a number of communication methods that aren't available when you're not in control. For example, we've already seen the important role that introductions, bodies, and conclusions play. You can use them with great purpose simply because *you* decide to order things that way—that is, you (not the audience) decide where to begin the presentation, what comes next (and then next and next), and ultimately where and how to end the presentation. Obviously, when the audience controls the order of information, you can't think in terms of introductions, bodies, and conclusions, because where to begin and when to end is *their* choice.[18]

Another sequential method we've discussed is to take advantage of the prägnanz principle. This principle works when you design the beginning of a presentation to work in tandem with the ending. Clearly, if you don't decide where things begin and end, purposely creating a sense of prägnanz (closure) isn't possible.

In addition to these methods, you can capitalize on three other techniques in developing the theme of a sequential presentation. The first two—transitions and foreshadowing—can be used in any form of sequential presentation. A third, what I call "assigning" a mental task, lends itself mainly to thematic guided tours.

Transitions—to Make Everything Easy

Because ending one main idea and beginning the next often involves a conspicuous change of topic, you might want to include **transitions** between them. Transitions don't need to be complicated. In fact, the best ones are short and simple. Their purpose is merely to indicate to the audience when you're going to quit talking about one main point and begin talking about the next one.

The simplest, most straightforward transition says to an audience:

> Okay, we're done talking about "A" and we're now going to talk about "B."

But depending on the context of things, you might need a slightly more elaborate transition. For example:

> So obviously, Darwin was thinking *way* outside the box of his time. But he wasn't the only one. Enter Alfred Wallace—someone you've probably never heard of.

This transition signifies to the audience that the speaker has finished (at least for the moment) talking about Charles Darwin. However, it also says that not only will she or he now begin talking about Alfred Wallace, but that the focus will be on how he, too, was thinking outside the box.[19] In this way, the audience is well "calibrated" for the next part of the presentation.

The Penny Suggestion

A talk given by Joe Gary, a US National Park Service interpreter at Ford's Theatre (in Washington, DC), artfully demonstrated how the conclusion of a sequential presentation can use a suggestion to trigger later reinforcement of a theme. Ford's Theatre is the playhouse in which the sixteenth president of the United States, Abraham Lincoln, was assassinated on April 14, 1865. Lincoln was president during the US Civil War, which was a painfully bloody four-year clash between the North and South over the issue of slavery. When the North eventually won, many Northerners wanted to punish the South for its atrocities. Lincoln, however, insisted on forgiveness and amnesty as a way to heal the nation's wounds. Although his death came before he could personally direct the South's reconstruction, the power of Lincoln's philosophy prevailed, and today he's credited both for abolishing slavery in the United States and having saved the Union.

The theme of Joe's talk was that:

> Abraham Lincoln was the perfect president for his time because he was a president for all Americans. Had anyone else been president, the United States might be a very different country today.

As Joe developed his theme, he brought out three key points about Lincoln: (1) It didn't matter if you were from the North or the South, he was your president; (2) it didn't matter if you were black or white, he was your president; and (3) it didn't matter if you were rich or poor, he was your president.

As he concluded his twenty-minute talk, Joe returned to his theme:

> So you can see, ladies and gentlemen, that regardless of what else you might know or think about Abraham Lincoln, one fact of history is clear: he was a president for *all* Americans, and if anyone else had been president then, the United States might be a very different country today.

Then he paused and added:

> But you don't need *me* to tell you that. You already know it. In fact, you have the proof in your pocket. All you've got to do is pull out a penny and look at it. There you'll have the story of Abraham Lincoln. On one side is an image of the man, and on the other is the monument in Washington, DC, that bears his name. A penny is a coin that's available to all people. It doesn't matter if you're from the North or the South; you can have a penny. And it doesn't matter if you're black or white or red or yellow or purple; you can have a penny; and you know, even the poorest person on earth can own a penny. So there you have it. I hope you enjoy the rest of your day in Washington.

You no doubt can appreciate how many of the people who listened to Joe's talk were thereafter reminded of his theme every time they looked at a one-cent coin. In the United States, it's still called the "Lincoln Penny."

Figure 9-2. *How a suggestion can trigger later reinforcement of a theme.*

> The purpose of a transition is to indicate when you're going to quit talking about one idea and begin talking about the next.

It's important to think carefully about your transitions—both how to phrase them and where to use them. They're simple statements, but they serve a *big* purpose: reducing the effort your audience must invest to follow your thinking.

Building transitions into a presentation makes your job easier, too. In fact, a lot of interpreters memorize their transitions because doing so helps them remember the rest of their commentary. In other words, it's much easier to remember the "color" underneath each major idea than it is to remember the entire body as one big narrative. It's as though you're telling a series of small stories held together with transitions, rather than one big story. Less experienced interpreters sometimes forget to plan their transitions, and their talks suffer as a result. If you sometimes have trouble remembering what you want to say, try using preplanned transitions between your main points. Chances are, you'll find this makes remembering much easier.

Foreshadowing—to Stimulate Curiosity

Foreshadowing involves hinting to an audience about what comes next (or later) in a presentation, and doing so in a way that creates curiosity or intrigue about what it might be.[20] That is, you give an *incomplete* description of what lies ahead, leaving out of your description some key detail of interest. In this way, foreshadowing creates a degree of uncertainty and a need to resolve it. You can think of it as sequential "teasing."

One of the great advantages of sequential communication is that *you* always know what comes next (or later) in your presentation, and your audience doesn't. *You* know, for example, what the next part of your talk is about, and the audience must wait to hear from you what it is. Similarly, *you* know what your tour group will see in the next room of the historic building you're guiding them through—they don't yet have a clue. And *you* know what lies ahead at the next stop on your guided nature walk, or what vista will suddenly appear when the group rounds the next bend on the trail. In

> Foreshadowing creates uncertainty and a need to resolve it. You can think of it as sequential "teasing."

Type of Foreshadowing	Example
Pure intrigue	"You can see that the Johnsons were actively religious. But that didn't stop them from having a little 'devilish' fun every now and then. You'll see what I mean when we go upstairs."
Exception to the norm	"It's obvious that an advantage birds have in an El Niño year is being able to fly away to better climes. But that's not always the way it works. Tomorrow when we visit Fernandina Island, you're going to see a vivid example of what happens when they *can't* fly away."
Comparative	"If you think *this* is a beautiful flower, don't put your camera away yet. I'm saving the best for our last stop—which is about twenty minutes from now."
Resolving a mystery / answering a question	"Owls can't easily digest bones and feathers any more than a human could. So how do they deal with this problem after a night of successful hunting? You'll see for yourself at our next stop—and it's probably *not* what you think."

Figure 9-3. *Four common types of foreshadowing.*

foreshadowing, you capitalize on this advantage by giving your group *just enough* information about some future part of the presentation that they'll want to know the rest.

Foreshadowing can take any number of forms. I've described a few common ones in Figure 9-3.

Mental Tasks—Keeping the Mind Engaged

I call this method "assigning"[21] a **mental task** because it involves giving the audience something to do and think about—usually between stops of a guided interpretive encounter such as a tour or guided walk.[22] The method involves not just hinting at what's to come (as foreshadowing does), it also asks people in the audience to engage in some sort of problem-solving activity—one that typically involves both observation and theme-related thinking. For example, an interpreter leading a guided walk on a forest trail might conclude his commentary at a particular stop by saying:

If there are no more questions, let's head up the trail. But while we're walking, pay attention to the forest on your left. It's going to change in three major ways. See if you can figure out what's happening, and we'll talk about it when we reach our next stop.

> In assigning a mental task, you ask your audience to engage in some sort of problem-solving activity.

After assigning this task (which involves observing the forest on the left and trying to determine which "changes" the interpreter is referring to), the group is now engaged and thinking in theme-related ways.[23] Since provoking theme-related thoughts is the whole idea of interpretation, using this method not only adds an element of fun for the audience—it's also good interpretive strategy.

Three Models for Sequential Theme Development

If you've taught or trained someone in thematic interpretation, you've probably been asked a question like this:

> Am I supposed to tell my audience the theme when I give my talk [or guided tour]?

Opinions abound as to whether interpreters should tell their audiences what their theme is, and if so, *when* during a presentation they should reveal it. Some argue you should state your theme at the very outset of a presentation; others argue you should save it for the end; others recall Thorndyke's (1977) studies that showed stating a theme both at the beginning and end of a story led to better audience recall of facts.[24] And some interpreters will tell you it's not necessary to state your theme at all.[25] So who's right?

In my experience, most of the opinions have merit. And indeed I've seen truly excellent presentations that fall into three of the four categories For reasons having mostly to do with their personal styles, different interpreters develop preferences for some approaches over others—and that's to be expected in any expressive art such as interpretation. So it's not surprising to hear conflicting opinions about which model is better or best.

While many would agree that stating your theme only in the beginning of a talk or guided tour might seem a little awkward to audiences (probably because it violates the prägnanz principle we reviewed earlier), the other three possibilities (both *beginning and end*, *end only*, and *never*) are used widely and effectively by all kinds of communicators. Each is a different model for

	Introduction	Body	Conclusion
Sandwich model	**State your theme**	Flesh out your theme	**State your theme**
Emergent model	Orient your audience to your theme	Flesh out your theme	**State your theme**
Implicit model	Orient your audience to your theme	Flesh out your theme	Reinforce your theme, but do not say it in words

Figure 9-4. *Three models of sequential theme development.*

developing a theme, and they differ from one another only in terms of where and when the theme is actually articulated in words to the audience. I call them, respectively, the *sandwich model, emergent model,* and *implicit model* of theme development.

Figure 9-4 shows where the theme is expressed in each model. In the case of the emergent and implicit models, note that even when you don't actually articulate your theme in the introduction, you still need to orient your audience to it (see the section on introductions earlier in this chapter). Note also that the purpose of the body remains the same in all three models: fleshing out your theme and bringing it to life. And finally notice that whether and where you express your theme is different in each model. Let's now look in more detail at how each model works.

Sandwich Model

In the **sandwich theme model**, you express your theme twice—both in the introduction and conclusion. Of course, the term *sandwich* comes from the fact that the body (or "meat" of the presentation) is sandwiched between the introduction and conclusion.[26] You might recall from our earlier discussions that this model of theme development has built-in prägnanz. If your theme is *strong*, it will be memorable due to the thinking it provokes. When the audience hears it for a second time in the conclusion, it's likely they'll remember you saying it the first time in the introduction. When they make this connection, things come full circle in their minds, and they sense your presentation is about to end. At this point, closure occurs (prägnanz).

> The sandwich theme model has built-in prägnanz.

In *Environmental Interpretation* (Ham, 1992), I presented only the sandwich model. My thinking then was that it seemed a good model for beginning interpreters because it followed the familiar advice to "tell your audience what you're going to say" (in the introduction), "then say it" (in the body), and finally, "tell them what you said" (in the conclusion). In addition, in those early days of thematic interpretation I was heavily influenced by studies such as Thorndyke's (1977) experiments, which showed that audience recall of facts was better if the theme of a story was revealed both at the beginning and end. At that time, however, research on the importance of provoking thinking (rather than memory of facts) was just beginning to flourish. Today, it's clear that if provoking an audience to think is your main goal, two additional models of theme development can also produce very good results.

Emergent Model

When you're following the **emergent theme model**, you state your theme just once—in the *conclusion*. If you develop it well, your theme will gradually take form and "emerge" at the end of your presentation. In this model of theme development, your theme works in much the same way as the punch line of a well-told joke. In fact, a joke is simply a short story that follows the emergent theme model. Think about the last time you told someone a joke. You no doubt began from the very first sentence to prepare your listener(s) for the punch line, and throughout the joke you added bits and pieces of information that would give the punch line its intended effect. But you didn't actually say the punch line until the end.

> A joke is simply a short story that follows the emergent model of theme development.

Like the punch line of a good joke, a strong theme expressed only near the end of a presentation provokes thinking because it suddenly shows the wisdom of everything that preceded it. You begin preparing your audience for this important statement in the introduction, and in the body you add selected information to give it fuller meaning. But you'll express the full theme in words only in the conclusion.

Implicit Model

In the **implicit theme model**, you never actually express your theme in words. But that's its only major difference from the other two models. As with any thematic communication product, you begin the design and preparation phase by first crafting a strong, thought-provoking theme. And as you normally would, you then rely on that theme to guide your creative thinking and decision making about what to include, what to emphasize, and what leave out or deemphasize. So nothing changes in the preparation stage when you're following the implicit model.

In other words, "not saying" your theme doesn't mean you didn't have one in mind as you planned and prepared your presentation, and it doesn't mean you're not consciously developing that theme. It's simply a theme you'll never share *in words* with your audience.

When you consider all forms of expressive communication, the implicit model of theme development is probably the most commonly used of the three. Most great movies, plays, poems, song lyrics, and fine artworks don't tell you the theme. As we saw in Chapter 8, William Shakespeare never wrote into his script for *Romeo and Juliet* any dialogue or other verbal reference about the power of love.[27] And yet many generations of readers and playgoers have extracted personal themes from his famous play that hover around that idea. And if Shakespeare were alive today to talk with people about their personal themes,[28] he'd probably feel that most are within his zone of tolerance. Indeed, they should be—he started with a very strong theme ("great love defies

> When you consider all forms of creative expression, the implicit model is probably the most commonly used of the three.

even death"), and then he developed his theme exceedingly well. This is *exactly* your approach when following the implicit theme model. Even though you don't articulate your theme in words, you develop it so well that your presentation provokes thoughts that are agreeable and consistent with your theme—despite the fact that relatively few of them will sound exactly like your actual theme.

As with the other two models, you orient your audience to your theme in the introduction, but usually in very broad terms. That is, you want to frame your theme in the introduction so that your audience begins thinking in the direction you're going to take them, but the path is wide and forgiving. For this reason, you'll often find that the implicit model suits itself better to general, all-encompassing (or even philosophical) themes than to very specific ones.

You'll also probably find that when you've presented a talk or guided tour following the implicit model, you instinctively allow more latitude in the kinds of thoughts you expect or

> An implicit theme model and a wider zone of tolerance often go hand in hand.

hope people will be provoked to think during and after the encounter. That is, your zone of tolerance will naturally be wider than it might otherwise have been. The two (an implicit theme model and a wider zone of tolerance) usually go hand in hand. (If this idea doesn't yet ring true, this would be a good time to review the unrestricted and wide zones of tolerance in Chapter 8.)

Some interpreters think it's never necessary to tell an audience their theme. This is tantamount to saying that the sandwich and emergent models should never be used. They feel that if they've done a good job of developing the theme, it should be obvious to the audience, and everyone should consequently think similar thoughts and extract pretty much the same morals of the story. But I don't think the evidence bears this out.

Even *Romeo and Juliet* is variously interpreted by different people. Obviously, not everyone takes away the specific idea that true love defies death, and some people will even get the wrong idea (e.g., that "we men should stay away from women because they'll just get us killed"). As we saw in Chapter 6, when a theme is well-developed and artfully presented, it can give rise to any number of personal themes in someone's mind. And we noted that not all (or even most) of these personal themes will necessarily match the one the interpreter tried to develop (see Figure 6-3 and Appendix 3 as examples).

However, if a sufficient number of the thoughts you provoked fall within your zone of tolerance (that is, if they're agreeable enough or consistent enough with what you'd hoped for), then you've achieved the most basic form of success in interpretation.[29] Although you never formally state your theme in the implicit model, you develop it so well that *if you sat people down afterward and asked them what they were thinking* as a result of your guided tour or talk, *the thoughts they expressed would fall largely in your zone of tolerance*—just as you'd expect had you instead used the emergent or sandwich model.

Which Model Is "Best?"

It's important to recognize that none of the three models is inherently better, more effective, or more "creative" than the others. And none of them is inherently more difficult or complicated to use. They are just *different*, and all three are available to you as you begin the task of developing a theme for a sequential presentation. I've personally employed all three dozens of times with comparable results, and I've seen all three used effectively not only by accomplished interpreters, but by storytellers, novelists, screenplay writers, poets, and musical composers. My observation is that the three models are equal in their ability to succeed or fail, and that it's mainly the style and communication skill of the presenter that makes the deciding difference.

> All three models are equal in their ability to succeed or fail.

How Would I Know Which Model to Use?—The 2-3-1 Rule

Having used all three theme development models so many times, I've found that I almost never know in advance of preparing a presentation which one I'm actually going to use.[30] The way I eventually settle on one is sort of backward. Instead of deciding ahead of time which of the three models to follow, the model is revealed to me during the process of thinking through what I'm going to say in each part of my talk or guided tour (i.e., the introduction, body, and conclusion). I call this process the "2-3-1 rule."

If we number the three parts of a sequential presentation in the order you'd present them, the introduction would be 1, the body would be 2, and the conclusion would be 3. The 2-3-1 rule tells you the order in which you should think about, plan, and *prepare* the three parts. That is, you should start with the body, then work out the conclusion, and finish by preparing your introduction (2-3-1).

Recall that the introduction, body, and conclusion of a thematic presentation serve different purposes when it comes to developing the theme. One of the distinguishing purposes of the introduction is preparing the audience for the conclusion—that is, setting the stage for a thought-provoking ending. A question you might ask yourself is whether you can realistically design an introduction to set the stage for the conclusion if you don't yet know what the conclusion will look like. Similarly, until you have at least a detailed outline for the body of your presentation, how could you know how to introduce *it*? For both these reasons, I recommend saving your preparation of the introduction until you have both the body and conclusion fairly well thought out.

It's in applying the 2-3-1 rule that your model of theme development will be revealed to you. You start by preparing a detailed outline of the body (indicating not only the flow of ideas and "color," but where to use transitions, where to foreshadow, and where to work in intangible connections, anecdotes, examples, analogies, and so forth). This process produces a detailed

> It's in applying the 2-3-1 rule that your model of theme development will be revealed to you.

picture of the body and will eventually lead you to a final transition to your conclusion.

As you prepare your conclusion, you'll get your first clue about which of the theme development models you're following. If at some point in drafting your final words it occurs to you to actually state your theme (that is, if in thinking through the words of your conclusion you suddenly feel the creative urge to articulate your theme), you'll then know you're following either the sandwich or emergent model, but not the implicit model. That's because both the sandwich and emergent models involve stating the theme in the conclusion. So if you find yourself expressing the core of your theme in your conclusion, you'll know you've eliminated the implicit model.[31] Whether you're using a sandwich or emergent model, however, remains to be determined.

Eventually, you'll proceed to the final step of the 2-3-1 rule: preparing your introduction. But now, of course, you'll enjoy the great advantage of knowing how both the body and conclusion will unfold. As you work through your design of the introduction, it may or may not occur to you to state your theme. If you find that you've finished preparing the introduction and still haven't been compelled to express your theme, you'll now (and only now) know that you've been following the emergent model of theme development. Of course, if you find yourself saying your theme in the introduction, you're using the sandwich model.

Like almost everything in creative expression, good ideas take effort and time to germinate. The main value of the 2-3-1 rule is that it gives you a process for getting there more quickly than you might otherwise have arrived.[32]

Thematic Packaging

I want to conclude the chapter with a few observations that, to some, might seem like a radical departure from conventional practice. For others, however, the possibilities I suggest might seem like a breath of creative fresh air. Since the issue has to do with the way you package a theme in an interpretive product, let's call it "thematic packaging."

By thematic packaging, I mean the conceptual container in which an interpreter develops a theme. In sequential communication, you can recognize a **thematic package** first by its all-too-familiar telltale *parts* (an introduction, a body, and a conclusion). A second feature is that the three parts are designed to develop a single strong *theme*. And a third important feature of a thematic package is that it always ends with reinforcement of the theme and final *closure*. That is, each package is defined by the same theme development process we've been talking about all along. So taking these three features together, you can think of a thematic package as a completed circle drawn around a strong theme. The circle begins with an introduction and concludes with closure (Figure 9-5).

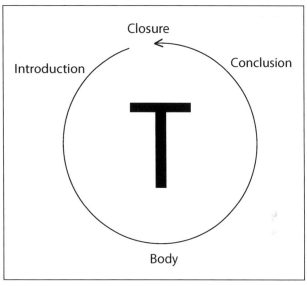

Figure 9-5. *Ingredients of a thematic package: a strong theme developed via an introduction, body, conclusion, and closure.*

In conventional practice, you design a given sequential interpretive product (such as a guided tour or talk) within just *one* thematic package. For example, an interpreter's twenty-minute talk should develop just a single overarching theme. Similarly, a one-hour guided tour would attempt to develop just one global theme. This "one-package-per-product" format has stood the test of time and continues to serve interpreters well. You probably can see that it's the one depicted in Figure 9-5.

Some interpreters, however, have explored additional creative options that don't conform neatly to the one-package-per-product approach. They entertain the possibility of situations in which a single interpretive product might consist of *more* than one thematic package. For example, is there any reason a twenty-minute talk shouldn't consist of two thematic packages, one in the form of a five-minute presentation (with a theme, introduction, body, conclusion, and closure), followed by a fifteen-minute package (with its own three-part theme development and closure)? Furthermore, is there any reason the two packages (the five-minute presentation and the fifteen-minute presentation) necessarily have to be connected to one another? Couldn't they be distinct and deal with completely different types of themes?

In conventional practice, you design a sequential interpretive product within just one thematic package.

The one-package-
per-product
format isn't the
only approach
that can lead to
thought-provoking
presentations.

In a similar vein, would there be anything wrong with a guided tour that consists of multiple thematic packages within a single tour route, such that multiple themes are introduced and concluded as part of that interpretive product? Might a new package even be introduced and concluded at each stop?

My personal reaction to such questions is "why not?" The conventional one-package-per-product format is by any measure a tried and proven approach, but it's not necessarily the only approach that can lead to interpretation's main outcome of interest: provocation. In fact, exploring other formats might well result in interpreters discovering new creative techniques suited to their specific circumstances, just as has happened with the evolution of new electronic technologies during the past 50-plus years.

Although there are, no doubt, numerous ways to package themes within a given interpretive product, I've outlined three fairly straightforward formats in Figures 9-6 through 9-8. These include the conventional one-package format, the serial-package format, and the nested-package format.

The **one-package format** represents the conventional approach to theme development shown in Figure 9-6. In this format, interpreters develop and bring closure to a single strong theme via an introduction, body, and conclusion. It's the format most thematic interpreters are accustomed to using.

In the **serial-package format** (Figure 9-7), interpreters develop two or more successive themes, *each* with an introduction, body, and conclusion, and *each* brought to closure. The themes might or might not be related to each other, but in either event, the interpreter makes no attempt to tie them together into a collective whole meaning. That is, each

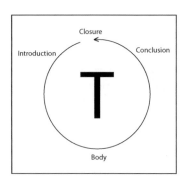

Figure 9-6. *A one-package format: a single theme is developed with an introduction, body, conclusion, and closure.*

package stands alone, thematically independent of the others. Put another way, the individual packages aren't simply subthemes of an overall global theme that links them together.[33] An example of this sort of design is a guided tour of a historic building in which the interpreter develops (and brings closure to) a different theme for each room and makes no attempt to tie them all together. In this sense, the tour consists of a series of short, unrelated thematic talks.

A **nested-package format** (Figure 9-8) is organized in the same way as a serial package, except that in this case you *do* tie the themes together within an overarching theme. In this way, each smaller thematic package is designed to develop (and bring closure to) a *subtheme* of the overarching global theme. That is, the smaller individual thematic packages collectively add up to the larger one. In this format, your development of the smaller themes is "nested" within your development of the overall theme. An example would be a four-hour interpretive hike that consists of a series of thematic packages you develop along the route. At the end, you'd then draw on the subthemes you developed in the smaller thematic packages to reinforce an overarching conclusion about the whole hike. Similarly, an evening program

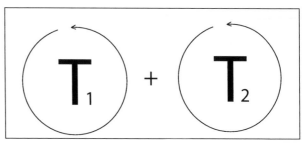

Figure 9-7. *A serial-package format: two or more successive themes are independently developed, each with its own introduction, body, conclusion, and closure.*

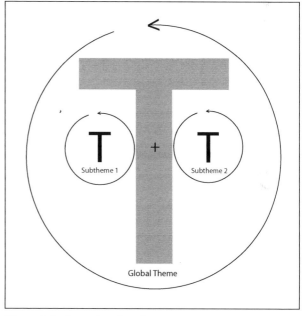

Figure 9-8. *A nested-package format: two or more related themes are developed as part of an overarching global theme. Closure to the global theme ties the smaller themes together.*

might be divided into three related talks (each with its own introduction, body, conclusion, and closure), followed at the end by an overall conclusion that connects the dots between the three subthemes. Obviously, *many* other nesting possibilities exist. Be sure to limit the number of subthemes in any nested theme package to four or fewer (recall the "magical number four" discussed in Chapter 2).

Summary and a Final Look Ahead

We've seen in this chapter that developing a theme for a sequential interpretive product means first and foremost designing the introduction, body, and conclusion to do what they're supposed to do—and to do it *well* ("good talks and tours have good parts"). We reviewed a number of creative options and found that each part can be designed to achieve its purposes in different ways.

A dilemma in face-to-face thematic interpretation is whether interpreters should reveal their theme to an audience—and if so, where in the presentation they should do it. We considered three models of sequential theme development and found that the answer to these questions is different depending on which of the models (sandwich, emergent, or implicit) an interpreter is using. Since all three models can produce excellent results, which of them you use on a given day will ultimately depend on your personal style and preference.

Finally, we considered some alternative creative formats for theme development. Traditionally, an interpretive product involves development of just a single theme. But we saw that other options might exist in which an interpreter could develop multiple themes in the same interpretive encounter. Among these alternative formats are the serial thematic package and the nested thematic package.

In Chapter 10, we'll see that developing a theme for a nonsequential communication device is different from the method described in this chapter. When audiences (rather than interpreters) control the order of information they receive, a different but simple approach to theme development is called for.

Glossary terms: closure, develop (a theme), emergent theme model, extrapolation, foreshadowing, implicit theme model, intangible meaning, mental task, nested-package format, nonsequential communication, one-package format, prägnanz, recapitulation, sandwich theme model, sequential communication, serial-package format, suggestion, tangible meaning, thematic package, transition

Additional Thoughts for Chapter 9

---

1   I emphasize *forefront* because the "color" has always been in the background. In fact, it's been at the center of your thinking all along. It consists of all the information and creative ideas you processed and worked through as you gradually arrived at your theme. It's easy to see you needed to do this in order to be able to write a strong theme in the first place. Indeed, by the time you have your theme

in finished form you'll have processed so much information that finding things to say in developing it won't be a challenge. As Lewis (1980: 38) promised, once you have a theme in mind, everything else will "tend to fall into place." I would estimate that at least 75 percent of the effort to develop a TORE-quality interpretive product goes into crafting the *T* itself. See Chapter 7 for a review.

2   Similarly, movies, novels, poems, stage plays, and songs are sequential since writer-composers determine the order of events and words. Some guides, particularly those who do expeditionary style guiding (for example, those who take their audiences whale watching, birding, or who lead tours along ocean beaches or in other dynamic environments) sometimes ask whether those sorts of interpretive products are actually sequential. Obviously, such guides can never be totally certain what they'll encounter on a given tour, or in what order—which makes sequential control difficult. Nevertheless, such guides will ordinarily know from their experience the range of possible features they might encounter, even if the exact sequence remains uncertain. This foresight is ordinarily adequate to prepare and present an introduction (or briefing) that builds curiosity and orients tourists to the range of possibilities. That is, although the body and conclusion of such an interpretive product will depend in part on what the group actually sees, the overall event is sequential because the guide can capitalize in the introduction on her or his knowledge about what groups typically encounter along the route. For the same reason, some ask whether Q & A sessions are nonsequential since the audience (not the interpreter) determines the order of the questions that are asked. The answer, of course, is that although the order of the questions is indeed determined by the audience, the interpreter decides how to structure her or his response to each question. Therefore, Q & A is a form of sequential communication from the interpreter's side of things.

3   In nonsequential communication, the audience (not you) has control over the sequence of information it receives. Nonsequential communication devices include such media as websites, most smartphone apps, exhibits, wayside exhibits, signs, and the individual stops on a self-guided tour. In Chapter 10, I outline a fundamental theme development strategy for nonsequential communication—using what I've called "theme titles" that, in conjunction with one or more major design elements, convey the essence of a theme to even a very brief audience.

4   I've been asked why preparing an introduction, body, and conclusion is necessarily the best way to approach a sequential presentation. My answer is that it's not *necessarily* the best way, but I'm still waiting for someone to show me a better one. These three basic parts of an oral presentation have been advocated by communication experts for twenty-one centuries. In fact, they were first identified in about 350 BC by Aristotle in *Poetics*. However, the introduction, body, and conclusion of a thematic presentation do not simply correspond to the beginning, middle, and end, as some claim Aristotle intended. In the TORE model, each part serves a different purpose than the other two with respect to developing the theme.

5   How specifically you orient them to your theme will depend on which model of theme development you've adopted for your presentation. In the most specific case, you'll actually state your theme

in the introduction (see the sandwich model later in the chapter). But sometimes you might only hint at your theme or introduce some broad thematic sideboards to frame the rest of your presentation (see emergent and implicit models later in the chapter).

6   If your theme is weak, this method probably won't work well for you. Stating your theme in both the introduction and conclusion is the sandwich model of theme development discussed later in this chapter.

7   In their superb volume, *Conducting Meaningful Interpretation*, Ward and Wilkinson (2006) contrast two approaches to presenting the body of a thematic talk. They call them, respectively, the "theme/subtheme style" and the "narrative style." In the theme/subtheme style, your development of a global theme and subthemes (if there are any) is explicit and conspicuous. The narrative style also develops the theme (and subthemes), but reference to them is vague or implicit. Ward and Wilkinson's theme/subtheme style follows the sandwich theme development model I discuss later in this chapter, whereas their narrative style would be either an emergent or implicit model (depending on whether you state your theme in the conclusion). Figure 9-4 shows how these three models of theme development (sandwich, emergent, and implicit) differ from one another.

8   You'll find good practical advice in Lisa Brochu and Tim Merriman's (2012) *Personal Interpretation*; Gil Field and Lotte Lente's (2000) *Developing Ecotours*; John Pastorelli's (2003) *Enriching the Experience*; and Carolyn Ward and Alan Wilkinson's (2006) *Conducting Meaningful Interpretation*.

9   In fact, great talks sometimes revolve entirely around an intangible meaning. A well-known example is Dr. Martin Luther King's immortal speech, "I Have a Dream." In some cases, an interpreter might introduce a talk with an intangible-tangible connection, or a talk might focus mainly on tangible ideas until the conclusion, when all the tangibles are linked to an intangible meaning. Likewise, as we saw in Chapter 7 ("Not All Themes Are Equal"), any theme that invokes a universal concept, by definition, makes a tangible-intangible connection.

10   Larsen (2003) and his colleagues have referred to these tangible things as "icons." See the thought-provoking article by Goldman, Chen, and Larsen (2001), "Clicking the Icon."

11   Recall from Chapters 2 and 7 the value universal concepts can bring to crafting a strong, thought-provoking theme. You probably can see that every universal concept is intangible—it refers to something that is widely important to human beings (sometimes in a visceral or emotive way), but the meanings evoked are subjective and symbolic.

12   For a vivid example, see the invited commentary by Shelton Johnson in Figure 2-5.

13   This fictitious story about the Chilkoot family is an example of a "narrative style" body. See Ward and Wilkinson (2006: 77-78).

14 The principle of prägnanz comes from Gestalt psychology which originated in Germany in the early 1900s. Today it remains a widely applied theory in the visual and oratory arts, among many other fields. Gestalt theory explains human thinking and behavior in terms of how we perceive the inherent organization and wholeness of things.

15 I want to thank to Professor Roy Ballantyne, University of Queensland, Australia, for giving me this idea. I've adapted it from a segment of *Tour Guiding*, a video training package I worked on with Roy and others in 1999.

16 I call it a "suggestion" because it works somewhat like a hypnotic suggestion. The key difference is that unlike a hypnotist who must first induce a *hypnotic state* before issuing the suggestion (i.e., something that will later trigger some sort of behavior from the hypnotized person), an interpreter must instead induce *a lot of thinking* (provocation) before this type of suggestion will trigger reinforcement of a theme.

17 I estimate twenty-four to forty-eight hours as the optimal time frame only because the strength of the suggestion will inevitably be diluted, both by forgetting and by people's processing of new information in the days following the presentation.

18 This is the case, for example, with audiences who view exhibits, signs, brochures, and websites, as well as for users of most smartphone apps. In Chapter 10, we'll look at a theme-development strategy for nonsequential communication.

19 Alfred Russel Wallace (yes, Russel with one *l*) independently developed his own theory of natural selection and evolution in 1858. Aware of his competition, Darwin hastened publication of *On the Origin of Species* in 1859.

20 In classic literature, Herman Melville arguably set the standard for foreshadowing in *Moby Dick* where omen after omen hinted at Captain Ahab's fate. But more contemporary readers (and those less inclined to read the classics) might consider Dan Brown (author of *The Da Vinci Code* and *Angels and Demons*) to be the present-day master. Almost every chapter ends with a foreboding description of what some bad guy is plotting against the persistent professor, Dr. Robert Langdon.

21 "Assigning" is in quotation marks as a reminder that your audience is probably noncaptive. If they don't want to participate, that's their choice.

22 This is because your audience will need time and freedom from distractions (one of which is your voice) to carry out the task and do the thinking you want them to do. The time people spend walking between stops on a guided tour naturally provides this opportunity. You might use the method in a talk, but in doing so you'd need to quit talking while they do their part. Anything is possible, but this might prove logistically complicated.

23 This assumes, of course, that the interpreter actually plans to link the changes to his theme.

24 See Ham (1992: 39-40) where I discussed Thorndyke's (1977) experiments. He found that if you're interested in an audience's ability to *recall factual information*, the best place to state a theme is at the beginning of a presentation, and the next best place is at the end. He also found that *factual recall* from a presentation in which the theme is never stated was no better than that following a presentation of those same facts in random order. So based on Thorndyke's results, I advised in *Environmental Interpretation* (p. 40) that in sequential communication "you should reveal the theme to your audience at the beginning of the presentation, and then reinforce it at the end." This became known as the sandwich model of theme development. Some twenty years later, however, things have changed quite a bit. We now know from dozens of studies that Tilden's advice about "provocation, not instruction" was valid, even if it came decades ahead of its time. Trying to provoke thought and trying to promote factual recall can be quite different. And studies have shown that high provocation doesn't necessarily mean good factual recall, or vice versa (Bucy, 2005; Cacioppo & Petty, 1989; Rand, 2010). While the sandwich model is still a perfectly good approach to theme development, it's not necessarily the only good model when the interpreter's goal is to *provoke thought* rather than memory of facts.

25 These interpreters argue that if you've done a good job of developing your theme, you shouldn't have to state it to your audience at all—that is, it will be so obvious to them they'll automatically "see" it. Although I appreciate this point of view and completely agree that it's not always necessary to state your theme, I cannot agree with the reason these interpreters give (i.e., that the theme will necessarily be obvious). I explain this in more detail later when we consider the implicit model of theme development.

26 A humorous fact of history (perhaps) is that because I've so often referred to this model as the "sandwich," some people now call it the "Ham Sandwich Model." When you have a name like mine, you have to retain your sense of humor.

27 Unlike Huey Lewis and the News, who did indeed reveal their theme in the hit single "The Power of Love" (1985): "The power of love is a curious thing; make-a one man weep, make another man sing."

28 In other words, Shakespeare is conducting a thought-listing exercise with people in his audience. If the thoughts they're having fall largely within his zone of tolerance, he can give himself a well-earned pat on the back for having developed his theme well. You'll find instructions for carrying out a simple thought-listing procedure in Chapter 8 (Figure 8-4).

29 I say "most basic" because you might have other objectives in mind (such as promoting a particular attitude or influencing a particular behavior). In such cases, a comprehensive evaluation would also want to examine whether the additional objectives were being met. But to achieve these ad-

ditional outcomes, you'd ordinarily need to succeed first in provoking thought. An exception, of course, is when a peripheral (quick path) impact occurs (see "Two Paths to Impacting Attitudes" in Chapter 5).

30 And even when I've finally decided on one, I sometimes find that the next time I actually make the presentation I've unconsciously slipped into a different model. Like a strong theme, the three models are simply tools we can use to make better decisions about program content and delivery. They aren't handcuffs intended to constrain our choices but rather keys that both liberate and guide our creative thinking. This is another way of saying that you shouldn't let your first choice of theme development model become an end in itself.

31 On the other hand, if you've finished preparing the conclusion and it *hasn't* occurred to you to state your theme, then by default, you've chosen the implicit model for that particular presentation.

32 As you work through the 2-3-1 process, you'll naturally find yourself referring repeatedly to your theme. After all, it's your main guide to deciding on content, emphasis, and creative approach. At some point in this process, however, your thinking might even lead you to see a way to improve the theme itself. Your first reaction to this possibility might be "Oh no! If I change my theme *now*, I'll have to change everything else I've already thought out and basically start over!" But in practice this almost never happens. Chances are, you're making only minor refinements to your theme, rather than taking it in an entirely new direction. So when this happens, don't hesitate to make the change. Remember, your theme isn't an end in itself—it's not some sort of jail intended to constrain your creative thinking. Rather, its purpose is to liberate your creativity and help you make good decisions. So if working through the 2-3-1 process helps you further strengthen your theme, all the better.

33 This is the only difference between a serial thematic package and a nested one. In a nested package, the interpreter *does* make connections between the individual themes and ties them together within an overarching global theme. In essence, this makes the themes developed in the individual packages subthemes of the global theme.

CHAPTER 10
Nonsequential Theme Development

When the audience controls the sequence of information, you need a quick way to reach them with a thought-provoking theme.

In Chapter 9, we saw that when you control the order in which your audience receives information, you have at your disposal several creative options for theme development. Among these are your ability to use introductions, bodies, and conclusions to strategic advantage; to purposefully design prägnanz into a presentation (for closure); to build in transitions; and to capitalize on other sequential techniques such as foreshadowing and assigning mental tasks between stops on a guided tour. We also saw that different models exist for developing the theme of a sequential presentation (sandwich, emergent, and implicit). All such methods are available to you in sequential communication simply because it's *you* who determines where things start, what comes next, and where things end. In this final chapter, however, *none* of these apply.

What's Different about Nonsequential Theme Development?

In nonsequential communication, each person in the audience determines what to pay attention to and in which order. Where one person begins, another might end—and a third person might not even "go there." This is the kind of challenge you face, for example, in developing the theme of an exhibit, a brochure, a website, or a nonsequential audio tour.[1] Similarly, theme development for smartphone apps, wayside exhibits, signs, and information kiosks is nonsequential. That is, in designing these types of devices, an interpreter can't know in advance which information (if any) the audience will pay attention to, *or* in what order.

> Where one person begins, another might end—and a third person might not even "go there."

Obviously, when the audience controls the order of information, you can't think in terms of introductions, bodies, and conclusions because where to begin and when to end is *their* choice, not yours. You also can't prepare an audience for closure or prägnanz in nonsequential communication because there is no definitive beginning or end. Likewise, it's impractical to plan transitions between main points, to foreshadow what comes next, or to give audiences something to do or think about between one thing and the next. Indeed, in nonsequential communication, concepts such as "beginning," "end," and "next" are vague or even meaningless.

This should tell you something important about nonsequential theme development—it requires a *different* approach than the one we considered in Chapter 9. What this strategy entails, and why it's necessary, will be our focus in this chapter.

The Constraint of Time

Another very real limitation in developing a theme for a nonsequential presentation is that your window of communication opportunity is a moving target, meaning it's never clear just how much time you have to get the job done. That's because it's impossible to predict how much time a given individual is going to invest in engaging with your interpretation.[2]

Consider, for example, three different people who all stop to view a museum exhibit. The first might engage with and fully process *everything* in your exhibit, reading every bit of text and exhausting herself of the entire presentation of ideas (I call these people "**studiers**" or "students"). But a second person viewing the same

> In a nonsequential presentation, your window of communication opportunity is a moving target.

The constraint of time—streakers, browsers, and studiers are equally important audiences in nonsequential theme development.

exhibit might be more selective—perusing things, stopping here and there to read a bit of this and a little of that, before leaving (I call them "**browsers**"). And yet a third person (I affectionately call these folks "**streakers**")[3] might simply glance at your exhibit, spending only enough time to locate and read the title while momentarily perceiving some predominant design element (such as a large photo or illustration, something three-dimensional or anything moving). All told, the streaker might invest anywhere from a fraction of a second to five or six seconds—but not much more.[4]

The question we need to ask is how you might approach developing a theme for this exhibit. Put another way, given that your purpose in developing your exhibit's theme is to provoke theme-related thinking, *whose* thinking do you wish to provoke? This is tantamount to asking who your primary audience is. Is it just the studiers who "earned" your favor by putting in all that "work?" Or would you like to reach everyone? It's a fair question.

If you're like most interpreters I know, you probably wouldn't be satisfied knowing that the only people impacted by your theme will be the studiers—the people who read (or listen to) everything. First, intuitively, you know the studiers are probably few in number, meaning your exhibit's reach will be limited. And second, you might justifiably assume that studiers are likely to already know more and care more about the topic of the exhibit—which means your exhibit might miss the very people you were most hoping to reach (see Figure 10-1).[5] Either way, you're probably thinking:

Data summarized by John Falk and Lynn Dierking (1992) illustrate why streakers are an important audience to consider in nonsequential theme development. Although they're certainly not the only audience, a one-to-six-second audience is often a prevalent audience for a given interpretive product.

The graph below depicts the typical pattern of reading times by museum exhibit viewers. As Falk and Dierking point out, the most common scenario is that visitors spend either very little time or a lot of time reading a particular exhibit. As the graph illustrates, the largest number of visitors will pass by a given display and read nothing (0 seconds reading time), while a fairly large group will invest between about 1 to 18 seconds. And another sizable group will read somewhere between about 40 seconds and a little more than a minute (the average being around 60 seconds).

What's noteworthy about the graph, however, is the large highlighted area ranging from about 1 to 6 seconds of reading time. These are the streakers we've discussed: viewers who engage only long enough with an exhibit to read its title and momentarily perceive a predominant design element. You probably can see that streakers are a sizable, if not predominant, audience for a typical museum or interpretive center exhibit.

When a theme title works in conjunction with design to communicate a quick but provocative message, a nonsequential interpretive product can achieve a degree of success with even a very brief audience. Viewers who invest more time will receive a richer development of the theme. But conveying the essence of your theme in the title gives you your best chance of reaching the greatest number of people.

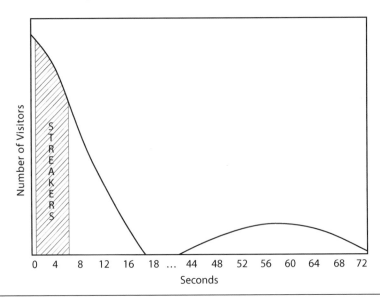

Figure 10-1. *Streakers are often a prevalent audience for nonsequential communication (adapted with permission from Falk and Dierking, 1992).*[6]

I have a strong theme that says something truly important, something I want everyone who views my exhibit to think about—even the streakers. Therefore, *everybody* is my audience, regardless of how much time they invest in viewing the exhibit.

This is the premise I assume about all forms of nonsequential theme development: that a well-developed theme should aim to stimulate the thinking of everyone in an audience, irrespective of the amount of time they put into processing it.[7] A recent study of 428 exhibit viewers in a German national park visitor center shows how important this way of looking at things can be. About 17 percent spent six seconds or less viewing exhibits, and over a quarter of them spent just 10 seconds or less.[8] Obviously, if an exhibit fails to communicate its theme quickly to these visitors, it's likely to miss a significant portion of the audience.

A Strategy for Nonsequential Theme Development

If it's important to reach everyone with your theme (including the streakers), your strategy for developing the theme has to deal head-on with the constraint of time. That is, you've got to figure out a way to communicate the theme in a thought-provoking way in about one to six seconds. That's where theme titles come into play.

When people encounter an interpretive product such as an exhibit or poster, they instinctively look for the title since they assume those words will give them a clue as to what the thing is about.[9] That is, they intuitively know the title will reveal the topic of the exhibit or poster and, based on their interests at that moment, help them decide whether to spend any more time with it. Understanding how this works, designers usually make sure that the most conspicuous words in a design space are those in the title.[10]

> If you want to reach the streakers, you have to deal head-on with the constraint of time.

At about the same time most viewers read the title of an exhibit or poster, they also perceive at least one other visually dominant design element—something that literally "catches their eye" and draws attention to itself (for example, large-scale background imagery, an interesting photograph or vivid illustration, anything three dimensional, anything moving, or objects illuminated with special lighting). When a viewer puts the two together (the words in the title and the visual element), it's natural to look for an association between them. And when this association is made, an impression, a thought, or an inference

THE MOST IMPORTANT REASON
FOR MAKING YOUR WORKPLACE SAFE,
IS NOT AT WORK AT ALL.

Figure 10-2. A theme title quickly conveys the essence of the theme in a thought-provoking way. Courtesy of The Shannon Company and WorkSafe Victoria, Australia.

of some sort often follows. It's at this moment that even a very brief audience can be provoked to think one or more theme-related thoughts—success.

In other words, the words in the title and the dominant nonword imagery are perceived as a unit, each part adding something to the other, and together culminating in a whole idea—that is, a personal theme. This is exactly the effect of The Shannon Company's award-winning occupational safety poster shown in Figure 10-2. Neither the words in the title nor the imagery, would, *alone*, communicate a clear or complete idea. But when you perceive them together as one conceptual unit, the poster's message is both clear and poignant.

It is this *combination* (of the words in the title and another predominant design element) that gives us our best strategy for nonsequential theme development. If the words, in conjunction with the other design element, communicate the central aspect of your theme in such a way that even a streaker is provoked to think about it, you've accomplished exactly what you hoped to accomplish: reaching everyone—even the *briefest* of audiences—with your theme. In thematic interpretation, when we refer to a "theme title," we're always referring to this verbal-visual *combination*, even in cases where the words might carry most of the meaning.[11]

Stated as a principle of thematic interpretation, the recommended strategy for nonsequential theme development is to display a **theme title** that combines words with another conspicuous design element to convey the essence of the theme in a thought-provoking way. In this way, even a person who spends only a few seconds engaging with the interpretive product can walk away provoked to think theme-related thoughts. Figure 10-3 summarizes the main differences in theme-development strategies for sequential and nonsequential interpretation.

Sequential Theme Development	Nonsequential Theme Development
✓ Strategic introduction, body, conclusion ✓ Beginning and ending work in tandem (closure) ✓ Transitions ✓ Foreshadowing ✓ Assigning mental tasks ✓ Sandwich, emergent, and implicit model Example applications: talks, guided tours, guided walks, sequential self-guided tours (trails, road tours, etc.), scripts for multimedia programs, stories, novels, stage plays, screenplays, song lyrics, etc.	✓ Theme title (a combination of words and visual support) that conveys the essence of the theme and provokes theme-related thinking Example applications: exhibits, signs, wayside exhibits, information boards, brochures, websites, smartphone apps, nonsequential self-guided tours, etc.

Figure 10-3. *Comparison of sequential and nonsequential theme-development strategies.*

Theme Titles versus Topic Titles

One way to understand what theme titles should do is to compare them with **topic titles**. Whereas a theme title conveys the essence of an interpretive product's theme, a topic title merely tells a viewer what the product (for example, an exhibit, website, or sign) is *about*—that is, its topic. This difference between theme titles and topic titles is all important in nonsequential theme development since only a theme title stands much of a chance of provoking theme-related thinking for a one-to-six-second audience.

As illustrated in Figure 10-4, even without visual accompaniment, the words in a theme title can quickly convey a thought-provoking whole idea. Topic titles, however, convey only the subject matter of an interpretive product. Consequently, to get some sense of what the theme might be, a viewer would have to read further, investing more time than a streaker is willing to spend.

Because everyone knows that a theme is a sentence, some interpreters think that a theme title also needs to be expressed in a sentence. But

> A theme title is a verbal-visual combination, even in cases where the words might carry most of the meaning.

Theme Titles Provoke Thought around a Whole Idea

Most people read the title of a nonsequential interpretive product before they read anything else. In fact, a lot them will read *only* the title. For this reason, the title is singularly important in developing a theme if you want it to reach even a very brief audience. Below are two lists of hypothetical titles. One shows conventional topic titles, and the other shows how a theme title for that topic might look. You can see that even if you read no more than just the title, you still extract a whole idea from the titles on the right. Can you say the same about the titles on the left?

Topic Title	Theme Title
A Famous Author	Steinbeck—Master of the Metaphor
Rioja Wines	Noble Grape from Our Ancestors—*Tempranillo*
Birds of This Park	You're Surrounded by 100,000 Beating Bird Hearts
Tropical Forests	Tropical Forests—Where Pharmacists Go to Shop
Water Contamination	We're Polluting the Water That Dinosaurs Drank
The Ocean	The Ocean—Powerful, yet Fragile

Figure 10-4. *A comparison of theme titles and topic titles.*

that's not necessarily the case. In fact, very short titles of just a word or two or three can, in combination with an appropriate visual, communicate powerful whole ideas.

To see how this can work, compare the two exhibit designs (A and B) shown in Figure 10-5. A few things are noteworthy about them. First, you can see they're essentially identical in every respect, except for their titles. Another thing you'll notice is that the topic of both exhibits is the same: polar bears. Finally notice that whereas Exhibit A has a topic title, Exhibit B has a theme title.

Now put yourself in the role of a streaker, and imagine yourself stopping in front Exhibit A for just a second or two—time enough only to read the title and connect it to the dominant visual (the photograph of the polar bear). Now quit looking at the exhibit and ask yourself, "What am I thinking now that I've glanced at this exhibit about polar bears? What connections am I making? What inferences am I drawing? What does this exhibit *tell* me?"[12]

Chances are, your answer is "not much." That's because the title of Exhibit A told you only its topic. Obviously, you'd have to read further into the text and explore the details below the title

Figure 10-5. *Effect of a theme title versus a topic title in an exhibit. Photo courtesy of Scott Kish, National Geographic.*

in order to extract any sort of personal theme about polar bears. Is the message that the bears are common around here? Does it tell you polar bears eat about any kind of animal they can catch? Does it tell you polar bears need floating ice to use as hunting platforms? The fact is, you have no idea. You're a streaker, and you were gone long before you could get answers to such questions.

Now, take the same brief glance at Exhibit B and ask yourself the same question: "What am I thinking now that I've glanced at this exhibit about polar bears?" If you're like most people, the result is different because the theme title of this exhibit made you *think*. As we discussed earlier, you likely did three things simultaneously: You saw the photograph of the bear, read the one-word title "Goodbye?," and put the two together, forming one whole idea—thereby extracting a personal theme from the exhibit. A theme most people take away (in one form or another) is that things don't look good for the polar bear—it's a threatened species. Some viewers interpret the question mark in the title as implying there's still hope; some extend the hope idea to a sort of "call to action" (i.e., we can still turn things around); some viewers will take "goodbye?" as coming from an anonymous narrator (i.e., the exhibit itself), while others infer that it's the *bear* asking whether this is "goodbye?" (which, for some, results in an emotional dimension to the theme). And all this thinking resulted from just a couple of seconds of processing—which is *precisely* what a good theme title (consisting both of words and visual support) should accomplish.

A Good Theme Title Provokes Thoughts within Your Zone of Tolerance

The reason I can be fairly confident in saying that these are the thoughts "most people" viewing Exhibit B would be provoked to think is that I *asked* real people to tell me their thoughts. That is, I conducted a thought-listing exercise (using the procedures I listed in Figure 8-4). Specifically, I wanted to know what a broad cross section of people would be thinking after looking at the digital poster design shown in Figure 10-6.

The theme I wanted to develop in the poster was that:

> It's plausible that some people alive today will still be around to hear the sad news that the last polar bear in the wild has died.

Working with my graphic-designer spouse, I used this theme to arrive at the simplest possible design concept—one consisting only of a theme title that could be processed in a couple of seconds. In this way, I decided on the image of a polar bear and the one-word title (with question mark). The creative planning process took literally about two minutes and production about ten minutes. Although the design was quick and could have been improved with more time, it was only the theme title I was interested in testing. Likewise, whether the message would be emotive or merely informative was unimportant. I simply wanted to know what kinds of *thoughts* the theme title would provoke in viewers.

So, an hour later I emailed the poster design to seventy-two people in seven countries[13] and asked them (1) to look at the design and (2) to complete this sentence:

> The main thing I take from the image is that _____.

All but three of them responded. Their replies (see Appendix 3) were exactly what I described. However, what's most important about these replies (from a thematic communication perspective) is that almost all of them fell within my zone of tolerance. That is, the vast majority of them seemed to me to be consistent with or supportive of the theme I was trying to develop, even though only one of them expressed the idea pretty much the way I did.[14]

Only a few were thoughts I really *didn't* want to provoke—such as the bear saying a casual goodbye to a tourist/visitor (Respondent 10), "We've given up the fight" to save the polar bear (Respondent 26), and "We shouldn't be afraid of bears" (Respondent 62). Were these kinds of thoughts more prevalent, however, I'd be wise to go back to the drawing board and ask myself what I could change to increase the number of thoughts falling within my zone of tolerance.

As you'd expect, some of the thoughts people expressed were unanticipated. For example, when I decided on the title "Goodbye?," in my mind an anonymous narrator was talking.[15] However, when several people replied that in their minds the *bear* was talking, I realized that although I hadn't initially expected that reply, I was pleased with the emotional

Figure 10-6. *"Theme-title-only" design tested with seventy-two people (see Appendix 3). Photo courtesy of Scott Kish, National Geographic.*

impact it had on these people. It fell within my zone of tolerance. One person, in fact, suggested I replace the photo with one of a mother polar bear and her cubs in order to strike an even more poignant emotional chord—a good idea, perhaps.[16]

On the whole, these results tell me I'm on the right track but also that room for improvement remains. Getting this kind of feedback is exactly the purpose of doing a thought-listing exercise. The results tell you not only how much thinking your interpretation is provoking but also specifically what people in your audience are thinking about. With this kind of insight, what you can do to improve becomes clearer.

> A thought-listing exercise will give you insight into ways to improve.

Summary

In this final chapter, we've considered the special challenges of developing themes for nonsequential interpretive products. We saw that the many methods you can capitalize on in sequential theme development aren't available when you don't control the order of information an audience receives.

In nonsequential communication, audiences (not interpreters) determine the sequence of information flow. This means that no two people are likely to receive the same information in the same order. We also saw that different people will devote different amounts of time to processing the information presented. In fact, in most situations, a sizable group of these people will spend as little as a few seconds. Based on the assumption that an interpreter's theme should aim to provoke thinking even for the briefest of audiences, theme titles emerged as the centerpiece of nonsequential theme development strategy.

It's important to note that this chapter has emphasized an approach to developing themes for interpretive products such as exhibits, signs, posters, websites, and other nonsequential devices. We haven't, however, considered the equally important issues of artistic design and layout. Here, I refer readers to three excellent sources: *Interpretation by Design*, by Paul Caputo, Shea Lewis, and Lisa Brochu (2008); *Signs, Trails and Wayside Exhibits*, by Michael Gross, Ron Zimmerman, and Jim Buchholz (2006); and *Designing Interpretive Signs*, by Gianna Moscardo, Roy Ballantyne, and Karen Hughes (2007).

Glossary terms: browser, streaker, studier, theme title, topic title

Additional Thoughts for Chapter 10

1   Nonsequential audio tours are increasingly common in large museums and historic sites. They're nonsequential in the sense that visitors carry the audio device with them and selectively activate recorded messages where and when they want to. Some of the best nonsequential audio tours I've seen (well, *heard*) are those offered at the Prado Museum in Madrid, Edinburgh Castle in Scotland, and Alcatraz in the United States. Note, however, that whereas the overall tour is nonsequential, any given recorded segment is sequential (since a script writer and producer decided the sequence in which each segment would unfold).

2   In sequential communication, we assume interpreters determine the amount of time they have for developing the theme. This is because we assume they'll use the power of interpersonal communication and the many advantages of sequential control to hold an audience's attention for an allotted time.

3   Of course, the name "streakers" is in honor of Ray Stevens's (1974) smash hit single, "The Streak": "Oh yes, they call him the streak…fastest thing on two feet."

4   It's important not to think of streakers, browsers, and studiers as if they were kinds of people. You probably know from your own experience at museums and interpretive centers that you can be a streaker at one exhibit, a browser at the next, and then instantly become a studier when the next exhibit presents something you're deeply interested in or you know something about.

5   Readers familiar with the 3-30-3 rule (which says that exhibits should be designed hierarchically for a 3-second audience, a 30-second audience and a 3-minute audience) might draw some inter-

esting conclusions from the graph in Figure 10-1. First is that a 3-second audience does indeed fall in the center of what I've called the "streakers." In my opinion, this is what is best and most important about the 3-30-3 rule—it stresses the need to quickly convey a theme. However, you can also see from the graph that very few exhibit viewers actually spend 30 seconds engaging with an exhibit, and a 3 minute audience doesn't exist at all. This is not to say that some people might not spend 30 seconds or 180 seconds reading an exhibit or sign; it simply means that people who actually invest those amounts of time are probably pretty rare. You can see in the graph, for example, that the average viewing time by the most interested readers is only around 1 minute and that almost no viewers invested even as much as 72 seconds. So the "30" and the second "3" in the 3-30-3 rule might not correspond as well to real-world audiences as the first "3." Despite these discrepancies, however, I've always been a fan of the 3-30-3 rule because it tells writers and designers not to overlook or underestimate the importance of the streakers.

6   You'll notice in Figure 10-1 that I haven't indicated where the browsers and studiers begin and end on the graph. There are two reasons for this. First is that nobody actually knows what *empirically* constitutes a browser or a studier in the context of exhibit viewing. These are simply words I subjectively invented to describe two audiences, each of which spends progressively more time than streakers (which I defined as a one-to-six-second audience). And the second reason is that it really doesn't matter where the browsers or studiers fit into the data. It's the streaker we're concerned with most. Our thinking is that if you can reach even the briefest of audiences, then you're almost guaranteed to reach the rest with an even more complete development of the theme. So the idea in nonsequential theme development is to convey *very quickly* the essence of a theme in a way that provokes thinking around the theme. If you do this successfully, your theme has the potential to reach virtually every viewer regardless of whether they're streakers, browsers, or studiers. Of course, if you've designed the rest of the interpretive product in a hierarchy, as most experts suggest, you can be fairly certain that the browsers and studiers will receive an even richer, more contextualized development of the theme. On hierarchical design see Caputo, Lewis, and Brochu (2008); Gross, Zimmerman, and Buchholz (2006); and Moscardo, Ballantyne, and Hughes (2007).

7   Even in sequential communication, we know that not all people in an audience are going to pay equal attention to everything, or actively engage with it. Yet interpreters design every sequential presentation fully expecting to provoke thought in everyone—not just in those few who process every byte of information from beginning to end.

8   This study by von Ruschkowski, Arnberger, and Burns (forthcoming) tells pretty much the same story as the data in Figure 10-1, which were published 20 years earlier by Falk and Dierking (1992). Streakers potentially represent a large and important audience for most nonsequential communication situations. The von Ruschkowski, et al. study was conducted in July 2012 at the Torfhaus Visitor Center, Harz National Park in northern Germany.

9   Famed educational psychologist David Ausubel (1960) coined this effect an "advance organizer" more than a half century ago.

10   When it comes to titles, "bigger is better," advise Gianna Moscardo, Roy Ballantyne, and Karen Hughes in *Designing Interpretive Signs* (2007). Only rarely would a title be smaller than other words in a design. And in such exceptions, some other visual quality of the letters—such as color or dimensionality—would be accentuated or exaggerated so that a viewer's eye would be drawn *first* to the title.

11   In some cases, the words alone carry most or all the meaning and may or may not require any visual support—for example, "Pesticides Kill" or "Our Ocean—Powerful yet Fragile." But even in these cases, a design will usually include a visual element to reinforce or add context to the words.

12   You probably recognize this as a thought-listing interview—in this case, one you're doing with yourself. See more on the thought-listing method in Chapters 8 and 9. I provided instructions for conducting a simple thought-listing procedure in Figure 8-4.

13   Australia, Canada, New Zealand, Spain, Sweden, United Kingdom, and United States. Many of the people were colleagues in the heritage tourism field, but many others had no connection to interpretation or the environment. They included accountants, marketing experts, academics, researchers, nursing home administrators, salespeople, health professionals, bartenders, waiters, carpenters, and local government officials, among others.

14   See Respondent 6 in Appendix 3.

15   I decided on the overall concept and the "Goodbye?" title *before* we actually had the polar bear image shown in Figure 10-6. Up until then, I was imagining a polar bear profile, not a frontal view with those eyes staring back at me. What a difference a visual can make—worth 1,000 words indeed.

16   It bears mentioning (no pun intended) that another person remarked that the concept was over the top, describing it as "a transparent attempt to manipulate my emotions." As we've seen so many times throughout this book, all things in communication are audience dependent.

APPENDIX 1

Summaries of Two Key Theories behind the TORE Model of Thematic Interpretation

Elaboration Likelihood Model of Persuasion

Reasoned Action Model

Elaboration Likelihood Model (ELM)

Essence: The more we think about ("elaborate") a message, the more influence it can have on our attitudes and behavior. The less we elaborate, the more important are other factors (or "cues"), such as source credibility and trustworthiness. The central route to persuasion occurs when the likelihood of elaboration is high (when the audience is both motivated and capable of processing the arguments contained in the message). Central route persuasion can be enduring. The peripheral route to persuasion occurs when the audience is either unmotivated or less capable of processing the message, but attends to other aspects of the communication. Peripheral route persuasion can be quite effective, but it's often short-lived. With either route, the more favorable (pro) thoughts that are stimulated in the audience's mind, the stronger the message is and the more effective it will be in impacting attitudes.

Key Variables

Elaboration is the process of thinking about and processing a message. Processing involves generating two kinds of arguments in our minds: those in favor of and supportive of the argument and those that are counter to it. You can think of these, respectively, as thoughts that fall inside and outside a zone of tolerance.

Attitude is our positive or negative evaluation of or feeling about something.

Message strength is determined by the number of favorable arguments a message generates in the receiver's mind (as compared to the number of counterarguments). The greater the ratio of favorable arguments to counterarguments, the stronger the message is.

Message relevance determines the degree to which an audience is motivated to process the message. Things important to us are highly relevant. Things unimportant to us are irrelevant. Ease of processing is determined mainly by organization and appropriatetness of language among other factors.

Application: People in just about any audience are diverse. Some might have quite a lot of theme-related knowledge and see a lot of personal relevance in a given message. Others will either lack knowledge, see little personal relevance, or both. According to the ELM, the first group will arrive with high elaboration likelihood (EL), whereas the second group will be in the low EL category. Persuasion is possible via both routes if you have a strong theme to promote central-route processing *and* provide peripheral cues (credible source, attractive message presentation, and so forth) for people not inclined to process centrally. In Chapter 5 and elsewhere, we've used "provocation path" and "strong path" to describe the central route and "quick path" or "weak path" to describe the peripheral route to persuasion. We've used the phrase "provocation likelihood" to mean "elaboration likelihood."

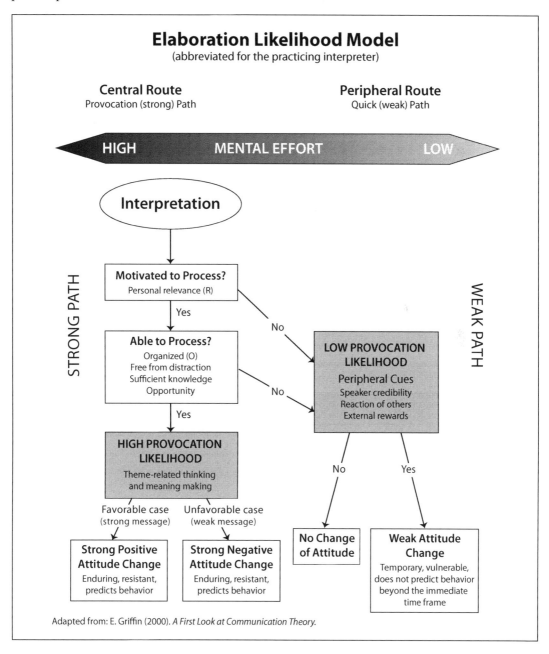

Elaboration Likelihood Model
(abbreviated for the practicing interpreter)

Central Route
Provocation (strong) Path

Peripheral Route
Quick (weak) Path

HIGH   MENTAL EFFORT   LOW

STRONG PATH

WEAK PATH

Interpretation

Motivated to Process?
Personal relevance (R)

Yes

No

Able to Process?
Organized (O)
Free from distraction
Sufficient knowledge
Opportunity

No

Yes

LOW PROVOCATION LIKELIHOOD
Peripheral Cues
Speaker credibility
Reaction of others
External rewards

HIGH PROVOCATION LIKELIHOOD
Theme-related thinking and meaning making

Favorable case
(strong message)

Unfavorable case
(weak message)

No   Yes

Strong Positive Attitude Change
Enduring, resistant, predicts behavior

Strong Negative Attitude Change
Enduring, resistant, predicts behavior

No Change of Attitude

Weak Attitude Change
Temporary, vulnerable, does not predict behavior beyond the immediate time frame

Adapted from: E. Griffin (2000). *A First Look at Communication Theory.*

Reasoned Action Model

Essence: Human behavior is rational and consistent with the *beliefs* we have about a behavior. Our beliefs give rise to *attitudes* that are consistent with the beliefs. Our attitudes give rise to *intended ways of behaving* that are consistent with those attitudes. Our behavioral intentions give rise to overt behaviors that are consistent with our intentions. Likewise, our sense of social pressure and capacity to perform the behavior also influence what we intend to do and how we ultimately behave. [Note: the current reasoned action model (Fishbein & Ajzen 2010) is an extension of the theory of planned behavior (Ajzen 1985, 1991), which, in turn, is an extension of the theory of reasoned action (Fishbein and Ajzen 1975)].

Key Variables: Three Kinds of Beliefs

Behavioral beliefs describe what we think will result or happen if we perform a given behavior (i.e., perceived consequences) and whether we think each consequence is good or bad (i.e., evaluation).

Normative beliefs describe what we think important others will think if we perform a given behavior (i.e., perceived social pressure) and whether most other people perform or do not perform the behavior (i.e., perceived normality).

Control beliefs describe our perceptions of whether we have the ability and opportunity to perform the behavior (i.e., perceived self-efficacy).

Application: Every theme expresses a belief about something. In thematic communication, implanting in a person's mind a new or modified belief that supports a desired behavior encourages the person to behave in ways that are consistent with the belief. "Desired behaviors" may be things we want people to *do* (actions) or *not do* (inactions).

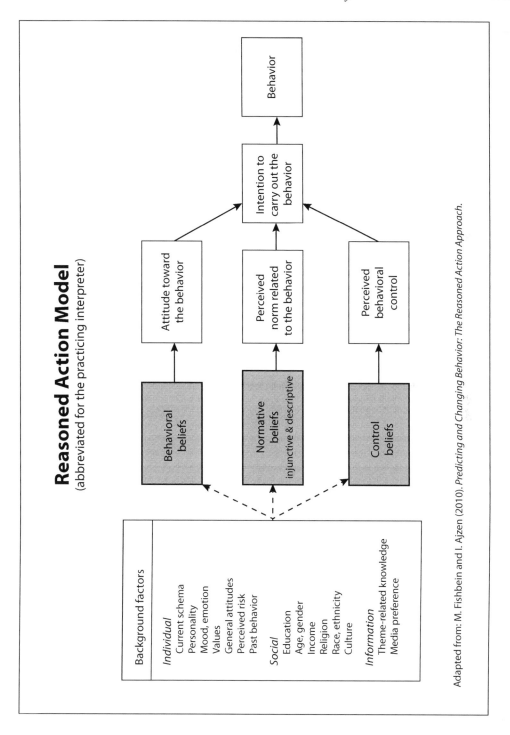

Reasoned Action Model
(abbreviated for the practicing interpreter)

Background factors

Individual
Current schema
Personality
Mood, emotion
Values
General attitudes
Perceived risk
Past behavior

Social
Education
Age, gender
Income
Religion
Race, ethnicity
Culture

Information
Theme-related knowledge
Media preference

Behavioral beliefs

Normative beliefs
injunctive & descriptive

Control beliefs

Attitude toward the behavior

Perceived norm related to the behavior

Perceived behavioral control

Intention to carry out the behavior

Behavior

Adapted from: M. Fishbein and I. Ajzen (2010). *Predicting and Changing Behavior: The Reasoned Action Approach.*

APPENDIX 2

Verbs for Stronger Themes and More Engaging Commentaries

Some Verbs to Try

In compiling this list, I've tried to select verbs that are simple, common, and understandable by most native-English-speaking adults. I've tried to include mainly verbs that describe easily imagined/easily visualized actions or which make interesting sounds. Notice how many interesting verbs begin with the letter *s*.

A

abandon abduct abhor abort absorb abuse accelerate accept accompany account ache act activate adapt adhere adjust admire adorn advance aerate affect aggravate aggregate agitate agonize aid ail aim alarm alert align allure alternate amass amaze amble ambush amplify amputate amuse analyze anchor anger angle anguish annihilate annoy appeal appear append applaud apply apprehend arch argue arise arm arouse arrest arrive ascend asphyxiate assassinate assault astound attach attack avalanche avenge awe axe

B

babble baby back backfire backhand backlash backslide badger bag bail bake balk balloon band bar bare barge bark barrel barricade bat bate bathe batter battle beam bear beat beckon befuddle beg behead belch belt bend bewitch bind bisect bite blanket blare blast blaze bleach bleed blend blister bloom blossom blur blurt blush bluster board bob bog (down) boggle bolt bombard bond bore bother bounce bow braid branch brave break breath breathe breeze brew brighten bristle broadside broil browse bruise bubble buckle bud budge bully bum bump bunch bundle bungle buoy (up) burden burn burnish burp burrow burst bury bustle butcher butt buzz bypass

C

cache cackle cage calm camouflage cannibalize canvass cap capsize captivate capture caress carpet cart carve cascade cast catalogue catapult catch cave (in) cease celebrate cement center chafe channel chap char charge charm chart chase cheapen cheat check cheer cherish chill chime chip chisel choke chop christen chronicle chuck chug churn circle clack clamber clamor clamp clang clash clasp claw cleanse clear cleave clench click climax climb clinch cling clink clip cloak clobber clock clog clothe cloud clown club cluster clutch clutter coast coat coerce coil collapse collar comb combat combust comfort compact compress conceal concoct condemn condense confine congeal connect conquer console conspire constrain constrict consume contrast converge convulse cool cope copulate corner corral corrode couple court cover cower crack (down) crackle cradle craft cram crane crank crash crave crawl creak crease creep cremate crest cringe crinkle cripple crisscross croak crook croon cross crossbreed crouch crow crowd crown crucify cruise crumble crumple crunch crush crust cry crystallize cuddle cup curb curl curve cushion cuss cut cycle

D

dab dabble dam dampen dance dangle dare darken dart dash daub dawn daze dazzle deaden deafen decapitate decay decelerate decimate decorate decoy deepen defecate defend deflate deflect deflower defoliate deforest deform defy degenerate degrade demand demolish demonstrate den dent denude deodorize depict deplete deposit deprive derail descend desert desiccate despoil destroy detach detect detonate detour devastate devour dice die dig digest dim dip dirty disable disarm discover disengage disentangle disintegrate dislodge dismember dismount disperse displace disrobe dissect dissolve disturb dive divide dodge dog dominate doodle doom dot double douse dovetail doze drag drain dramatize drape dream dredge drench dribble drift drill drink drip drive drizzle drone drool droop drop drown drum dry dry-run duck duel dull dump dunk dust dwarf dwindle dye

E

ease eat eavesdrop echo eclipse edge (away) eject eke (out) elate elbow electrify elevate elude emancipate embark embarrass embed embellish embody embrace embroil emerge emit empower empty enable enact enamor encase enchant enclose encompass encounter encroach endanger endow endure energize engage enhance enlarge enliven enrich enslave entangle enthuse entomb entrap entrench entwine envelop envision equip eradicate erase erode erupt escalate escape escort etch evacuate evade evaporate evict excavate excise excite exclude excrete exhale exhaust exhilarate exhume expand expel expire explode exploit explore expose exterminate extract exude eye eyeball

F

fabricate face fade fail fake fall fan fancy fantasize farm fascinate fashion fasten father fatigue favor fear feast feature feed feel feign fell fend (off, for) ferret (out) ferry fertilize fester fetch fetter feud fight file fill filter find finesse finger fire fish fit fix fizz fizzle flake flame flank flare (up) flash flatten flaunt flavor flee flex flicker flinch fling flip flirt float flock flog flood floor

flop flounder flourish flow flower fluff flush flutter fly foam focus fog foil fold fondle fool
(with, around) forage forbear force foresee foretell forge fork form fortify fossilize fracture
frame frazzle free freeload freeze freshen frighten frolic frost froth frown fruit fudge fuel
fumble fume funnel fuse fuss

G

gab gabble gaff gag gallop gamble (on) gape garble gas gash gasp gather gauge gawk gaze
gel generate germinate gesture giggle girdle glance glare glaze gleam glide glimmer glisten
glitter glow glue glut gnarl gnash goad gobble goof gore gorge gouge grab grapple grasp
grate gratify gravitate graze grease greet grieve grill grin grind grip gripe grit groan groom
groove grope group growl grub grumble grunt guard guide gulp gum (up) gurgle gush gut
guzzle gyrate

H

hack haggle halt halve hammer hamper hand handcuff handle hang harbor harden harm
harmonize harness harp hassle hatch hate haul haunt hawk hazard haze head heal heap heat
heave heckle hedge heighten herd hew (out) hiss hit hitch hobble hog hogtie hoist hollow
(out) hone hood hoof hook hoot hop horrify horse (around) hose hound house hover howl
huddle hug hum humidify humiliate hunger (for) hunt hurdle hurl hurt hush hustle hydrate
hydroplane hypnotize

I

ice ignite illuminate image imagine imbue imitate immerse immigrate immobilize impair
impale impede implant implode implore imprint imprison improvise inbreed incapacitate
incarcerate inch incite incubate induce indulge inebriate infect inflame inflate inflict infuriate
infuse ingest inhale inhibit inject injure ink inlay inoculate inscribe insert inspect install
instill insulate intensify interact interbreed intercept interfere interfold interlace interlink
interlock interplay interrupt intersperse intertwine interweave intoxicate intrude inundate
invade invert investigate invigorate ionize irrigate irritate isolate itch

J

jab jabber jack jacket jackknife jail jam jangle jar jaunt jaw jeer jell jerk jest jet jiggle jimmy
jingle jitter jog join jolt jostle jot (down) journey juggle jumble jump junk jut (out) juxtapose

K

kayak kick kill kink kiss knead knee kneel knife knit knock knot knuckle (down, under)

L

label labor lace lacerate ladle lag lance land lap lash (out) lasso latch lather laugh launch layer leach lead leak lean leap lecture leer leg (out) level liberate lie lift light limp line linger lip litter liven load lob lock lodge log long (for) loom loop loosen lounge love lower lubricate lug lull lumber lump lunge lurch lure lurk

M

madden magnify maim mangle map mar march marinate mark (up) marry martyr marvel mash mask masquerade massacre massage master mate mature maul meander meet meld mellow melt mend merge mesh mesmerize migrate milk mill (around) mime mimic mince mingle miniaturize moan mob mock model moisten mold molest molt monkey (with, around) mop (up) mother motion motor mottle mount mourn mouth move mow muck (around) muddle muffle mug mulch mumble munch murder murmur muscle mush mushroom muster mute mutilate mutter muzzle mystify

N

nab nag nail nap narrow navigate near needle nest nestle net nibble nip nod nose notice nourish nudge numb number nurse nurture nuzzle

O

oar obscure obstruct offend oil ooze open operate oppose orbit originate ornament orphan oscillate ostracize oust outclass outcrop outdistance outdo outfit outgrow outlive outmaneuver outmatch outrage outreach outrun outshine outsmart outsoar outspeak outspread outstay outstretch outstrip outtalk outwear outweigh outwit outwork overact overcome overcrowd overdo overdress overexpose overflow overhang overhear overindulge overlap overlay overload overlook overnight overpower overproduce overreact overrun oversee overshadow overshoot oversleep overtake overtax overthrow overturn overuse overwhelm overwork

P

pace pacify pack package pad paddle pain paint pair pale palm pamper pan panhandle panic pant pantomime parade parallel paralyze parch pare park part partition party paste pat patch patrol patter pause pave pawn peak peck pedal peddle peel peep peer peg pellet pelt pen pencil penetrate pepper perch percolate perforate perform perfume perish perk (up) permeate persevere persist personify perspire perturb peruse pervade pester pet petrify pickle picture piddle pierce piggyback pile pilfer pillage pilot pin pinch pine pioneer pipe pirate pitch pivot place plague plant plaster plate platoon play plead please plot plow pluck plug plummet plump (up, out) plunder plunge plunk poach pocket point poise poison polish pollute pommel ponder pool pop pore portage portion pose position post pounce pound pour powder power powwow pray preach preen press pressure prevail prey prime prize probe prod project prop (up) propel protect protrude prowl prune pry pucker puff pull pulsate pulverize pummel pump punch punish purge purify purr push pussyfoot putrefy puzzle

Q

quack quadruple quaff quake quarantine quarrel quarry quarter quash quaver quell quench quibble quicken quiet quintuple quip quit quiver quiz

R

race rack radiate raft rage raid rail rain raise rake rally ram ramble rampage ramrod ranch rankle ransack rant rap rape rasp rat rattle ravage rave ravel ravish razz react ream reap rebel rebound rebuke recede recline recoil recover recuperate reduce reek reel reflect reforest refresh refuel regain regenerate regret regulate regurgitate rehabilitate rehash rehearse reign reinforce rejuvenate relax release relent relieve relinquish relish remain remedy remodel remove render renew renounce renovate reopen repair repeat repel replace replenish replicate reply report repress reprieve reproach reproduce repulse rescue research resemble reshape reside resist resonate respond rest restore restrain restrict resume resurrect retain retake retaliate retard retire retort retouch retrace retract retreat retrieve return reunite revamp reveal revel reverberate reverse revive revolt revolve reward rework rhyme rib ribbon ricochet rid riddle ride ridge ridicule riffle rifle rift rig right rim ring rinse riot rip ripen ripple rise risk rival rivet roam roar roast rob robe rock rocket roll roller-coaster romance romanticize romp room roost root rope rot rotate round rouse rout rove row rub (down) ruffle ruin rumble rummage run rupture rush rust rustle rut

S

sabotage sack sacrifice safeguard sag sail salivate salt salvage sample sand sandbag sandblast sandwich sanitize sap sass satiate satisfy saturate saunter sauté save savor saw scaffold scald scale scalp scamper scan scar scare scarf scathe scatter scavenge scent school scintillate scoff scold scoop scorch scorn scour scout scowl scrabble scram scramble scrap scrape scratch scrawl scream screech screen screw scribble scribe scrimp script scroll scrub scrunch scrutinize scuff scuffle sculpt sculpture scurry scuttle seal seam sear search season seat seclude second-guess secrete section secure sedate seduce seed seek seep seethe segment segregate seize send sense sensitize separate serenade serpentine serve set settle sever shackle shade shadow shake shampoo shape sharpen shatter shave shear shed sheer shell shelter shelve shepherd shield shift shim shimmer shin shine shingle shinny ship shiver shock shoot shore (up) short-circuit shorten shoulder shout shove shovel show shower shred shriek shrill shrink shrivel shroud shrug shuck shudder shuffle shun shush shut (up) shuttle shy (away) sicken sideline sideslip sidestep sidetrack sift sigh sight sign signal silence simmer simulate sin sing singe sink sip siphon sire sit situate size (up) sizzle skate skeletonize sketch skew skewer ski skid skim skin skip skirmish skirt skitter skunk sky slacken slam slant slap slash slaughter slay sled sledge sleep (on, off) sleigh slice slick(en) slide slime sling slip slit slither slobber slog slop slope slosh slouch slough slow slug slum slump slur slurp smack smart smash smear smell smile smirk smoke smooth smooth talk smother smudge snack snag snake snap snare snarl snatch sneak sneer sneeze snicker sniff sniffle snip snitch snoop snooze snore snorkel snort snow snowball snowshoe snuff (out) snuggle soak (up) soapbox soar sob sober (up) sock sod soft-pedal soften soil soldier solidify soot soothe sop sound sour souse sow space spade span spank spar spare spark sparkle spatter spawn spear speckle speed spell spellbind spend spew spice (up) spike spill spin spindle spiral spit splash splice splint split splotch spoil sponge spoof spoon spoon-feed spot spout sprawl spray spread spring springboard sprinkle sprout spruce (up) spume spur spurt sputter spy squabble squall squash squat squawk squeak squeal squeeze squelch squint squirrel (around) squirm squirt squish stab stabilize stack stage stagger stain stake stalk stall stammer stamp stampede stand stare starve stash station stay steal steam steep steepen steer stench step (up) sterilize stew stick stiff stiffen stifle still stimulate sting stink (up) stir (up) stitch stoke stomach stomp stone stonewall stoop storm stow straddle straggle straighten strain strand strap stray streak stream strengthen stress stretch strew stride strike string strip stroke stroll strong-arm struggle strut stub study stuff stumble stump stun stunt stupefy stutter stutter-step stymie subdivide subdue submarine submerge submerse submit (to) subside subvert succumb suck sucker suckle suffer suffocate sugarcoat sulk summer summon sun supercharge superimpose supply support suppress surf surface surge surmount surpass surprise surrender surround survey survive suspect suspend sustain suture swab swagger swallow swamp swap swarm swash swat sway swear sweat sweep sweeten swell swelter swerve swill swim swindle swing swipe swirl swish switch swivel swoop symbolize sympathize systemize

T

tack tackle tag tail tailor take tally tame tamp tamper (with) tan tangle tantalize tap tape taper target tarnish taste tatter tattle tattoo taunt tax taxi teach team (up) tear tear (up) [cry] tease teem teeter telegraph tell temper tempt tense (up) tent terminate terrace terrify terrorize test testify tether texture thatch thaw thicken thin think thirst thrash thread threaten thrill thrive throb throttle throw thrust thud thumb thump thunder thwart tick tickle tie tighten till tilt time ting tinge tingle tinker tint tip tiptoe tire titillate toast toboggan toddle toggle toil tolerate tomahawk tone (up, down) tongue tool toot top topple torch torment torpedo torture toss tote totter touch tour tow towel tower toy trace track traffic trail train tramp trample transcend transfer transform transmit transplant transport trap trash travel traverse tread treat tree trek tremble trench trespass trick trickle trigger trill trim trip triple trisect triumph trouble trounce trowel truck trudge trumpet truncate tuck tug tumble tune (up, out) tunnel turn tutor twang tweet twiddle twine twinge twinkle twirl twist twitch

U

unarm unbalance unbind unbolt unbox unbuckle unclench unclothe uncoil uncork uncouple uncover uncross undercut underdo underdress underfeed undergo underlay undermine underscore undress undulate unearth unfasten unfold unfurl unharness unhinge unhitch unhook unify unite unlace unlatch unleash unlink unload unlock unmask unmuffle unmuzzle unnerve unpack unpin unravel unroll unscramble unscrew unseat unsettle unsnap unsnarl unstick unstrap unstring untangle unthread untie untwist unveil unwind unwrap upraise uproot upset upstage upturn urge urinate usher usurp utter

V

vacate vaccinate vacillate validate vandalize vanish vanquish vaporize varnish vault veer vegetate veil vent ventilate venture (in, into) verbalize verify veto vex vibrate view vindicate violate visit visualize vitalize vivify vocalize voice void vomit vote vow voyage vulgarize

W

wad waddle wade waffle wag wager waggle wail wait waken wale walk wallop wallow wander wane want war warble ward (off) warm warn warp wash watch water wave wax weaken wean wear (in, on, out) weasel (out) weather weave wedge weed weep weigh weld well (up, forth) welt wet whack whap wheel wheeze whet whiff whimper whine whinny whip whir whirl whish whisk whisper whistle whitewash whittle whiz whoop widen widow wield wiggle wigwag wile (away) will wilt win wince winch wind wing wink winter winterize wipe wire witch withdraw wither withhold witness wobble wolf wonder woo word work worm worry wow wrack wrangle wrap wreathe wreck wrench wrest wrestle wriggle wring wrinkle write wrong

X

x-ray

Y

yak yammer yank yap yard yarn yawn yearn yellow yelp yen yield yip yodel

Z

zap zero (in) zigzag zing zip zone zonk (out) zoom

APPENDIX 3

Results of a Thought-Listing Procedure
for a "Theme-Title-Only" Message

Theme that guided development of this interpretive product:

It's plausible that some people alive today will still be around to hear the sad news that the last polar bear in the wild has died.

Respondent	Thoughts Expressed *The main thing I take away from the polar bear message is that …*	Within ZOT	Outside ZOT
1	the polar bear is suffering from climate change – likely to go for extinction in a not too distant future.	X	
	the polar bear is a strong symbolic animal for the giant loss of biodiversity following human impact on the ecosystems. "Extinct Is Forever" as it says on the t-shirts from WWF.	X	
2	the future of the Arctic and the earth's climate are both melting beneath the bear's paws.	X	
3	the bear is thinking "I'm standing on thin ice."	X	
4	this might be goodbye for the polar bear. With global warming and dissipating ice sheets / hunting grounds.	X	
	the bear is saying "goodbye and thanks for the fish."	X	
	friends are parting and one is wondering whether they'll see each other again.	X	
5	we are asking a question about whether or not polar bears will be around forever. "Goodbye?" Meaning, will they last?	X	
6	**I may live to see the polar bear become extinct.**	X	
7	the polar bear is on the verge of extinction for loss of habitat (due to global warming, melting of ice caps or other ice areas).	X	
8	polar bears may be extinct soon (due to climate change).	X	
9	I am overcome with a feeling of sadness due to the impending sense of doom.	X	

10	I'd think I was leaving Alaska or a national park and they were being friendly and saying goodbye		X
	if it were in a different location, I'd probably see it as a warning sign to stay away from bears.		X
	because of a WWF television advertisement here in Australia about climate change that uses polar bears I might also think it was trying to tell me that they were disappearing.	X	
11	we're losing control of our planet and now find ourselves facing great uncertainty.	X	
12	the polar bear is on the verge of extinction, and I will no longer see them in the wild.	X	
	I don't engage emotionally with the imagery or the typography enough to really move me.		X
13	it's too late and I will have to get used to a world without polar bears. Goodbye.	X	
	it could be an exit sign at a location that might provoke additional thought. Like on an Alaska cruise or a zoo trip.		X
14	we need to act!	X	
15	the human species too easily and too often disregards and downplays the effects that its actions (or inaction) have on the natural world and other species.	X	
16	we can avoid the polar bear's extinction.	X	
17	the polar bear may go extinct with global warming.	X	
18	the poor animal's world is about to disintegrate beneath its feet and it has nowhere else to go. Come to think of it, neither do we.	X	

19	I feel pain in the gut sadness if true, but then there must be something we can do.	X	
20	uncertainty about who is speaking and whether the word has been spoken, or heard, or whispered.	X	
21	the polar bear's environment is endangered.	X	
22	polar bears are facing problems with the melting Arctic ice, and I probably should have a closer look at my contribution to the greenhouse effect.	X	
23	someone is trying to provoke a conservation message.		X
24	polar bears must be threatened or endangered.	X	
25	climate change is adversely affecting polar bears, and their very existence as a species may even be threatened	X	
26	we have given up the fight and are now disconnected from the issues surrounding the survival of the bear.		X
27	polar bears may disappear, and I'd have to wonder why (if I didn't already know).	X	
28	the polar bear is disappearing along with its habitat.	X	
29	I'd like to know what the bear is thinking. Nature is incredible!		X
30	I feel sad upon seeing this.	X	
31	I'm sad and I need to fight for this bear.	X	
32	global warming is endangering polar bears to the point of possible extinction.	X	

33	man is such an arrogant animal.	X	
	this event was not started by anyone living today, but as we go forward, we who are here to witness it must pass the lesson along to those who come later.	X	
34	the bear is asking the human population whether they (the humans) are still working to save whatever ice/habitat remains. I see it as the bear asking whether he/she should say goodbye.	X	
	the bear's fate is in the hands of humankind; the bear is at the mercy of decisions made by humans.	X	
35	as the polar bear's environment becomes compromised, so does the polar bear.	X	
36	the polar bear is telling us their habitat is disappearing.	X	
37	polar bears are on thin ice and threatened as a species, as a consequence of global climate change.	X	
38	global warming is impacting the habitat of polar bears, and unless we do something, their future survival is under threat.	X	
39	extinction is looming (for the polar bear).	X	
40	polar bears as we know them will be extinct unless something changes. However, it doesn't look like it will.	X	
41	sad things are happening to wildlife, and I don't want to think about it.	X	
	sad things are happening to wildlife, and I need to do something about it.	X	
42	polar bears may be extinct soon, due to global warming.	X	
43	the loss of such an animal would be sad beyond description.	X	

44	the natural environment for polar bears is disappearing and that this species is endangered and could be on the verge of extinction if its habitat is not safeguarded.	X	
45	this might be the last polar bear on the planet.	X	
46	we know polar bears are in danger of going extinct. Do we still have time to prevent their habitat from disappearing altogether?	X	
47	polar bears are outta here if we don't do something soon.	X	
48	if humans don't stop what they're doing to this planet, this amazing animal will be gone forever.	X	
49	the bear is as sad to leave us as we will be to see it go.	X	
50	the bear wonders if we're telling it that it has to go (very sad)	X	
51	the polar bear is endangered.	X	
52	polar bears need people to do something about global warming and the melting of the polar ice.	X	
53	we don't have much time left to save the polar bear.	X	
54	the bear is possibly going to go extinct soon.	X	
55	the polar bear is close to being extinct for loss of habitat because of global warming caused by humans.	X	
56	without some drastic action soon, this incredible creature will be gone and my children will never see one (except in books)!	X	
57	polar bears are in danger.	X	
58	it doesn't have to turn out this way. We can still save the polar bear.	X	

59	polar bears will most likely be extinct soon if we don't get our act together.	X	
	we are such a dumb and arrogant species.	X	
60	the polar bear is in danger of going extinct.	X	
61	some animals are on thin ice.	X	
62	we shouldn't be afraid of bears.		X
63	somewhere along the line humans became the stupidest of all species.	X	
64	without our help, polar bears will probably be extinct in the very near future.	X	
65	global warming might cause the extinction of the polar bear.	X	
66	the future of the polar bear is in question.	X	
67	the bear is asking us to please help it.	X	
68	mankind erases another one.	X	
69	we are on the verge of losing this species.	X	

APPENDIX 4

Captive versus Noncaptive Audiences— How the Idea Originated

Captive and Noncaptive Audiences
A Story about How I Arrived at the Idea and What I Mean by It

ADAPTED FROM: Ham, Sam H. (2005). Captive and Noncaptive Audiences. A Story about How I Arrived at the Idea and What I Meant by It. *Journal of the Spanish Association for Heritage Interpretation* 13 (August): 2-4.

I invented the terms captive audience and noncaptive audience in 1971, when I was a twenty-year old undergraduate student taking my first interpretation course at Washington State University in the United States. One of our first assignments was to write a paper about what made interpretation "different" from other forms of information transfer. Even as a young student, I knew that this was a false premise. I saw nothing special or different about interpretation as a "kind" of communication. I reasoned that the human mind is the human mind. It doesn't change physiologically when we go from home to park to school to the supermarket to the movie to the beach to the museum. It is the same mind in every place. So communicating with that mind must too be the same in all of those places. Interpretation, as I saw it then and now, was not different in kind. Journalists, advertisers, marketers, teachers, salespeople, lawyers, politicians, preachers, song writers, play writers, screen writers, movie producers, poets, and novelists—anyone who communicates purposefully—is faced with the same human "mind-audience." Interpretation, I realized, was just another word to add to the list.

Yet, as an interpreter, I knew there was some other kind of difference that I just hadn't seen yet. Interpreters everywhere know that there is something different about interpretation! And so I continued looking for an answer until I found it in psychology. There I discovered something that has guided and informed my understanding of interpretation for more than three decades. I learned that what is different about interpretation isn't the audience or the "kind" of communication that takes place. What is different is how the audience sees things. It's their mind-set or mental state that distinguishes interpretation from some other forms of information transfer. Interpretation usually takes place where people go to have fun (parks, museums, zoos, botanical gardens, aquariums, theme parks, and so forth). It's their goal of enjoying themselves while learning that makes interpretation different from some other communication activities. This realization motivated me to continue working on the assignment.

Remembering Tilden's dichotomy that "interpretation is provocation, not instruction," and recalling that even his definition of interpretation stressed that it is "not simply communicating factual information," I found what I had been looking for in order to write my paper. Tilden was so emphatic about contrasting interpretation with teaching because he feared that fact-bearing interpreters would see it as "instruction." He knew that visitors would not respond well to that sort of interpretation because it didn't fit with their purpose for being in a park. They didn't see parks as classrooms but rather as pleasuring grounds. The difference I looked for lay not in the kind of communication that interpretation is, nor was it in the kinds of audiences that visitors are. Rather it lay in the psychological state they brought with them to the interpretive encounter.

Thinking more deeply about it, I envisioned a single human being, a woman, in many different communication environments. I instantly realized that this same woman could, in a single (albeit very long) day, attend class at the university, read a magazine at home, be a member of a jury, be approached by a salesperson, listen to a song on the car radio, and attend an interpretive program in a local park that evening. One cannot refute the fact that in each case, it was the same person with the same mind. But obviously, many things were different about the communication environments. The context was different (classroom versus courtroom versus home, car, or park). The kinds of outcomes the communicator sought were different in each case (academic performance, entertainment with words or music, purchase of the product, a vote to convict or acquit, and of course, for the interpreter, provocation). And finally, the rules of engagement were different (teachers and students are expected to interact in certain ways and not others, lawyers must follow strict rules about argumentation and presenting evidence, the writers of the magazine and song could not even see their audiences, and the interpreter would face an informal pleasure-seeking audience who would be accepting of many communication styles as long as it could be inspired about the park).

As I thought more about these differences of contexts, outcomes and "rules" of communication, I began to put them into categories of "alike" and "different," based on the role the person played in each environment. When I was done categorizing them, I was left with a result similar to this:

Alike: jury member, reader at home, driver of a car, and park visitor

Different: student

At first not even realizing what criteria I had applied in making the lists, I was dumbfounded by how much work it had taken me to arrive at such a simple solution, one that would surely earn me a high mark on my paper. When the same woman was in any of the "alike" roles, she didn't have to have to worry about grades and marks and qualifications. She could even ignore the communication, or let her mind wander, without fear of punishment. In each of these cases, she would choose of her own free will to pay attention, or not at all. Her reward for attention paying came from within her: it was internal. But in the classroom, if she failed to pay attention she would be punished by a system external to her, and if she paid close attention she would be rewarded by the same system. At this point, the notion of external versus internal rewards had become a sort of "axis" in my thinking. But where would I take it from there?

Being a student at the time, I realized that the promise of reward or threat of punishment was like a prison. We are held captive by an external reward system (such as grades and academic assessment), whereas when we don't have to worry about punishments and external rewards, it is only our intrinsic satisfaction with the communication itself that leads us to attend to it. In one instance we are "captive" and in the other we are "noncaptive." This difference is psychological. It is not the reward or punishment itself that makes an audience "captive." It is the person's understanding and acceptance of it that creates the prison. I thought of one of my classmates, a good guy, but he didn't care about his grades. This was the "rebellious" 70s, and he was in the class purely for his intrinsic enjoyment of the subject matter—even if he failed, it mattered little to him. Sitting next to him in class a few days after turning in my paper, I realized that he was a noncaptive audience and I was a captive one, even though we were in the same class learning from the same teacher. The external rewards I sought (a good grade, a job recommendation from my teacher, and being respected as a "good" student) were literally of no interest to him. He was just there to be stimulated by the information regardless of what kind of evaluation he received. At the end of the semester, we both earned very high marks in the class, and both of us have enjoyed long careers as interpreters.

The key difference I had been looking for had turned out to be psychological, not physical in any way. It is how the audience sees the communication environment that makes interpretation different from some (but not all) other forms of communication. And so the communicator must understand the mental state of the audience and adjust his or her approach according to the way the person's mind sees the context of the communication environment. In the case of the noncaptive audience, we must work diligently to capture and hold attention if we want to achieve our goal of provocation.

At some point the night I began writing my paper, I typed the words captive and noncaptive for the first time in my life. And they have been part of my vocabulary ever since. I wrote briefly about the concept in a 1983 journal article on cognitive psychology and interpretation, but I did not introduce it in writing to practicing interpreters until 1992, when I published *Environmental Interpretation.*

Since publication of that book, I have been amazed with the amount of confusion that this simple concept has sometimes created. The biggest error interpreters make with the idea is that they think that captive and noncaptive refer to different kinds of people. They clearly are not kinds of people. As you saw in my little story, the same person can be both kinds of audiences in a single day. A second mistake interpreters make is thinking of captive and noncaptive as though they were different kinds of places. They clearly are not places either. The person in our example could attend the evening interpretive program as a visitor and then return to the same park the next day with her university biology class as a student—noncaptive the night before and captive the next morning. And, of course, my classmate and I sat next to each other in the same classroom, one of us captive and one of us noncaptive at the same moment in time. Finally, and this is most important, interpreters must not make the error of assuming that only park interpretation audiences are noncaptive. This is not true. All audiences who are free to ignore us (without fear either of punishment or having to forfeit a reward), are noncaptive. This includes virtually every audience outside of academia or other instructional setting in which people are held accountable to demonstrate their own learning (e.g., to earn a grade or mark of some kind, a qualification, formal certificate, or license, and so on). In this sense, all the great novelists, journalists, song writers, advertisers, and the rest are interpreters. They just work in different contexts than most heritage interpreters work in.

In ending, I want to share a little secret. But it is a secret that will come as no surprise to many of you. Every audience—even the student in a classroom preparing for an exam—is biologically noncaptive. Our brains have programmed themselves through eons of evolution to seek the most gratifying stimuli they can find, and they engage during every moment throughout our lives in a never-ending quest for enjoyment of some kind—pleasurable thought. This is why students who are bored by their teacher have to work so hard to pay attention. They must overcome what their minds are programmed to do—provide enjoyable stimulation. And when their minds prevail in the battle, they may find themselves daydreaming in class. So to my fellow educators, I want to leave you with this piece of advice: Even though your students are a captive audience who are held prisoner by the external rewards academia imposes on them, you will teach them more, and they will love you forever, if you treat them every day as if they were a noncaptive audience. Work hard to make them want to learn from you, as if they had a choice—as they would if they were park visitors attending your interpretive program. Some of the best interpreters on earth are classroom teachers who simply choose to see things this way.

Post-script: I recall that my teacher liked the paper.

Sam H. Ham, Ph.D.

Professor of Communication Psychology

Director of the Center for International Training and Outreach, University of Idaho

September 1, 2005

Moscow, Idaho, United States

References

Ham, S. (1992). *Environmental interpretation—A practical guide for people with big ideas and small budgets.* Golden, Colorado, USA: Fulcrum Publishing.

Ham, S. (1983). Cognitive psychology and interpretation—synthesis and application. *Journal of Interpretation* 8(1): 11-27.

Tilden, F. (1957). *Interpreting our heritage.* Chapel Hill, North Carolina, USA: University of North Carolina Press.

GLOSSARY OF KEY TERMS

Glossary terms appear in **boldface** in each chapter.

Analogy: A bridging technique that shows many similarities between an object of interest and something else that's already familiar to an audience.

Attitude: A person's positive or negative evaluation of something (e.g., as good or bad, desirable or undesirable). The "something" is called the attitude object.

Attitude object: A specific thing, person, place, or concept toward which a person can have an attitude. Since people have attitudes about doing or not doing certain things, a specific behavior can also be an attitude object.

Audience side of theme: The impact a communicator's well-developed theme can have in an audience member's mind. Also called "results side."

Belief: A person's perception that a particular thing has certain attributes or characteristics. In the reason action model, a *behavioral* belief is a person's perception that a given behavior will lead to a certain consequence and that person's evaluation of the consequence; a *normative* belief is an individual's perception of (1) whether important others approve or disapprove of a given behavior, (2) the extent to which the individual's social referents themselves engage in the behavior, and (3) how motivated the individual is to comply with the wishes of important others; and a *control* belief is a person's perception as to whether certain factors or circumstances exist that would make performing the behavior easier or more difficult and how much easier or more difficult each factor makes doing the behavior.

Browsers: An audience segment assumed to spend more than six and up to about twenty or thirty seconds viewing or reading a nonsequential interpretive product.

Captive audience: An audience consisting of people who feel obligated to pay attention to a presentation even if it requires a lot of effort or bores them.

Closure: The point at which people in an audience sense a sequential presentation has ended and that nothing remains to be said (i.e., there are no loose ends). See also "prägnanz."

Contrast: A bridging technique that compares the major similarities and/or differences between the thing you're talking about and something else that can easily be related to it.

CREATES: An acronym developed by Ward and Wilkinson (2006) to help interpreters remember the elements of an effective message. Respectively, the letters stand for *Connects, Relevant, Enjoyable, Appropriate, Thematic, Engaging,* and *Structured.*

Develop (a theme): To substantiate or flesh out a theme by presenting information that supports and expands on it.

Difference: TORE-quality interpretation typically is claimed to be able to make three kinds of differences: (1) enhancing audience experiences, (2) creating appreciative attitudes about something, and (3) influencing audience behavior.

Edutainment: Education that is entertaining (ORE), or alternatively, entertainment that is educational. See also "entertainment" and "infotainment."

Elaboration: A term used in psychology to refer to effortful thought. Synonyms are *pondering*, *contemplating*, *deliberating*, and *wondering*. Provocation leads to elaboration.

Emergent theme model: A model of sequential theme development in which a communicator expresses the theme itself *only* in the conclusion.

Endgame: A term used to describe the status or condition of things when some process or event has reached a successful conclusion.

Enjoyable: A quality interpretation has when it's pleasing to an audience to attend to and process.

Entertainment: Information that is O, R, and E (organized, relevant, and enjoyable to process). Information that strongly holds attention, literally "engaging" an audience. See also "edutainment" and "infotainment."

EROT framework: An acronym developed by Ham (1992) to help interpreters remember the four qualities communication must have in order to hold an audience's attention and make a compelling point. Respectively, the letters stand for *Enjoyable, Relevant, Organized,* and *Thematic.*

EROTIC: An acronym developed by Ross, Siepen, and O'Connor (2003) to help distance educators remember the qualities of a good distance education program.

Example: A bridging technique wherein an interpreter quickly refers to something or someone that is like or in some way represents that kind of thing or person he or she is talking about.

Extrapolation: A type of conclusion that attempts to provoke audiences to think beyond the theme, and to extend the theme to a bigger picture or wider sphere of things.

Foreshadowing: A sequential technique in which a communicator hints at what is to come next or later in a presentation. Foreshadowing is often used to create curiosity or a sense of anticipation about what follows.

Global theme: The overall or overarching theme of an interpretive product. A subtheme develops some aspect or dimension of a global theme. That is, the subthemes of an interpretive product (should you include any at all) "add up to" the all-encompassing global theme.

Implicit theme model: A model of sequential theme development in which a communicator fully develops a theme but *never* expresses it in words to the audience.

Infotainment: Information that is entertaining (ORE), or alternatively, entertainment that is informative. Infotainment has high provocation likelihood but lacks a thematic focus. In its original usage, *infotainment* referred to "soft news." See also "edutainment" and "provocation likelihood."

Intangible meaning: An attribute of something that cannot be objectively verified through one of the senses. Intangible meanings are symbolic; they describe what something represents to a person, and they rely more on metaphor and subjective association than logic.

Intention side of theme: Refers to a communicator's use of a theme to guide decisions about content and focus—what to include, what to exclude, what to emphasize, and what to deemphasize. Also called "interpreter's side."

Interpretainment: A phrase coined by US National Park Service interpreter Bob Roney to mean interpretation designed primarily to entertain park visitors. See Larsen (2003).

Interpretation: Defined in this book as: A mission-based approach to communication aimed at provoking in audiences the discovery of personal meaning and the forging of personal connections with things, places, people, and concepts.

Interpreter: Anyone who does any kind of communication (face-to-face or nonpersonal) following the approached outlined in this book. Interpreters can include speakers, writers, designers, artists, staff at parks, zoos, museums, historic sites, tour operators, cruise ship companies, science centers, botanical gardens, forests, aquariums, wineries, breweries, theme parks, and manufacturing plants, as well as guides, expedition leaders, docents, storytellers, composers, musicians, dramatists, directors, actors, and performers of all kinds.

Interpreter side of theme: Refers to a communicator's use of a theme to guide decisions about content and focus—what to include, what to exclude, what to emphasize, and what to deemphasize. Also called "intention side."

Interpretive approach: A way of communicating that strives to make information thematic, organized, relevant, and enjoyable to process (TORE).

Interpretive encounter: Any act of communication following the interpretive approach (both face-to-face and nonpersonal).

Interpretive product: Any finished interpretive program or device.

Knockan theory: A tool for adding interest to topics that are low in inherent interest for a given audience. Applying Knockan theory involves connecting a low-interest topic to something else considered to be more inherently interesting for the audience.

Labeling: A communication technique in which new information is presented to people in the context of some social group they either associate themselves with or disassociate themselves from.

Magical number 4: According to studies by Cowan (2001), the maximum number of separate ideas most people can manage simultaneously without getting lost or being overwhelmed is four.

Meaningful: Information is meaningful when people in an audience can understand it in terms of something they already know.

Mental task: A sequential technique in which a communicator gives the audience something to do and think about—usually between stops of a guided interpretive encounter such as a tour or guided walk.

Metaphor: A statement that describes something with a word or phrase that is ordinarily used to describe a very different thing.

Nested-package format: A sequential presentation in which multiple themes are fully developed (each with an introduction, body, and conclusion) *within* the development of an overall (global) theme. Closure occurs following development of each smaller theme as well as following development of the global theme.

Noncaptive audience: An audience consisting of people who voluntarily choose to pay attention to a presentation because they find it gratifying to do so.

Nonsequential communication: Presentations in which people in the audience determine the sequence of information they pay attention to. Most forms of nonpersonal interpretation such as exhibits, websites, signs, and so forth involve nonsequential communication.

One-package format: A sequential presentation in which a communicator develops and brings closure to a single strong theme via an introduction, body, and conclusion. It's the conventional format most thematic interpreters are accustomed to using.

One-sentence rule: A guideline that says every theme should be expressed in a single sentence. Following the one-sentence rule is often a good idea, but *not* always.

Organized: Information is organized when it's presented in a way that's easy for an audience to follow. Information presented in four or fewer relevant ideas is said to be organized.

Personal: Information is personal when it makes a connection to something an audience cares about. The more the thing matters to them, the more personal the information is.

Personal theme(s): The subjective meaning(s) an individual makes as a result of exposure to an interpretive encounter. Synonyms include thoughts, morals of the story, conclusions, inferences, impressions, messages, ideas, main points, and so forth. A strong, well-developed theme can give rise to many personal themes in an individual's mind.

POETRY: An acronym developed by Brochu and Merriman (2008, 2012) to help interpreters remember the elements of professional interpretation. Respectively, the letters stand for *Purposeful, Organized, Enjoyable, Thematic, Relevant,* and *You.*

Prägnanz: A type of closure in which audiences feel things have come full circle, as when the ending of a sequential presentation reminds them in some way of something they heard or saw in the beginning. See also "closure."

Principle of Compatibility: A principle from social psychology saying that for communication to impact a person's attitude about virtually anything it must succeed in impacting the person's belief(s) about that same thing. See also "attitude object."

Provocation: The point at which a person is stimulated to think personal thoughts about something being presented. It can also mean "high elaboration likelihood."

Provocation likelihood: The probability that interpretation will provoke an audience to think. Also, the probability that a theme will provoke thinking. When a theme is both easy to process and relevant for the audience, provocation likelihood is high. See also "strong theme."

Provocation path: A pathway to impacting attitudes that involves effortful thought (i.e., elaboration) from the audience. Same as "strong path." (Called the "central route to persuasion" in the elaboration likelihood model and "systematic processing" in the heuristic-systematic processing model.)

Quick path: A pathway to impacting attitudes that involves relatively little thought (i.e., low elaboration) from the audience. Same as "weak path." (Called the "peripheral route to persuasion" in the elaboration likelihood model and "heuristic processing" in the heuristic-systematic processing model.)

Recapitulation: A type of conclusion that summarizes the key points made earlier in the body.

Relevant: A quality information has when it connects to something we already care about. In other words, relevant information is both meaningful and personal.

Results side of theme: The impact a communicator's well-developed theme can have in an audience member's mind. Also called "audience side."

Sandwich theme model: A model of sequential theme development in which a communicator expresses the theme itself *both* in the introduction and conclusion. A sequential presentation developed using the sandwich model has built-in prägnanz. See "prägnanz."

Self-referencing: A communication technique in which new information is presented to people at the same time they're asked to think about their own experiences related to it.

Sequential communication: Any presentation in which a communicator controls the order in which the audience receives information. Almost any kind of face-to-face interpretive encounter is sequential.

Serial-package format: A sequential presentation in which an interpreter develops two or more successive themes, *each* with an introduction, body, and conclusion, and *each* brought to closure. The themes might or might not be related to each other, but in either event, the interpreter makes no attempt to tie them together into a larger global theme (as in a nested-theme package).

Simile: A bridging technique in which you make a comparison between two things using words such as *like* or *as*.

Streakers: A very brief audience that typically devotes less than six seconds to viewing or reading a nonsequential interpretive product. Streakers are often a prevalent audience.

Strong path: A pathway to impacting attitudes that involves effortful thought (i.e., elaboration) from the audience. Same as "provocation path." (Called the "central route to persuasion" in the elaboration likelihood model and "systematic processing" in the heuristic-systematic processing model.)

Strong theme: A theme that is both easy to process and relevant. A strong theme has high "provocation likelihood."

Studiers: An audience segment that spends the most time viewing or reading a nonsequential interpretive product (typically more than about thirty seconds).

Subtheme: Part of a global theme. Note that sub*themes* are not sub*topics*. As with any theme, a subtheme is always expressed in a complete declarative sentence.

Suggestion: A type of conclusion that attempts to trigger later reinforcement of a theme by linking it to something people in the audience are likely to encounter or experience within a day or two following a presentation.

Tangible meaning: An attribute of something that can be objectively verified through one of the senses (seeing, hearing, smelling, tasting, or touching). The tangible meanings interpreters impart usually have to do with the scientific, cultural, or historic significance of something they're interpreting (i.e., the reason the thing is special and worthy of attention).

Thematic package: In sequential communication, the conceptual container in which an interpreter develops a theme. Every thematic package involves an introduction, a body, and a conclusion, followed by closure.

Theme: For the interpreter, a theme is the overarching idea she or he is trying to develop. Synonyms are *message*, *main point*, *moral to the story*, and *premise*. For the audience, themes are the thoughts they're provoked to think as a result of interpretation—that is, the conclusions they draw, the inferences they make, the impressions they form, and the personal morals of the story they extract from an interpretive encounter (see also "personal theme").

Theme title: In nonsequential communication, a title or main heading that, in combination with another conspicuous design element, quickly conveys the essence of the theme in a thought-provoking way. A good theme title accomplishes this within a few seconds at most.

Thought listing: A method for assessing the extent to which an interpretive product provokes thoughts in an audience. The greater the number of thoughts falling within your "zone of tolerance," the more successful your interpretive product is. See also "zone of tolerance."

Topic: The subject matter of an interpretive product.

Topic title: A title or main heading that communicates only the subject matter of a nonsequential presentation (such as an exhibit, website, or brochure).

TORE model: A model of thematic communication developed by Ham (2007). The acronym TORE refers to the four qualities communication must have in order to hold an audience's attention and make a compelling point. Respectively, the letters stand for *Thematic*, *Organized*, *Relevant*, and *Enjoyable*.

TORE-quality: Interpretation that (1) has a strong theme, (2) is organized for easy processing, (3) is relevant to the audience, and (4) is enjoyable to process. Only TORE-quality interpretation can *purposefully* (strategically) make the three kinds of differences interpreters usually want to make (i.e., enhancing experiences, impacting attitudes, and influencing behavior).

Transition: A simple connector in a sequential presentation. Transitions tell an audience when the focus of the presentation is going to change. They're important throughout any sequential presentation, but especially between the introduction and body and between the body and the conclusion.

Universal concepts: Intangible or symbolic connections to notions that (as far as we know) have always had special significance to humans everywhere and for all time. Universal concepts include extreme emotions such as love, hate, fear, elation, and sorrow; basic biological imperatives such as birth, death, hunger, and thirst; human fascinations with uncertainty, the cosmos, mystery, and suspense; and many other intangibles.

Weak path: A pathway to impacting attitudes that involves relatively little thought (i.e., low elaboration) from the audience. Same as "quick path." (Called the "peripheral route to persuasion" in the elaboration likelihood model and "heuristic processing" in the heuristic-systematic processing model.)

Zone of tolerance: A subjective area within which an interpreter judges the thoughts provoked by an interpretive product to be acceptable. Thoughts that fall within a communicator's zone of tolerance are considered to be supportive or consistent in some way with the theme the communicator was trying to develop. See also "thought listing."

References

Absher, J. & Bright, A. (2004). Communication research in outdoor recreation and natural resources. In Manfredo, M., Vaske, J., Bruyere, B., Field, D., & Brown, P. (Eds.), *Society and natural resources: a summary of knowledge*. Jefferson, Missouri, USA: Modern Litho, 117-126.

Ajzen, I. (2005). Laws of human behavior: symmetry, compatibility, and attitude-behavior correspondence. In A. Beauducel, A., Biehl, B., Bosniak, M., Conrad, W., Schönberger, G., & Wagener, D. (Eds.), *Multivariate research strategies*. Maastricht, Netherlands: Shaker Publishers, 3-19.

Ajzen, I. (1992). Persuasive communication theory in social psychology: a historical perspective. In Manfredo, M, (Ed.), *Influencing human behavior*. Champaign, Illinois, USA: Sagamore Publishing Co., Inc., 1-27.

Ajzen, I. (1991). The theory of planned behavior. *Organizational Behavior and Human Decision Processes* 50: 179-211.

Ajzen, I., & Driver, B. (1992). Application of the theory of planned behavior to leisure choice. *Journal of Leisure Research* 24(3): 207-224.

Ajzen, I., & Fishbein, M. (2005). The influence of attitudes on behavior. In Albarracín, D., Johnson, B., & Zanna, M. (Eds.), *The handbook of attitudes*. Mahwah, New Jersey, USA: Erlbaum, 173-221.

Ajzen, I. & Fishbein, M. (1980). *Understanding attitudes and predicting social behavior*. Englewood, New Jersey, USA: Prentice-Hall.

Alderson, W. & Low, S. (1976). *Interpretation of historic sites* (2nd edition). Nashville, Tennessee, USA: American Association for State and Local History.

Alvord, V. (2000). Auschwitz disco draws outrage. *USA Today* (October 25): 22A.

Ames, K., Franco, B. & Frye, L. (1997). *Ideas and images—developing interpretive history exhibits.* Creek, California, USA: AltaMira Press.

Anderson, R. & Pitchert, J. (1978). Recall of previously unrecallable information following a shift in perspective. *Journal of Verbal Learning and Verbal Behavior* 17(1): 1-12.

Armstrong, E. & Weiler, B. (2003). They said what to whom?! In Black, R. & Weiler, B. (Eds.), *Interpreting the land down under—Australian heritage interpretation and tour guiding.* Fulcrum Applied Communication Series. Golden, Colorado, USA: Fulcrum Books, 109-127.

Arnould, E. & Price, L. (1993). River magic—extraordinary experience and the extended service encounter. *Journal of Consumer Research* 20: 24-45.

Asociación para la Interpretación del Patrimonio (Spanish Association for Heritage Interpretation). (2012). http://www.interpretaciondelpatrimonio.com/

Association for Heritage Interpretation. (2012). http://www.heritage-interpretation.org.uk/

Ausubel, D. (1960). The use of advance organizers in the learning and retention of meaningful verbal material. *Journal of Educational Psychology* 51: 267-272.

Baars, B. (2002). The conscious access hypothesis: origins and recent evidence. *Trends in Cognitive Sciences* 6(1): 47-52. http://www.nsi.edu/users/baars/other/BaarsTICS2002.pdf

Baars, B. & Franklin, S. (2003). How conscious experience and working memory interact. *Trends in Cognitive Sciences* 7(4): 166-172. http://csrg.cs.memphis.edu/csrg/assets/papers/TICSarticle.pdf

Baddeley, A. (2001). The concept of episodic memory. In Baddeley, A., Conway, M., & Aggleton, J. (Eds.), *Episodic memory—new directions in research.* Oxford: Oxford University Press, 1-10.

Baddeley, A., Conway, M., & Aggleton, J. (Eds.). (2001). *Episodic memory—new directions in research.* Oxford: Oxford University Press.

Ballantyne, R. & Packer, J. (2005). Promoting environmentally sustainable attitudes and behaviour through free-choice learning experiences: what it the state of the game? *Environmental Education Research* 11(3): 281-295.

Ballantyne, R. & Uzzell, D. (1999). International trends in heritage and environmental interpretation—future directions for Australian research and practice. *Journal of Interpretation Research* 4(1): 59-75.

Bamberg, S. (2003). How does environmental concern influence specific environmentally related behaviors? A new answer to an old question. *Journal of Environmental Psychology* 23: 21-32.

Barney, S. (2006). Capitalizing on the self-reference effect in general psychology: A preliminary study. *Journal of Constructivist Psychology* 20: 87-97.

Bass, J, Manfredo, M., Lee, M. & Allen, D. (1989). Evaluation of an informational brochure for promoting charter boat trip opportunities along the Oregon Coast. *Journal of Travel Research* 27(3): 35-37.

Batten, B. (2005). A shared history? Presenting Australia's post-contact indigenous past. *Journal of Interpretation Research* 10(1): 31-48.

Bazeley P. (2007). *Qualitative data analysis with NVivo*. London: Sage Publications.

Beaumont, N. (2001). Ecotourism and the conservation ethic—recruiting the uninitiated or preaching to the converted? *Journal of Sustainable Tourism* 9(4): 317-341.

Beck, L. (2005). Wicked interpretation—lessons from Broadway. *The Interpreter* 1(4): 14-17.

Beck, L. & Cable, T. (2002). The meaning of interpretation. *Journal of Interpretation Research* 7(1): 7-10.

Beck, L. & Cable, T. (1998). *Interpretation for the 21st century—Fifteen guiding principles for interpreting nature and culture*. Champaign, Illinois, USA: Sagamore Publishing.

Beck, L. & Cable, T. (2011). *The gifts of interpretation—Fifteen guiding principles for interpreting nature and culture*. Champaign, Illinois, USA: Sagamore Publishing.

Beckett, S. (1958). *Endgame*. New York: Grove Press.

Bitgood, S. (2000). The role of attention in designing effective interpretive labels. *Journal of Interpretation Research* 5(2): 31-45.

Bitgood, S. (1988). Museum fatigue—early studies. *Visitor Behavior* 3(1): 4-5.

Bitgood, S. & Patterson, D. (1993). The effect of gallery changes on visitor reading and object viewing time. *Environment & Behavior* 25(6): 761-781.

Bitgood, S., Patterson, D. & Benefield, A. (1988). Exhibit design and visitor behavior: Empirical relationships. *Environment and Behavior* 20(4): 474-491.

Bixler, R. (2001). Why we must 'preach to the choir.' *Legacy* 12(6): 33-34.

Blackburn, M. (2004). History, memory and interpretation. *Legacy* 15(5): 32-34.

Blizzard, T. & Ellis, R. (2006). Interpreting slavery in Virginia's colonial capital. *Legacy* 17(1): 24-31.

Bridal, T. (2004). *Exploring museum theatre*. Walnut Creek, California, USA: AltaMira Press.

Brochu, L. (2012). *Interpretive planning* (2nd ed.). Fort Collins, Colorado, USA: Heartfelt Publications.

Brochu, L. & Merriman, T. (2012). *Personal interpretation—connecting your audience to heritage resources* (3rd ed.). Fort Collins, Colorado, USA: Heartfelt Publications.

Brochu, L. & Merriman, T. (2008). *Personal interpretation—connecting your audience to heritage resources* (2ⁿᵈ ed.). Fort Collins, Colorado, USA: Interpress, National Association for Interpretation.

Brody, M., Hall, R., Tomkiewicz, W., & Graves, J. (2002). Park visitors' understandings, values and beliefs related to their experience at Midway Geyser Basin, Yellowstone National Park, USA. *International Journal of Science Education* 24(11): 1119-1141.

Brown, F. & Koran, J. (1998). Learning from ruins—a visitor study at Uxmal. *Curator* 41(2): 121-131.

Brown, P. & Hunt, J. (1969). The influence of information signs on visitor distribution and use. *Journal of Leisure Research* 1(1): 79-83.

Brown, T., Ham, S. & Hughes, M. (2010). Picking up litter: An application of theory-based communication to influence tourist behaviour in protected areas. *Journal of Sustainable Tourism* 18(7): 879-900.

Bryson, B. (2000). *In a sunburned country*. New York: Broadway Books.

Bucy, D. (2005). Applying communication theory to design, location and evaluation of interpretive signs. Ph.D. thesis. Moscow, Idaho, USA: University of Idaho, Department of Conservation Social Sciences.

Cable, T., Knudson, D. & Theobald, W. (1986). The application of the theory of reasoned action to the evaluation of interpretation. *Journal of Interpretation* 11(1): 11-25.

Cable, T., Knudson, D., Udd, E., & Stewart, D. (1987). Attitude change as a result of exposure to interpretive messages. *Journal of Park and Recreation Administration* 5(1): 47-60.

Cacioppo, J. & Petty, R. (1989). Effects of message repetition on argument processing, recall, and persuasion. *Basic and Applied Social Psychology* 10(1): 3-12.

Cameron, C. & Gatewood, J. (2003). Seeking numinous experiences in the unremembered past. *Ethnology* 42(1): 55-71.

Cameron, C. & Gatewood, J. (2000). Excursions into the un-remembered past: what people want from visits to historical sites. *The Public Historian* 22(3):107-127.

Capra, D. (2006). Seven words interpreters should know. *The Interpreter* 2(2): 6-7.\

Caputo, P., Lewis, S., & Brochu, L. (2008). *Interpretation by design: Graphic design basics for heritage interpreters*. Fort Collins, Colorado, USA: InterpPress.

Carter, J. (Ed.). (1997). *A sense of place: An interpretive planning handbook*. Inverness, Scotland: Tourism and Environment Initiative.

Chaiken, S. (1980). Heuristic versus systematic information processing and the use of source versus message cues in persuasion. *Journal of Personality and Social Psychology*, 39(5): 752-766.

Cherry, C. (1966). *On human communication* (2nd ed.). Cambridge, Massachusetts, USA: Massachusetts Institute of Technology.

Cialdini, R. (1996). Activating and aligning two kinds of norms in persuasive communication. *Journal of Interpretation Research* 1(1): 3-10.

Cialdini, R., Kallgren, C., & Reno, R. (1991). A focus theory of normative conduct: A theoretical refinement and reevaluation of the role of norms in human behavior. *Advances in Experimental Social Psychology* 24: 201-234.

Cohen, E. (1985). The tourist guide: the origins, structure and dynamics of a role. *Annals of Tourism Research* 12(1): 5-2.

Colquhoun, F. (Ed.). (2005). *Interpretation handbook and standard—distilling the essence.* Wellington: New Zealand Department of Conservation.

Cowan, N. (2005). *Working memory capacity: Essays in cognitive psychology.* New York, New York, USA: Psychology Press.

Cowan, N. (2001). The magical number 4 in short-term memory: A reconsideration of mental storage capacity. *Behavioral and Brain Sciences* 24: 87-185.

Craik, F. & Tulving, E. (1975). Depth of processing and the retention of words in episodic memory. *Journal of Experimental Psychology* (General) 104: 268-294.

Crocker, J. (1984). A schematic approach to changing consumers' beliefs. *Advances in Consumer Research* 11: 472-477.

Csikszentmihalyi, M. (1996). *Creativity—Flow and the psychology of discovery and invention.* New York, USA: HarperCollins Publishing.

Cunningham, M. (2004). *The interpreter's training manual for museums.* Washington, DC: American Association of Museums.

Curry, A. (2002). The better angels: why we are still fighting over who was right and who was wrong in the Civil War. *US News & World Report* 133(12): 56-63 (September 30).

Curtis, J. (2008). Influencing visitor use of alternative transportation systems in Australian national parks: An application of the theory of planned behaviour. Ph.D. thesis. Berwick, Victoria, Australia: Monash University.

Curtis, J., Ham, S., & Weiler, B. (2010). Identifying beliefs underlying visitor behaviour: A comparative elicitation study based on the theory of planned behaviour. *Annals of Tourism Research* 13(4): 564-589.

Curtis, J., Weiler, B. & Ham, S. (2006). Gaining visitor acceptance of alternative transportation systems in Australian national parks. In O'Mahony, G. & Whitelaw, P. (Eds.), *To the City and Beyond*. Proceedings, Council for Australian University Tourism and Hospitality Education Conference (CAUTHE), 1027-1031.

DeMares, R. & Kryka, K. (1998). Wild-animal-triggered peak experiences. *The Journal of Transpersonal Psychology* 30(2): 161-177.

Dierking, L., Ellenbogen, K., & Falk, J. (2004). In principle, in practice: perspectives on a decade of museum learning research (1994-2004). *Science Education* 88 (Supplement 1): S1-S70.

Doering, Z., Bickford, A., Darns, D. & Kindlon, A. (1999). Communication and persuasion in a didactic exhibition: The *Power of Maps* study. *Curator* 42(2): 88-107.

Egri, L. (1946). *The art of dramatic writing—its basis in the creative interpretation of human motives*. New York: Simon and Schuster.

Eveland, W., Cortese, J., Park, H., & Dunwoody, S. (2004). How website organization influences free recall, factual knowledge, and knowledge structure density. *Human Communication Research* 30(2): 208-233.

Falk, J. (1997). Testing a museum exhibition design assumption—effect of explicit labeling of exhibit clusters on visitor concept development. *Science Education* 81(6): 679-687.

Falk, J. & Dierking, L. (2000). *Learning from museums—visitor experiences and the making of meaning*. Walnut Creek, California, USA: AltaMira Press.

Falk, J. & Dierking, L. (1992). *The museum experience*. Washington, DC: Whalesback Books.

Falk, J., Koran, J., Dierking, L., & Dreblow, L. (1985). Predicting visitor behavior. *Curator* 28(4): 249-257.

Falk, J. & Storksdieck, M. (2005). Using the contextual model of learning to understand visitor learning from a science center exhibition. *Science Education* 89: 744-778.

Fallon, L. & Kriwoken, L. (2003). Experiences from the Strahan visitor center, Tasmania. In Black, R. & Weiler, B. (Eds.), *Interpreting the land down under—Australian heritage interpretation and tour guiding*. Fulcrum Applied Communication Series. Golden, Colorado, USA: Fulcrum Books, 41-72.

Fazio, R. (1995). Attitudes as object evaluation associations: determinants, consequences, and correlates of attitude accessibility. In Petty, R. & J. Krosnick (Eds.), *Attitude strength: antecedents and consequences*. Mahwah, NJ: Erlbaum, 247-282.

Fazio, R. (1986). How do attitudes guide behavior? In Sorrentino, R. & Tory, E. (Eds.), *Handbook of motivation and cognition: Foundations of social behavior*. New York, USA: Guilford Press, 204-243.

Fazio, R. & Towles-Schwen, T. (1999). The MODE model of attitude-behavior processes. In Chaiken, S. & Trope, Y. (Eds.), *Dual-process theories in social psychology*. New York: Guilford, 97-116.

Fennell, R. (2004). The National Park Service: de-kitsching souvenirs. *Legacy* 15(2): 28-29.

Field, G. & Lente, L. (2000). *Developing ecotours and other interpretive activity programs*. Perth, WA, Australia: Western Australia Department of Conservation.

Fishbein, M. & Ajzen, I. (2010). *Predicting and changing behavior—The reasoned action approach*. New York, USA: Psychology Press.

Fishbein, M. & Ajzen, I. (1975). *Belief, attitude, intention and behavior: an introduction to theory and research*. Reading, USA: Addison-Wesley. http://www-unix.oit.umass.edu/~aizen/f&a1975.html

Fishbein, M., & Ajzen, I. (1974). Attitudes towards objects as predictors of single and multiple behavioral criteria. *Psychological Review* 81: 59-74.

Fishbein, M. & Manfredo, M. (1992). A theory of behavior change. In Manfredo, M, (Ed.), *Influencing human behavior*. Champaign, Illinois, USA: Sagamore Publishing Co., Inc., 29-50.

Fishbein, M. & Yzer, M. (2003). Using theory to design effective health behavior interventions. *Communication Theory* 13(2): 164-183.

Fiske, S. & Taylor, S. (1991). *Social cognition* (2nd ed.). New York: McGraw-Hill, 96-141.

Flesch, R. (1949). *The art of readable writing*. New York: Harper & Row.

Forrest, J. (2006). Evaluation of effectiveness of interpretation at six visitor centres—Knockan Crag. Battleby, UK: Scottish Natural Heritage.

Fosnot, C. (2005). Constructivism revisited: Implications and reflections. *The Constructivist* 16(1). Retrieved from http://users.otenet.gr/~dimigo/files/fosnot.pdf

Franklin, S., Baars, B., Ramamurthy, U., & Ventura, M. (2005). The role of consciousness in memory. *Brains, Minds and Media* 1: bmm150 (urn:nbn:de:0009-3-1505). http://www.brains-minds-media.org/archive/150/index_html/?searchterm=Franklin

Frick, R. (1992). Interestingness. *British Journal of Psychology* 83: 113-128.

Frost, W. (2005). Making an edgier interpretation of the Gold Rushes: contrasting perspectives from Australia and New Zealand. *International Journal of Heritage Studies* 11(3): 235-250.

Fudge, R. (2003). Interpretive themes—what's the big idea? In Larsen, D. (Ed.), *Meaningful interpretation—how to connect hearts and minds to places, objects and other resources*. U.S. National Park Service. Fort Washington, Pennsylvania, USA: Eastern National, np.

Gatewood, J. & Cameron, C. (2000). Measures of numen-seeking at Gettysburg National Military Park. 99th Meeting of the American Anthropological Association, San Francisco.

Geva, A., & Goldman, A. (1991). Satisfaction measurement in guided tours. *Annals of Tourism Research*, 18: 177-185.

Glen, M. (1997). Tackling taboos—the interpretation of crime, strife, belief and relief. *Legacy* 8(2): 18-19, 26-28.

Gobet, F. & Clarkson, G. (2004). Chunks in expert memory: Evidence for the magical number four... or is it two? *Memory* 12: 732-747.

Goldman, T., Chen, W., & Larsen, D. (2001). Clicking the icon: exploring the meanings visitors attach to three national capital memorials. *Journal of Interpretation Research* 6(1): 3-30.

Goulding, C. (2001). Romancing the past: Heritage visiting and the nostalgic consumer. *Psychology & Marketing* 18(6): 565-592.

Goulding, C. (2000). The commodification of the past, postmodern pastiche, and the search for authentic experiences at contemporary heritage attractions. *European Journal of Marketing* 34(7): 835–853.

Goulding, C. & Domic, D. (2008). Heritage, identity and ideological manipulation: The case of Croatia. *Annals of Tourism Research* 36(1): 85-102.

Gramann, J. (2000). Protecting park resources using interpretation. *Park Science* 20 (Spring): 34-36.

Griest, D. (1981). Factors contributing to and effects of manager-interpreter conflict: an analysis of US Fish and Wildlife Service support for interpretation. Columbus, Ohio, USA: Masters Thesis, The Ohio State University, School of Natural Resources.

Griffin, E. (2000). *A first look at communication theory* (4th edition). Boston: McGraw-Hill.

Gross, M. & Zimmerman, R. (2002). *Interpretive centers: the history, design and development of nature and visitor centers*. Stevens Point, USA: University of Wisconsin, Stevens Point Foundation Press.

Gross, M., & Zimmerman, R. and Buchholz, J. (2006). *Signs, trails, and wayside exhibits: Connecting people and places* (3rd ed.). Stevens Point, USA: University of Wisconsin-Stevens Point Foundation Press.

Hall, T., Ham, S., & Lackey, B. (2010). Comparative evaluation of the attention capture and holding power of novel signs aimed at park visitors. *Journal of Interpretation Research* 15(1): 15-36.

Hall, T. & Roggenbuck, J. (2002). Response format effects in questions about norms: implications for the reliability and validity of the normative approach. *Leisure Sciences* 24: 325-337.

Ham, S. (2009a). From interpretation to protection: Is there a theoretical basis? *Journal of Interpretation Research, 14*(2): 48-58.

Ham, S. (2009b). The role of interpretation in profound visitor experiences. Keynote address to the World Federation of Tourist Guide Associations, Bali, Indonesia, January 12.

Ham, S. (2008). Enhancing visitor experiences and making a difference on purpose. Keynote address to the National Association for Interpretation Conference, Arcata, USA, March 7.

Ham, S. (2007). Can interpretation really make a difference? Answers to four questions from cognitive and behavioral psychology. In *Proceedings, Interpreting World Heritage Conference,* March 25-29, Vancouver, Canada. Fort Collins, USA: National Association for Interpretation, 42-52.

Ham, S. (2004). The psychology of giving: Lessons learned for travelers' philanthropy. Presentation to the Conference on Travelers' Philanthropy. Palo Alto, USA: Stanford University, Institute for International Studies, April 14.

Ham, S. (2002a). Meaning making—the premise and promise of interpretation. Keynote address to Scotland's First National Conference on Interpretation, Royal Botanic Gardens, Edinburgh, April 4.

Ham, S. (2002b). Cognitive psychology and interpretation. In Hooper-Greenhill, E. (Ed.), *The educational role of the museum* (2nd edition). London: Routledge, 161-171.

Ham, S. (1992). *Environmental interpretation—a practical guide for people with big ideas and small budgets.* Golden, Colorado, USA: Fulcrum Publishing.

Ham, S. (1983). Cognitive psychology and interpretation—synthesis and application. *Journal of Interpretation* 8(1): 11-27.

Ham, S., Brown, T., Curtis, J., Weiler, B., Hughes, M., & Poll, M. (2009). *Promoting persuasion in protected areas—A guide for managers.* Gold Coast, Australia: Collaborative Research Centre for Sustainable Tourism: http://www.crctourism.com.au/BookShop/BookDetail.aspx?d=656

Ham, S. & Ham, B. (2010). *The 2010 LEX/NG Fund for Galapagos: Report of research findings and recommended communication strategy.* Final report to Lindblad Expeditions and National Geographic Society. New York, USA: Lindblad Expeditions.

Ham, S., Housego, A., & Weiler, B. (2005). *Tasmanian thematic interpretation planning manual.* Hobart, Australia: Tourism Tasmania. http://www.tourismtasmania.com.au/tasind/thematic/thematic.htm

Ham, S. & Krumpe, E. (1996). Identifying audiences and messages for non-formal environmental education: A theoretical framework for interpreters. *Journal of Interpretation Research* 1(1): 11-23.

Ham, S. & Shew, R. (1979). A comparison of visitors' and interpreters' assessments of conducted interpretive activities. *Journal of Interpretation* 4(2): 39-44.

Ham, S. & Weiler, B. (2007). Isolating the role of on-site interpretation in a satisfying experience. *Journal of Interpretation Research* 12(2): 5-24.

Ham, S. & Weiler, B. (2006). *Development of a research-based tool for evaluating interpretation outcomes.* Gold Coast, Australia: Final Research Report to the CRC for Sustainable Tourism. http://www.crctourism.com.au/bookshop

Ham, S. & Weiler, B. (2003). Interpretation is persuasive when themes are compelling. *Interpret Scotland* 8 (Autumn): 1.

Ham, S. & Weiler, B. (2002). Toward a theory of quality in cruise-based nature guiding. *Journal of Interpretation Research* 7(2): 29-49.

Ham, S., Weiler, B., Hughes, M., Brown, T., Curtis, J., & Poll, M. (2008). *Asking visitors to help: Research to guide strategic communication for protected area management.* Final Technical Research Report (Project 80039). Gold Coast, Australia: Collaborative Research Centre for Sustainable Tourism. http://www.crctourism.com.au/BookShop/BookDetail.aspx?d=586

Harwit, M. (1996). *An exhibit denied: Lobbying the history of the Enola Gay.* New York: Copernicus.

Heberlein, T. (2012). *Navigating environmental attitudes.* New York: Oxford University Press.

Hockett, K. & Hall, T. (2007). The effect of moral and fear appeals on park visitors' beliefs about feeding wildlife. *Journal of Interpretation Research* 12(1): 5-27.

Holland, R., Verplanken, B., & Van Knippenberg, A. (2002). On the nature of attitude-behavior relations: the strong guide, the weak follow. *European Journal of Social Psychology* 32: 869-876.

Hooper, J. & Weiss, K. (1991). Interpretation as a management tool—a national study of interpretive professionals' views. *Legacy* 2(1): 10-16.

Hooper-Greenhill, E. (1999). *The educational role of the museum* (second edition). London, UK: Routledge.

Hovland, C., Janis, I., & Kelley, H. (1953). *Communication and persuasion.* New Haven, Connecticut, USA: Yale University Press.

Hovland, C. & Weiss, W. (1951). The influence of source credibility on communication effectiveness. *Public Opinion Quarterly* 15: 635-650.

Hughes, C. (1998). *Museum theatre—communicating with visitors through drama*. Portsmouth, New Hampshire, USA: Heinemann.

Hughes, M., Ham, S., & Brown, T. (2009). Influencing park visitor behavior: A belief-based approach. *Journal of Parks and Recreation Administration* 27(4): 38-53.

Hughes, M. & Morrison-Saunders, A. (2002). Impact of trail-side interpretive signs on visitor knowledge. *Journal of Ecotourism* 1(2): 122-132.

Hwang, S., Lee, C. & Chen, H. (2005). The relationship among tourists' involvement, place attachment and interpretation satisfaction in Taiwan's national parks. *Tourism Management* 26: 143-156.

Interpretation Australia Association. (2012). http://www.interpretationaustralia.asn.au/

Interpretation Canada. (2012). http://www.interpscan.ca/

Interpret Europe. (2012). http://www.interpret-europe.net/top/heritage-interpretation/benefits-from-interpretation.html

Kahneman, D. (2011). *Thinking fast and slow*. New York, New York, USA: Farrar, Strauss, Giroux.

Kardash, C., Royer, J., & Greene, B. (1988). Effects of schemata on both encoding and retrieval of information from prose. *Journal of Educational Psychology* 80(3): 324-29.

Klingberg, T. (2009). *The overflowing brain: Information overload and the limits of working memory*. New York, New York, USA: Oxford University Press.

Knapp, D. (2003). Interpretation that works. *Legacy* 14(6): 26-33.

Knapp, D. & Barrie, D. (1998). Ecology versus issue interpretation—the analysis of two different messages. *Journal of Interpretation Research* 3(1): 21-38.

Knapp, D. & Benton, G. (2005). Long-term recollections of an environmental interpretive program. *Journal of Interpretation Research* 10(1): 51-53.

Knapp, D. & Yang, L. (2002). A phenomenological analysis of long-term recollections of an interpretive program. *Journal of Interpretation Research* 7(2): 7-17.

Knudson, D., Cable, T., & Beck, L. (1995). *Interpretation of cultural and natural resources*. State College, Pennsylvania, USA: Venture Publishing.

Kohen, R. & Sikoryak, K. (2005). *A guide to comprehensive interpretive planning*. Denver, Colorado, USA: US National Park Service.

Kohl, J. (2004). Mighty messages make memorable presentations. *Legacy* 15(1): 42-44.

Kumkale, T. & Albarracı´n, D. (2004). The sleeper effect in persuasion: A meta-analytic review. *Psychological Bulletin* 130(1): 14-172.

Lackey, B. & Ham, S. (2004). Assessment of communication focused on human-black bear conflict at Yosemite National Park. *Journal of Interpretation Research* 8(1): 25-40.

Lackey, B. & Ham, S. (2003). Contextual analysis of interpretation focused on human-black bear conflicts in Yosemite National Park. *Applied Environmental Education and Communication* 2(1): 11-21.

Lampinen, J., Copeland, S., & Neuschatz, J. (2001). Recollection of things schematic: room schemas revisited. *Journal of Experimental Psychology: Learning, Memory and Cognition* 27(5): 1211-1222.

Langer, E. (1989). *Mindfulness*. Reading, Massachusetts, USA: Addison-Wesley.

Larsen, D. (2005). Personal communication. August 24.

Larsen, D. (Ed.). (2003). *Meaningful interpretation—how to connect hearts and minds to places, objects and other resources*. U.S. National Park Service. Fort Washington, Pennsylvania, USA: Eastern National.

Larsen, D. (2002). Be relevant or become a relic. *Journal of Interpretation Research* 7(1): 17-23.

Lee, T. & Balchin, N. (1995). Learning and attitude change at British Nuclear Fuel's Sellafield Visitors Centre. *Journal of Environmental Psychology* 15(4): 283-298.

Leinhardt, G., Crowley, K., & Knutson, K. (Eds.). (2002). *Learning conversations in museums*. Mahwah, New Jersey, USA: Lawrence Erlbaum Associates.

Leinhardt, G. & Knutson, K. (2004). *Listening in on museum conversations*. Walnut Creek, California, USA: AltaMira Press.

Leinhardt, G., Knutson, K., & Crowley, K. (2003). Museum learning collaborative redux. *Journal of Museum Education* 28(1): 23-31.

Leiper, N. (1990). Tourist attraction systems. *Annals of Tourism Research* 17(3): 367-384.

Levy, B., Lloyd, S., & Schreiber, S. (2001). *Great tours! Thematic tours and guide training for historic sites*. Walnut Creek, California, USA: AltaMira Press.

Lewis, W. (1980). *Interpreting for park visitors*. Philadelphia: Eastern National Park and Monument Association, Eastern Acorn Press.

Livingstone, P., Pedretti, E., & Soren, B. (2002). Visitor comments and the socio-cultural context of science: public perceptions and the exhibition *A Question of Truth*. *Museum Management and Curatorship* 19(4): 355-369.

Lonie, N. (1998). *Practice and profile of interpretation in Scotland.* http://www.scotinterpnet.org.uk/pdfs/fulllonie.pdf

Loomis, R. (1996). How do we know what the visitor knows?—learning from interpretation. *Journal of Interpretation Research* 1(1): 39-45.

Lundberg, A. (1997). Toward a thesis-based interpretation. *Legacy* 8(2): 14-17, 30-31.

Manfredo, M, (Ed.). (1992). *Influencing human behavior.* Champaign, Illinois, USA: Sagamore Publishing.

Manhart, K. (2005). Likely story—myths persist in modern culture because of the brain's biological need to impose order on the world. *Scientific American MIND* (December): 58-63.

Manning, R. (2003). Emerging principles for using information/education in Wilderness management. *International Journal of Wilderness* 9(1): 20-27.

Marler, L. (1972). A study of anti-litter messages. In Schoenfeld, C. (Ed.), *Interpreting environmental issues: research and development in conservation communications.* Madison, Wisconsin, USA: Dembar Educational Research Services, 178-179.

McKee, R. (1997). *Story—substance, structure, style, and the principles of screenwriting.* New York: Harper-Collins.

McLuhan, M. (1967). *The medium is the message.* New York: Bantam Books.

McManus, P. (1993). Memories as indicators of the impact of museum visits. *Museum Management and Curatorship* 12: 367-380.

McManus, P. (1989). Oh yes they do—how museum visitors read labels and interact with exhibit texts. *Curator* 32(3): 174-189.

Mead, G. (1934). *Mind, self and society.* Chicago: University of Chicago Press.

Medved, M. (2000). Remembering exhibits at museums of art, science, and sport: A longitudinal study. Ph.D. thesis. Toronto: University of Toronto.

Medved, M. & Oatley, K. (2000). Memories and scientific literacy: remembering exhibits from a science centre. *International Journal of Science Education* 22(10): 1117-1132.

Merriman, T. & Brochu, L. (2005). *Management of interpretive sites.* Fort Collins, Colorado, USA: InterpPress.

Miller, G. (1989). George A. Miller. In Gardner, L. (Ed.), *A history of psychology in autobiography* (Volume 8), Palo Alto, California, USA: Stanford University Press, 391-418.

Miller, G. (1956). The magical number seven, plus or minus two: Some limits on our capacity for processing information. *Psychological Review* 63(2): 81-97.

Moody, R. (2005). *The joy and enthusiasm of reading*. National Public Radio, Morning Edition, USA. Retrieved August 29, 2005 from. www.npr.org/templates/story/story.php?storyId=4816313

Morales, J. (1998). *Guía práctica para la interpretación del patrimonio—el arte de acercar el legado natural y cultural al público visitante*. Sevilla, Spain: Junta de Andalucia, Consejería de Cultura.

Moray, N. (1959). Attention in dichotic listening: Effective cues and the influence of instructions. *Quarterly Journal of Experimental Psychology* 11(1): 56-60.

Morgan, M., Absher, J., Loudon, B., & Sutherland, D. (1997). The relative effectiveness of interpretive programs directed by youth and adult naturalists in a national forest. *Journal of Interpretation Research* 2(1): 13-26.

Morgan, M., Absher, J., & Whipple, R. (2003). The benefits of naturalist-led interpretive programs—implications for user fees. *Journal of Interpretation Research* 8(1): 41-54.

Moscardo, G. (1999a). Communicating with two million tourists—a formative evaluation of an interpretive brochure. *Journal of Interpretation Research* 4(1): 21-37.

Moscardo, G. (1999b). *Making visitors mindful—principles for creating sustainable visitor experiences through effective communication*. Champaign, Illinois, USA: Sagamore Publishing.

Moscardo, G. (1996). Mindful visitors—heritage and tourism. *Annals of Tourism Research* 23(2): 376-397.

Moscardo, G., Ballantyne, R., & Hughes, K. (2007). *Designing interpretive signs—Principles in practice*. Applied Communication Series. Golden, Colorado, USA: Fulcrum Publishing.

Museums Australia. (2012). http://www.museumsaustralia.org.au/

National Association for Interpretation. (2012). http://www.interpnet.com/

Novey, L. & Hall, T. (2007). The effect of audio tours on learning and social interaction: An evaluation at Carlsbad Caverns National Park. *Science Education* 91(2): 260-277.

Oliver, S., Roggenbuck, J., & Watson, A. (1985). Education to reduce impacts in forest campgrounds. *Journal of Forestry* 83(4): 234-236.

O'Mahony, B., Hall, J., Lockshin, L., Jago, L., & Brown, G. (2006). The impact of winery tourism on later wine consumption. In O'Mahony, G. & Whitelaw, P. (Eds.), *To the City and Beyond*, proceedings, Council for Australian University Tourism and Hospitality Education Conference (CAUTHE), 1816-1831.

Orams, M. (1997). The effectiveness of environmental education—can we turn tourists into 'greenies'? *Progress in Tourism and Hospitality Research* 3(4): 295-306.

Pastorelli, J. (2003). *Enriching the experience: an interpretive approach to tour guiding.* Frenchs Forest, Australia: Hospitality Press.

Pearce, P. & Moscardo, G. (1998). The role of interpretation in influencing visitor satisfaction: a rainforest case study. In Faulkner, W., Tidswell, C., & Weaver, D. (Eds.), *Progress in tourism and hospitality research, 1998, Part 1.* Proceedings of the Eighth Australian Tourism and Hospitality Research Conference, Gold Coast. Canberra: Bureau of Tourism Research, 309-319.

Peart, B. (1984). Impact of exhibit type on knowledge gain, attitude change and behavior. *Curator* 27(2): 220-237.

Pettus, A. (1976). Environmental education and environmental attitudes. *Journal of Environmental Education* 8: 48-51.

Petty, R. & Cacioppo, J. (1986). *Communication and persuasion: central and peripheral routes to attitude change.* New York: Springer-Verlag.

Petty, R. & Cacioppo, J. (1979). Issue involvement can increase or decrease persuasion by enhancing message-relevant cognitive processes. *Journal of Personality and Social Psychology* 37: 1915-1926.

Petty, R., Cacioppo, J., & Goldman, R. (1981). Personal involvement as a determinant of argument-based persuasion. *Journal of Personality and Social Psychology* 41: 847-855.

Petty, R., Cacioppo, J., & Heesacker, M. (1981). The use of rhetorical questions in persuasion. A cognitive response analysis. *Journal of Personality and Social Psychology* 40: 432-440.

Petty, R., Cacioppo, J., & Schumann, D. (1983). Central and peripheral routes to advertising effectiveness—the moderating role of involvement. *Journal of Consumer Research* 10: 134-148.

Petty, R., McMichael, S., & Brannon, L. (1992). The elaboration likelihood model of persuasion: applications in recreation and tourism. In Manfredo, M. (Ed.), *Influencing human behavior: theory and applications in recreation, tourism and natural resources management.* Champaign, USA: Sagamore Press, 77-101.

Petty, R., Rucker, D., Bizer, G., & Cacioppo, J. (2004). The elaboration likelihood model of persuasion. Seiter, J. & Gass, R. (Eds.), *Perspectives on persuasion, social influence, and compliance gaining.* New York, USA: Pearson, 65-89.

Pine, J. & Gilmore, J. (1999). *The experience economy—work is theatre & every business a stage.* Boston: Harvard Business School Press.

Pinker, S. (1997). *How the mind works*. New York, USA: W.W. Norton & Co.

Powell, R. & Ham, S. (2008). Can ecotourism interpretation really lead to pro-conservation knowledge, attitudes and behaviors? Evidence from the Galapagos Islands. *Journal of Sustainable Tourism* 16(4): 467-489.

Rand, A. (2010). Examining cognitive outcomes from exposure to interpretive materials at the Menor's Ferry Historic District in Grand Teton National Park. Masters thesis. Moscow, Idaho, USA: University of Idaho, Department of Conservation Social Sciences.

Ratey, J. (2001). *A user's guide to the brain: perception, attention, and the four theaters of the brain*. New York: Vintage Books.

Regnier, K., Gross, M. & Zimmerman, R. (1994). *The interpreter's guidebook—techniques for programs and presentations* (3ʳᵈ ed.). Stevens Point, Wisconsin, USA: University of Wisconsin-Stevens Point Foundation Press.

Reidy, J. & Riley, R. (2002). Who should interpret indigenous cultures and sacred places? *Legacy* 13(4): 26-28.

Rennie, L. & Johnston, D. (2004). The nature of learning and its implications for research on learning from museums. *Science Education* 88(S1): S4-S16.

Reno, R., Cialdini, R., & Kallgren, C. (1993). The transsituational influence of social norms. *Journal of Personality and Social Psychology* 64(1): 104-112.

Rivis, A. & Sheeran, P. (2003). Descriptive norms as an additional predictor in the theory of planned behaviour: A meta-analysis. *Current Psychology: Developmental, Learning, Personality, Social* (Fall) 22(3): 218-233.

Roggenbuck, J. (1992). Use of persuasion to reduce resource impacts and visitor conflicts. In Manfredo, M, (Ed.), *Influencing human behavior*. Champaign, Illinois, USA: Sagamore Publishing, 149-208.

Roggenbuck, J. & Ham, S. (1986). Information and education in wildland recreation management. In, *A literature reviewthe president's commission on Americans outdoors*. Washington, D.C., USA: US Government Printing Office, 59-71.

Ross, A., Siepen, G., & O'Connor, S. (2003). Making distance learning E.R.O.T.I.C. Applying interpretation principles to distance learning. *Environmental Education Research* 9(4): 479-495.

Roxborough, S. (2004). *'Downfall' breaks taboo, portrays Hitler's human side*. http://www.hollywoodreporter.com/thr/article_display.jsp?vnu_content_id=1000624963

Savage, G. & James, J. (2001). *A practical guide to evaluating natural and cultural heritage interpretation—exit interviews, observation methods, focus group discussions.* Adelaide, Australia: Flinders University Press.

Schank, R. (1979). Interestingness—controlling inferences. *Artificial Intelligence* 12: 273-297.

Scherbaum, P. (2008). *Handles: A compendium of interpretive techniques to help visitors grasp resource meanings.* U.S. National Park Service. Fort Washington, Pennsylvania, USA: Eastern National.

Schramm, W. (1971). *The process and effects of mass communication.* Urbana, Illinois, USA: University of Illinois Press.

Schulhof, R. (1990). Visitor response to a native plant habitat exhibit. *Visitor Behavior* 5(4): 11-12.

Scottish Interpretation Network. (2006). http://www.scotinterpnet.org.uk/

Serrell, B. (1999). *Paying attention—visitors and museum exhibitions.* Washington, DC: American Association of Museums.

Serrell, B. (1977). Survey of visitor attitudes and awareness at an aquarium. *Curator* 20: 48-52.

Sharpe, G. & Gensler, G. (1978). Interpretation as a management tool. *Journal of Interpretation* 3(2): 3-9.

Shiner, J. & Shafer, E. (1975). *How long do people look at and listen to forest-oriented exhibits?* USDA Forest Service Research Paper NE-325. Upper Darby, Pennsylvania, USA: Northeast Forest Experiment Station.

Shuman, D. and Ham, S. (1997). Toward a theory of commitment to environmental education teaching. *Journal of Environmental Education* 28(2): 25-32.

Simon, J. (2003). In their own voice—the delicate matter of speaking for others. *Legacy* 14(1): 12-21.

Smith, L., Ham, S., & Weiler, B. (2011). The impacts of profound wildlife experiences. *Anthrozoos* 24(1): 51-64.

Smith, L. (2004). A qualitative analysis of profound wildlife encounters. Masters thesis. Melbourne, Australia: Monash University, Department of Management.

Smith-Jackson, T. & Hall, T. (2002). Information order and sign design: a schema-based approach. *Environment & Behavior* 34(4): 479-492.

Solso, R., MacLin, M., & MacLin, O. (2008). *Cognitive psychology* (8th edition). Needham Heights, Massachusetts, USA: Allyn & Bacon..

Spock, M. (Ed). (2000). *Philadelphia stories—a collection of pivotal museum memories.* Washington, DC: American Association of Museums.

Starkey, P. (2009). Effect of persuasive messages on campers' littering behavior in Wenatchee National Forest, Washington. Masters thesis. Moscow, Idaho, USA: University of Idaho, Department of Conservation Social Sciences.

Stern, M., Powell, R., Martin, E., & McLean, K. (2012). *Identifying best practices for live interpretive programs in the United States National Park Service.* Research report. Blacksburg, VA, USA: Virginia Tech University, Department of Forest Resources and Environmental Conservation.

Stevens, R. & Hall, R. (1997). Seeing *Tornado:* How video traces mediate visitor understandings of natural phenomena in a science museum. *Science Education* 81(6): 735-747.

Stevenson, J. (1991). The long-term impact of interactive exhibits. *International Journal of Science Education* 13(5): 521-531.

St. John, F., Edwards-Jones, G., & Jones, J. (2010). Conservation and human behaviour: lessons from social psychology. *Wildlife Research* 37: 658-667.

Stokes, A., Cook, S., & Drew, D. (2003). *Geotourism—the new trend in travel.* Washington, DC, USA: Travel Industry Association of America.

Storksdieck, M., Ellenbogen, K., & Heimlich, J. (2005). Changing minds? Reassessing outcomes in free-choice environmental education. *Environmental Education Research* 11(3): 353-369.

Strauss, S. (1996). *The passionate fact—storytelling in natural history and cultural interpretation.* Fulcrum Applied Communication Series. Golden, Colorado, USA: Fulcrum Books.

Symons, C. & Johnson, B. (1997). The self-reference effect in memory: A meta-analysis. *Psychological Bulletin* 121: 371-394.

Tardona, D. (2005). Exploring evolved psychological underpinnings of universal concepts and meaningful connections. *Journal of Interpretation Research* 10(1): 69-74.

Tarlton, J. & Ward, C. (2006). The effect of thematic interpretation on a child's knowledge of an interpretive program. *Journal of Interpretation Research* 11(1): 7-31.

Thorndyke, P. (1977). Cognitive structures in comprehension and memory of narrative discourse. *Cognitive Psychology* 9(1): 77-110.

Tilden, F. (1957). *Interpreting our heritage.* Chapel Hill, North Carolina, USA: University of North Carolina Press.

Tourism Tasmania. (2003). *Tasmanian experience strategy—creating unforgettable natural experiences.* Hobart, Australia: Tourism Tasmania. www.tourismtasmania.com.au/tasind/t_experience/

Trapp, S., Gross, M., & Zimmerman, R. (1994). *Signs, trails, and wayside exhibits: Connecting people and places.* Stevens Point, Wisconsin, USA: University of Wisconsin-Stevens Point Foundation Press.

Tubb, K. (2003). An evaluation of the effectiveness of interpretation within Dartmoor National Park in reaching the goals of sustainable tourism development. *Journal of Sustainable Tourism* 11(6): 476-498.

Tuckey, M. & Brewer, N. (2003). How schemas affect eyewitness memory over repeated retrieval attempts. *Applied Cognitive Psychology* 17: 785-800.

Tulving, E. (2001). Episodic memory and common sense—how far apart? In Baddeley, A., Conway, M., & Aggleton, J. (Eds.), *Episodic memory—new directions in research.* Oxford: Oxford University Press, 269-287.

Tulving, E. (1983). *Elements of episodic memory.* Oxford: Clarendon Press.

Tulving, E. (1972). Episodic and semantic memory. In Tulving, E. & Donaldson, W. (Eds.), *Organization of memory.* New York: Academic Press, 381-403.

US National Park Service. (2012). Interpretive development program. www.nps.gov/idp/interp/

Uzzell, D. & Ballantyne, R. (1998). Heritage that hurts: interpretation in a post-modern world. In Uzzell, D. & Ballantyne, R. (Eds.), *Contemporary issues in heritage and environmental interpretation—problems and prospects.* London: The Stationery Office, 152-171.

Vander Stoep, G. & Gramann, J. (1987). The effects of verbal appeals and incentives on depreciative behavior among youthful park visitors. *Journal of Leisure Research* 19(2): 69-83.

von Oech, R. (1990). *A whack in the side of the head—How you can be more creative.* New York, USA: Warner Books.

von Ruschkowski, E., Arnberger, A., & Burns, R. (forthcoming). Visitor center exhibit use and visitor behaviour at Torfhaus, Harz National Park, Germany. *Visitor Studies.*

Vygotsky, L. (1978). *Mind in society.* Cambridge, Massachusetts, USA: Harvard University Press.

Vygotsky, L. (1962). *Thought and language.* Cambridge, Massachusetts, USA: MIT Press.

Wagar, J. (1976). *Cassette tapes for interpretation.* USDA Forest Service Research Paper PNW-207. Portland, Oregon, USA: Pacific Northwest Forest and Range Experiment Station.

Ward, C. & Roggenbuck, J. (2003). Understanding park visitors' responses to interventions to reduce petrified wood theft. *Journal of Interpretation Research* 8(1): 67-82.

Ward, C. & Wilkinson, A. (2006). *Conducting meaningful interpretation—a field guide for success*. Fulcrum Applied Communication Series. Golden, Colorado, USA: Fulcrum Books.

Washburne, R. & Wagar, J. (1972). Evaluating visitor response to exhibit content. *Curator* 15(3): 248-254.

Weigel, R. (1983). Environmental attitudes and the prediction of behavior. In N. R. Feimer, N. & Geller, E. (Eds.), *Environmental psychology: Directions and perspectives*. New York, USA: Praeger, 257-287.

Weigel, R. & Newman, L. (1976). Increasing attitude-behavior correspondence by broadening the scope of the behavioral measure. *Journal of Personality and Social Psychology* 33: 793-802.

Weiler, B. & Ham, S. (2002). Tour guide training: a model for sustainable capacity building in developing countries. *Journal of Sustainable Tourism* 10(1): 52-69.

Weiler, B. & Ham, S. (2001). Tour guides and interpretation. In Weaver, D. (Ed.), *The encyclopedia of ecotourism*. Wallingford, UK: CAB International, 549-563.

Werner, C., Rhodes, M., & Partain, K. (1998). Designing effective instructional signs with schema theory: case studies of polystyrene recycling. *Environment & Behavior* 30(5): 709-735.

Widner, C. & Roggenbuck, J. (2001). Reducing theft of petrified wood at Petrified Forest National Park. *Journal of Interpretation Research* 5(1): 1-18.

Widner, C. & Roggenbuck, J. (2003). Understanding park visitors' responses to interventions to reduce petrified wood theft. *Journal of Interpretation Research* 8(1): 67-82.

Wiles, R. & Hall, T. (2005). Can interpretive messages change park visitors' views on wildland fire? *Journal of Interpretation Research* 10(2): 18-35.

Winter, P. (2006). The impact of normative message types on off-trail hiking. *Journal of Interpretation Research* 11(1): 35-52.

Winter, P., Cialdini, R., Bator, R., Rhoads, K., & Sagarin, B. (1998). An analysis of normative messages in signs at recreation settings. *Journal of Interpretation Research* 3(1): 39-47.

Witteborg, L. (1981). *Good show! A practical guide for temporary exhibitions*. Washington, DC: The Smithsonian Institution.

Woods, B. & Moscardo, G. (2003). Enhancing wildlife education through mindfulness. *Australian Journal of Environmental Education* 19: 97-108.

World Association of Zoos and Aquaria. (2012). http://www.waza.org/

Yamada, N. & Ham, S. (2005). Impact assessments for interpretation: their advantages, disadvantages, and applications. *Japanese Journal of Environmental Education* 15(1): 2-10.

Subject Matter Index

About the Author

Sam H. Ham is a professor of communication psychology and conservation social sciences at the University of Idaho, USA. Sam's work has taken him throughout the USA and Canada, and to nearly fifty other countries, where his approach to thematic communication is considered best practice in a wide variety of communication fields. Today, Sam's thematic communication principles are put into daily practice by thousands of interpreters of cultural heritage and nature, as well as by museums, tour operators, zoos, botanical gardens, aquariums, national parks, and protected areas. Government bodies and private enterprises across the world have incorporated his theme-based principles into communication programs ranging from municipal sustainability and conservation education, to tourism marketing, philanthropy and interpretation of wine, beer, chocolate and art. His nearly 400 publications include the best-selling book, *Environmental Interpretation—A Practical Guide for People with Big Ideas and Small Budgets*, which was published in four languages. He also has edited six books on interpretation, storytelling and journalism for Fulcrum Publishing's Applied Communication Series.

Sam and his wife, Barbara, live in Moscow, Idaho, USA.

Made in the USA
Coppell, TX
22 June 2020